Sustainability Leadership

"In today's uncertain times, the examples of how Swedish business leaders have weathered turbulent times, re-defined their businesses and sought new ways to amplify value for all stakeholders is a precious and timely source of inspiration."
—Lim Boon Heng, Chairman, *Temasek*

"Henrik Henriksson and Elaine Weidman Grunewald have issued a stirring call to action that cannot be ignored. The authors provide a roadmap for how companies can define their purpose and live by it—something we need more than ever in these challenging times. The candid stories of how Swedish CEOs have risen to those challenges is inspiring. I urge every business leader to read this book and share it widely among their teams."
—N. Chandrasekaran, Chairman, *Tata Sons*

"Not only do Grunewald and Henriksson demonstrate how sustainability ambitions must be realized through business action, they also show how such business action can be achieved and provide a plan of action for sustainability leadership through concrete and inspirational cases from the Nordics."
—Kristin Skogen Lund, CEO, *Schibsted*

"This book is a treasure chest: It reveals the secrets behind Sweden's success and how corporations can thrive on sustainability while being part of the solution for the big challenges of our time."
—Georg Kell, Founder, UN Global Compact and Chairman, *Arabesque*

"Sweden is a powerhouse of sustainable industrial transformation. This book describes the management approach behind it. Henrik Henriksson and Elaine Weidman Grunewald invite change- makers in Swedish business to tell their stories. And they tell their own story, not least about Scania, a company that shows how sustainability and profitability can go together. The core message: Global challenges like the climate crisis require clear entrepreneurial values: integrity, responsibility, effectiveness. We have no time to lose!"
—Herbert Diess, Chairman of the Board of Management, *Volkswagen AG*

"In this valuable book, Elaine Weidman Grunewald and Henrik Henriksson provide an easy to read, inspiring and practical guide to sustainability leadership. The examples are compelling and show that sustainability is an integral part of the strategy of profitable, successful businesses – and will be even more so going forward."
—Stephanie O'Keefe, CEO, *International Women's Forum*

"Sweden has offered the world so many valuable lessons over the years; and this excellent book is the latest contribution - timely and valuable business insight explained with clarity and humility. It reminds us that purposeful leadership is both essential in today's highly unpredictable, challenging business environment and must be approached with energy, method and expansive imagination. It should be read by every leader who wishes to eschew incrementalism and confront the most pressing of contemporary questions, namely, how to deliver a step-change in sustainable growth, balancing the interests of all stakeholders without trade off, compromise or delay."

—Rick Haythornthwaite, Chairman, *Mastercard and Xynteo*

"Nordic countries and companies are globally recognized for their sustainability leadership. In their informative new book, Elaine Weidman Grunewald and Henrik Henriksson reveal "the secret sauce" that gives Swedish companies their inherent sustainability advantage. In translating to a global business audience, they offer a powerful three-step leadership model that any CEO or business leader can put in practice wherever they may find themselves in the world. This book provides definitive thinking on sustainability leadership for the twenty-first century—all with a wonderfully distinctive Swedish twist."

—Robert Strand, Executive Director & Lecturer, *Center for Responsible Business, Haas School of Business, University of California, Berkeley, USA*

Henrik Henriksson
Elaine Weidman Grunewald

Sustainability Leadership

A Swedish Approach to Transforming your Company, your Industry and the World

Foreword by Johan Rockström

palgrave
macmillan

Henrik Henriksson
Scania AB
Stockholm, Sweden

Elaine Weidman Grunewald
AI Sustainability Center
Stockholm, Sweden

Foreword by
Johan Rockström
Potsdam Institute of Climate Impact Research
University of Potsdam
Stockholm, Germany

ISBN 978-3-030-42290-5   ISBN 978-3-030-42291-2   (eBook)
https://doi.org/10.1007/978-3-030-42291-2

This Palgrave Macmillan imprint is published by the registered company Springer Nature Switzerland AG.
The registered company address is: Gewerbestrasse 11, 6330 Cham, Switzerland

Foreword

This is written in the beginning of April 2020. The world is fighting the coronavirus pandemic and the outcome is still very uncertain. The world economy is shaking, the number of confirmed deaths has just passed 80,000, and the mortality curve is still pointing upward, while the big fear is to what degree COVID-19 hits countries in the developing world.

In this turbulent time, science, politics, business, and civil society need to work together, to handle both short- and long-term challenges in a collaborative fashion. It is already clear that there is so much to learn from the coronavirus crisis. One lesson is the need to build resilience in a world that is, and will continue to be, characterized by turbulence, surprise, and shocks, from social, economic, and ecological changes, that moreover form part of a connected web of interactions in a big world on a small planet.

Businesses around the world face a new reality. And it is a deeper reality than the pandemic alone. I am not talking here about globalization or the digital revolution of exponential change in technology and innovation. Nor is it about social instabilities and rising inequities. The global health crisis is a manifestation of something bigger. It is a manifestation of the fact that we, the modern world of today, now constitute the dominant force of change of the entire planet. Driven by globalization, dense population pressures, and unsustainable production and consumption, and causing impacts on health, conflict, insecurity, and development, the fact that we are now in the Anthropocene, the new geological epoch triggered by our unsustainable exploitation of nature and climate, is the mother of all challenges.

And it changes everything. We have had zoonotic disease outbreaks—when infectious diseases are passed from animals to humans—in the history of mankind (think Spanish flu after World War I). But the frequency is on the increase, and both the source and impacts can be attributed to human pressures in the Anthropocene. The coronavirus crisis, however devastating in terms of human loss, is an alarm bell for us, signaling that our recovery must be a transformation to a resilient future where people and planetary health go hand in hand.

Scientifically, we can now say with a high degree of certainty that we have changed the living conditions on Earth as they have been since we left the last Ice Age, 12,000 years ago. We are following a path, if we continue burning fossil fuels and degrading nature as we do today, that will take us to global warming exceeding 3°C in only 80 years, when your children have grown-up children. In a geological blink of time, we are at risk of pushing our home, Earth, back to a climatic point She has not been in for the past four million years.

Our only chance to meet the Paris climate agreement of limiting global warming to 1.5°C, or at least stay well below 2°C, is to bend the curve of global emissions within the next few years, and then cut emissions by half each decade, until we reach a largely fossil-fuel-free world economy by mid-century, in 30 years. This is what we scientifically call the "Carbon Law," as it must trigger the same level of exponential innovation as "Moore's Law," which in 1965 predicted an exponential innovation pace of doubling the speed in computer transistors every 18–24 months. This led to a self-fulfilling prophecy driving the innovation that we have seen in the digital industry through the present day.

But this will not be enough. Stabilizing the global climate at a level that will not generate unmanageable risks will also require that we halt the destruction of nature. Today we have reached the sixth mass extinction of species on Earth, the first to be caused by another species: ourselves. We have wiped out 60 percent of animal populations since the 1970s and are on track to lose one million out of eight million known species on Earth.

The overall conclusion is that we have reached a state of planetary emergency. We have rising evidence that global warming, deforestation, and loss of ecosystems increase the risk of zoonotic disease outbreaks, which can transform into pandemics in the globalized world of the twenty-first century. We now need to mobilize all human ingenuity, leadership, and action for our common future on Earth. What we do over the coming decade is likely to determine the future for all coming generations in the world.

Business plays a fundamental role in this context, as a major source of unsustainable pressures on the planet, from use of natural resources to ecosystem change and greenhouse gas emissions. Yet, the private sector also represents the ability to provide solutions and be a leader in climate action. We are starting to see examples of that leadership today, which we direly need to see scaled and accelerated. My personal conclusion is that business, across a wide range of sectors from food, to energy and transport, injected pivotal support that provided the political leadership a significant portion of the confidence and courage to take the Paris climate negotiations in 2015 all the way to a successful global accord.

Business has continued to play a very important and constructive role on climate action. Immediately after Paris, hundreds of international businesses stepped up to adopt science-based targets (SBTs) for climate action, first to meet the 2°C target, and increasingly to reach 1.5°C. Right now, business is rallying to move from climate to planetary boundaries, by engaging in the Science-Based Targets (SBTs) for Earth initiative under the Global Commons Alliance, initiated by the Global Environment Facility (GEF) together with science (Future Earth) and business (We Mean Business).

All this is really important. Even more fundamental, though, is the narrative framing this action; the fact that climate action is increasingly moving from an environmental agenda to becoming a part of core business. Here Henrik Henriksson, as CEO of Scania and Elaine Weidman Grunewald, sustainability leader and innovator with long experience in the technology business, represent two global leaders. When they argue for making sustainability core to the business, they do it with empirical evidence and profound conviction, in a way that few leaders can. And it is here that they provide a really important piece of strategic advice for all business leaders, applicable to all sectors: making sustainability the core of your business is not a moral agenda; it is the pathway to profits and business success. As they point out, purpose-driven leadership is the most important business asset, as it generates innovation and gives a competitive edge.

Together, Henrik and Elaine provide what I consider the most important business advice one can get today—to embed the core business in a culture of sustainability. They do so by representing two of the most important sectors in the transformation to sustainable development, namely decarbonizing the transport sector and making digitalization work for sustainability. This makes the voice of these two business leaders so valuable and timely at a juncture where we must accelerate and scale innovations and solutions toward a prosperous and equitable future for humanity within planetary boundaries.

Potsdam Institute of Climate Impact Research   Johan Rockström
University of Potsdam, Potsdam, Germany

Preface

Many people have asked us how we came to write this book together. One rainy Swedish afternoon in early spring 2019, Elaine and Kershini Henriksson, Henrik's wife, were sitting down for that quintessential Swedish ritual, the *fika*, a coffee-and-cake break that is more of a state of mind than a time of day. Elaine had recently left her position leading the sustainability work at Information and Communication Technology (ICT) company Ericsson and was embarking on the next chapter in her journey. The discussion turned to climate change, and why it was a game-changing moment for companies to step up on sustainability. "You know," Kershini mused, thinking of family chats around her own dinner table, "Henrik shares our passion for sustainability; he really burns for it just as much as you and is frustrated over the lack of action. You two should write a book."

Kershini's idea resonated with both of us. Like a core theme described in this book, we were unconventional partners, with distinctly different backgrounds. Yet we share two fundamental beliefs: (1) that the world faces unprecedented and urgent global challenges and that business needs to step up, and (2) that, while not perfect, Sweden is brimming with great examples of how companies are working profitably and meaningfully to move the needle on sustainability.

So, we've opened up our toolbox and shared our experience, along with that of other leaders who share our passion for sustainability leadership. The Swedish companies and business leaders we interviewed in the book represent a broad spectrum, from startups to large industrial giants with 100-year-plus histories.

We wrote this book to use our own platforms and, in our own way, help to accelerate that momentum and catalyze change. The question business leaders face is not just *why* to act—but *how*: how to best engage others on the same journey, and how every leader can maximize his or her impact. Over the course of our careers, we have figured out some of the answers to those questions. That led us to spend many hours creating and discussing a leadership model with sustainability at its core, and a formula, for that all-important *how*.

Since we began writing this book, we've been encouraged by the progress we've seen and the commitments that are being made by business leaders all over the world. The tides seem to be shifting toward greater recognition of the importance of sustainability. It is no longer a race to the bottom but rather a race to the top.

The desire to write this book also comes from a very personal place for both of us. Anyone who has ever worked with Elaine knows that she is nothing if not persistent—for the things that she believes in and is passionate about, and how she is driven to see results. She has worked for small non-profits and large multinationals, but what most inspires her is the private sector's powerful platform for positive sustainability impact. Her work has taken her from the corridors of the United Nations to refugee settlements in South Sudan, visiting the poorest, seemingly forgotten, parts of the world, often without hope, but where the strongest hope often emerges: "Whether you're in the developed world with the most advanced technology or in the developing world with access to only the most basic technology, the capacity of the private sector, and the power of an individual leader, to wield influence, is bottomless, if the will, or ambition, is there."

Elaine is all about building coalitions of the willing—those, who, like her, embrace the "yes, and," not the "no, but" way of getting things done. She sums it up this way:

> Greater collaborations, partnerships, sharing of ideas. That's what we need to achieve the exponential impact that can move the needle on so many sustainable development challenges. Adopting the UN Sustainable Development Goals (SDGs) was a powerful moment of coming together. But without greater engagement of the private sector, without that exponential impact, there will be no future to sustain. This book has also been about creating a vision for the next generation of the coalition of the willing, the ones that want to go for something greater than business as usual.

For Henrik, the "why" of his journey in sustainability leadership is crystallized in an actual place, his summer cottage on the island of Blidö in the Stockholm archipelago.

That is our sanctuary, that is where my wife and I have raised our two daughters. Now nine and eleven years old, the place in the archipelago—close to the nature, the fresh air and the clear water—has been the place that has started to shape them as global citizens, shaped their values and their beliefs. It is that sanctuary that I want to save and protect today and for the future generations. And it's there that I think about the legacy I would like to leave for them one day.

Henrik continues:

I've always felt that at the end of the day the true judge of my legacy are my daughters. I have this picture in my head when I'm retired and sitting on my favorite bench on Blidö, at age 70, and my two grownup daughters come to sit with me. Two scenarios unfold. In the first they ask: "Weren't you the CEO of that company called Scania? Didn't you see what was going on? Why didn't you take your responsibility? Were you blind or stupid?" In the second scenario, they ask: "How did you find the strength, the courage and the drive to transform not only that company but a small piece of the world?" And of course, I want it to be the second scenario. This book is an opportunity to tell the story, not about me, but about all the great people in my company and how they build a better world. The Scania family. We are great, but our journey has just begun, and we can do better.

With this book we want to encourage you and others to start your journey. Use your ambition and drive to create your legacy. This is a perfect time to start!

Stockholm, Sweden   Henrik Henriksson
                                                Elaine Weidman Grunewald

Acknowledgments

We dedicate this book to our children—and to all children—so that they might inherit a planet worth inhabiting, and so that they might have a guide to carry forth the torch for sustainability leadership into the next generation.

First and foremost, we want to thank our families, for their patience and support as we spent many, many days, weekends, and evenings working on this book. Thank you Kershini. Thank you Per. And, of course, our children: Oscaria and Isabella, and Lukas, Knut, Felix, and Mira.

Thank you to the following individuals who shared their time with us in many hours of interviews, and without whose contributions and support this book would not have been possible: Niklas Adalberth, Founder of Norrsken Foundation; Åsa Bergman, CEO of Sweco; Elsa Bernadotte, President and Chief Operating Officer, Karma; Osvald Bjelland, Founder and Chairman of Xynteo; Anna Borgström, CEO, NetClean; Mark Boutros, Executive Vice President and Global Strategist; Omnicon Group; Peter Carlsson, CEO, Northvolt; Johan Dennelind, CEO, du; former CEO, Telia Company; John Elkington, Founding Partner and Chief Pollinator, Volans; Ulf Ewaldsson, Senior Vice President, Technology Transformation, T-Mobile; Anna Felländer, Co-Founder, AI Sustainability Center; Georgi Ganev, CEO, Kinnevik; Göran Gennvi, CEO, Nature Academy Learning Lab; Mats Granryd, Director General, GSMA; Per Grunewald, Founding Partner, Pegroco Invest AB (and Elaine's husband); Rickard Gustafson, CEO, SAS; Eva Karlsson, CEO, Houdini; Georg Kell, Chairman of the Arabesque Group; Mia Brunell Livfors, CEO, Axel Johnson; Sam Manaberi, CEO, Trine; Sue Reid, Principal Advisor, Finance, Mission 2020; Jeffrey Sachs, University Professor and Director of the Center for Sustainable Development at Columbia University; Jonas Samuelsson, CEO, Electrolux; Christian Sinding, CEO, EQT; Robert Strand,

Executive Director of the Center for Responsible Business and Lecturer at the Berkeley Haas School of Business; Michael Treschow, Director, Board of Directors, Knut and Alice Wallenberg Foundation; Hans Vestberg, Chairman and CEO, Verizon; and Jacob Wallenberg, Chair, Investor AB.

Thank you to the following reviewers, who challenged us, tested our logic, and gave valuable feedback to our ideas and propositions: Osvald Bjelland; Mark Boutros; Felix Grunewald, Project Manager, Northvolt; Stephanie Huf, Head of Marketing & Industries, Telia Global & Division X, Telia Company; Jonas Kjellstrand, Executive-in-residence, Universal Consulting Company; Lars Löfgren, former Artistic Director, Royal Dramatic Theatre of Sweden; Joanna Rubinstein, President and CEO, World Childhood Foundation, Childhood USA; Lisen Schultz, Programme Director, Executive Programme, Stockholm Resilience Centre; Martin Sköld, Associate Professor at the Centre for Innovation and Operations Management, Stockholm School of Economics; Birger Steen, Principal, Summa Equity; and David Stone, Chief Marketing Officer, Xynteo. We'd also like to thank the team at Scania for their reviews and support: Eva Skeppström-Jansson, Andreas Follér, Åsa Pettersson, Jakob Thärnå, Susanna Berlin, Erik Ljungberg, and Karin Hallstan. A special thank you to Johan Rockström, Professor in Earth System Science, University of Potsdam and Director, Potsdam Institute of Climate Impact Research, who captured this pivotal moment in time so well in his Foreword.

We also want to thank our editorial and production team: Amy Brown, our fearless, dedicated, always-on lead copywriter and editor, whose writing skills never wavered; Andrea Spencer-Cooke, Founding Partner, One Stone Advisors, supporting editor and reviewer, working the time zones creatively; our researchers—Sasha Quahe, Ida Pehrson, and Alexander Deimel—all starting their own sustainability journeys, and the illustrations provided by Andreas Malm, Form åt folket.

Lastly, thank you to Sweden, for being the kind of place where sustainability thrives.

Contents

Contents xvii

List of Figures

List of Tables

1

Introduction: The Case for Action
Expönentiality Cheat Sheet

We're just a few months into a new and pivotal decade, and the global coronavirus pandemic has changed life as we know it. Turning a crisis into an opportunity is of course a cliché—and before the coronavirus crisis we were already on the brink of another, slower sustainability disaster—climate change. Somehow it is easier to mobilize resources to solve the critical, short-term, immediate problems, as opposed to the climate crisis which has been underway for decades. The pandemic has created an unprecedented, terrible reality that will change us in ways we can't even anticipate. But it's also a wakeup call, and a chance to rethink how we conduct business. It has presented a *tabula rasa*—a clean slate—an opportunity to restart business based on sustainable principles.

Business cannot thrive on economic returns alone. As we lay out in this book, we need to measure success beyond profit to motivate change. And just as health workers, fire departments, police forces, and many others have been on the front lines of the COVID-19 pandemic, it's time for business leaders to step up to the front lines of the sustainability crisis.

COVID-19 has created a lot of fear and uncertainty—but this means that it is a leadership imperative. In reaction to the pandemic, companies can demonstrate in unprecedented ways their commitment to purpose and society. The businesses that are authentic will build trust, loyalty, and resilience.

The pandemic also highlights the importance of science and facts, a point we underscore in this book. In this case, COVID-19 has shown us that human health and the health of the planet are inseparable, that we must resist fake news and convenient truths, and that partnerships are key to solving major

© The Author(s) 2020
H. Henriksson, E. Weidman Grunewald, *Sustainability Leadership*,
https://doi.org/10.1007/978-3-030-42291-2_1

challenges. Now more than ever, concerted global action for a more sustainable world is urgently needed.

While we grapple with the seismic shifts in our society and economy brought on by the pandemic—the full consequences of which we can't yet predict—we cannot lose focus on the myriad challenges that the planet and humanity are facing. Climate change, rising inequality, and unsustainable resource use continue to demand our attention and action. This is not a head-in-the-sand moment. It is an invitation for the world to change direction—faster and more decisively than ever. It is also an opportunity for the private sector to exercise much-needed leadership in finding solutions rather than adding to the problems. With just ten years left to achieve the UN Sustainable Development Goals (SDGs) agreed by the world's nations in 2015, all sectors of society need to mobilize for a decade of action.[1]

Courageous and visionary business leaders are already heeding that call, inspiring others to set big, bold goals. There has also been a remarkable shift among investors, including influential mainstream investors, toward prioritizing sustainability and factoring the impact of climate change into investment decisions. Citizens around the world have been raising their voice for change, in ever larger numbers. Business leaders can no longer turn away. This book is a wake-up call because there is simply no time to lose.

Sweden may be a small country, but it has long punched above its weight. It is admired around the world for its progressive actions on sustainability, both as a nation and within the business sector. In this book, we share some of the essential ingredients in Sweden's "secret sauce" for corporate sustainability leadership. We draw extensively on our own leadership platforms and experience as well as that of other business leaders who share the same commitment to sustainability.

There Is No Business as Usual in a Turbulent World

Concerted global action for a more sustainable world is urgently needed and the challenges we face are more complex than ever. While it is encouraging to see that setting sustainability targets has become business as usual for many companies, most targets are still based on achieving incremental improvements. Leaving a better world for our children requires not just some action from the business world, but exponential solutions. Sustainability is not a trend; it is a condition for future business success, and we need to up the game.

It's important to keep in mind that sustainability is *not* philanthropy. It is much broader than environmental impact, corporate citizenship, or corporate social responsibility. It is not a stand-alone issue but affects every aspect of a company, and therefore must be connected to the core business and aligned with overall corporate strategy. We define sustainability, in the business context, as an integrated approach to minimize a company's negative impacts and maximize its positive social, environmental, and economic impacts, while creating long-term value for all stakeholders. We see sustainability as critical to the success of today's companies.

Over the next 30 years the world population will likely reach ten billion people, all wanting the same opportunities for a decent life. Despite global economic gains, more than 700 million people—some 10 percent of the world's population—still live in extreme poverty.[2] At least two billion people worldwide live in areas affected by fragility, conflict, and violence, where the intersection of poverty, high population growth, environmental degradation, natural hazards, and protracted conflict leaves them especially vulnerable.[3] Unprecedented mass migration and movements of people have led to some 150 million people being displaced (equivalent to the world's tenth largest country), due to conflict and humanitarian crises. The current geopolitical instability, economic turbulence, protectionism, and polarization exacerbate global inequality and threaten peace and prosperity. While globalization has opened up new markets it has also contributed to supply chain complexity and risks of labor exploitation.

People and planet depend on one another—but this mutual dependency is not reflected in current measurements of economic growth. Gross domestic product (GDP) is an increasingly inadequate indicator of growth, productivity, and value from the perspective of sustainable development, and the relentless pursuit of higher GDP has resulted in environmental destruction and a narrow notion of human wellbeing netted at the expense of a fair and inclusive society. The UN Sustainable Development Goals, the world's plan to build a better world for people and the planet by 2030, call for a recalibration, with only a decade left to shift direction.

As many Swedish business leaders in this book point out, they are well aware of the privilege of birthright, coming from a country where basic needs are met, and where they can rely on the benefits of social democracy—the right to free education, healthcare, and other aspects of a stable, well-functioning society. Part of their passion for creating purpose-driven companies stems from a recognition of the importance of balance: the drive for profitability is tempered with a sense of responsibility to create positive impact in the world, and leave a worthy legacy, with sustainability as a central, defining aspect.

As CEO of Scania, Henrik knows that transport is a big part of the problem, responsible for 24 percent of direct CO_2 emissions from fuel combustion, according to the International Energy Agency, and road vehicles account for nearly three-quarters of transport CO_2 emissions.[4] But he is also convinced that Scania can be part of the solution, by driving the shift to fossil-free commercial transport. This book is partly the story of that journey. For her part, Elaine's years of experience with technology and digitalization have brought her to the same point of deep commitment to act, to realize the substantial sustainability benefits Information and Communication Technology (ICT) can deliver, but also to raise awareness around—and preempt—its emerging challenges.

Our case for action is for business leaders, the primary audience for this book. Business has more influence and power than ever before. In the past 20 years, the number of companies with a market capitalization above $100 billion has more than doubled from 37 in 1999 to 98 companies in 2019[5] and many companies today are larger than governments. CEOs and other executives are expected to step up and do their share to contribute to sustainability. While we are seeing the welcome appearance of individual CEO activists, this needs to become the norm—not the exception.

Encouragingly, the financial world is waking up to the climate crisis and the costs of sustainability inaction. The financial risks of climate change are now firmly on the agenda of many banks, insurers and other financial institutions and growing numbers are putting a stop to investment in the fossil fuel economy. In 2019, the European Investment Bank announced it would cease funding fossil fuel projects by the end of 2021. Sustainable investing and Environmental Social Governance (ESG) investing is no longer niche but rather one of the signature financial shifts of the past decade, obliging more companies to focus on sustainability as well as profits.

The urgency to act is there: to be a leading company and business leader today requires sustainability leadership. But what does it take? Do you have the ambition and the tools to take your organization on the journey and make a credible, meaningful contribution to the sustainable development challenges the world faces? What can you learn from how Sweden is rising to the challenge?

The Sustainability Leadership Model

This book attempts to answer some of those questions and point you in the right direction. It starts and ends with emphasizing the importance of leadership. Based on our combined decades of experience in moving the needle in our respective industries, we've developed a simple but powerful Sustainability Leadership Model (i.e., the journey to sustainable Expönentiality, with a Swedish flair) (Fig. 1.1).

The three steps of the model consist of the following elements:

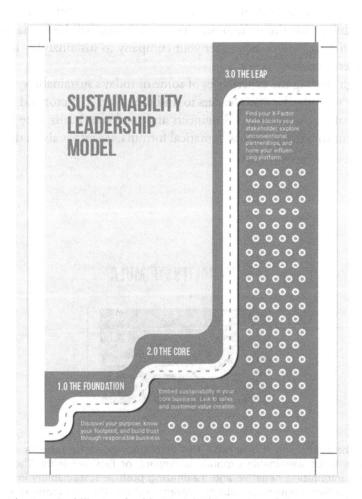

Fig. 1.1 The Sustainability Leadership Model. This consists of three steps that include setting the Foundation (1.0), embedding sustainability into the Core (2.0), and making the Leap (3.0)

- *The Foundation*: Discover your purpose, know your footprint, and build trust through responsible business.
- *The Core*: Embed sustainability in your core business. Make it real by linking it to sales and customer value creation.
- *The Leap*: Find your X-Factor. Adopt a societal and planetary lens, seek unconventional partnerships, and hone your influencing platform.

The entire model is a journey toward sustainable exponential impact, or Expönentiality, which is the destination. A simple formula shows how individual leaders can reach that destination, and find their X-Factor. Think about the X-Factor as your level of ambition on steroids; what differentiates you as a sustainability superhero. Your ambition as a leader will be fundamental to guide the necessary actions to steer your company to sustainability leadership and market success.

Through sharing the experiences of some of today's sustainability pioneers, our goal is to nudge business leaders to find their own X-Factor and start their Expönentiality journey today. Engineers and mathematicians, take note: this is not meant to be a precise mathematical formula; it's rather about directional leadership (Fig. 1.2).

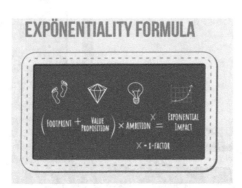

Fig. 1.2 The Expönentiality Formula. This simple but powerful formula shows how leaders can reach sustainable exponential impact, or Expönentiality. The *footprint* focuses on minimizing negative and maximizing positive sustainability impacts. The *Value proposition* is how sustainability is integrated into the core business. By upping their *ambition*, leaders can discover their *X-Factor* through a set of unique tools and accelerators. The *exponential impact* you create delivers long-term value for business and for society

A Reader's Guide

We recognize readers will be at different stages of the sustainability leadership journey. Some will be just setting out and others may be well on the way to becoming exponential in their reach and ambition. Our intention is to provide guidance for business leaders at every stage. By business leader we mean first and foremost CEOs, but also the C-suite (other senior executives) such as chief sustainability officers, or anyone trying to lead a sustainability transformation in the company. The book is structured to allow readers to begin where they like—to sample the *smörgåsbord* (that famed Swedish buffet meal), according to their own preferences and appetite. The book is divided into three parts, in line with the Sustainability Leadership Model:

Part 1.0 The Foundation includes three chapters:

- *Purpose-driven leadership*, describing how a leader can discover their purpose or "north star" to guide their sustainability leadership journey (Chap. 3);
- *A stake in the ground*, knowing the basics, and outlining how to use stakeholder insights to help set your level of commitment or ambition (Chap. 4); and
- *How to earn trust*, underlining the importance of responsible business practices in building trust—a vital ingredient for successful partnerships and stakeholder relationships (Chap. 5).

In *Part 2.0 The Core*, the focus is on business integration for sustainable value creation. The three chapters in this section include:

- *Embedding sustainability in the core business*, analyzing the strategy, business model, and value proposition to identify the challenges and opportunities that matter most and where you can have the greatest impact (Chap. 6);
- *It all comes down to sales*, making the all-important link between sustainability commitment and your customer (Chap. 7); and
- *Measuring impact beyond profit*, how to use robust sustainability metrics to measure what matters and support your progress (Chap. 8).

Part 3.0 The Leap is where business leaders define their level of ambition. These five final chapters are intended to help leaders aim higher and set their sights on changing the world. It is here that the Expönentiality Formula can help visualize where the greatest transformational business potential lies.

- *The Path to Expönentiality* introduces the societal ecosystem approach, and how using societal and planetary lenses helps you understand your impact on society (Chap. 9).
- *Society as a Stakeholder* applies the Expönentiality Formula and helps you to find your X-Factor, in part through unconventional partnerships (Chap. 10).
- *Making Business Sense of the SDGs* is about understanding how you fit into the broader sustainable development agenda, and how to make the UN Sustainable Development Goals purpose-fit for business, and be on the alert for "SDG-washing" (Chap. 11).
- *The Next Sustainability Frontier Is Digital* explores how digitalization is a powerful accelerator but why caution is needed to avoid some of the inherent risks in data-driven societies, that is., data pollution (Chap. 12).
- *Find Your Personal Influencing Platform* sets out why the key to advancing a leadership vision for sustainability transformation begins and ends with leadership and that the true test of purpose is having an authentic, impactful voice on the issues a leader is most passionate about (Chap. 13).

The three stages of the model in their entirety comprise the journey to Expönentiality. By the end of Part 3.0, we hope leaders will have identified new possibilities for their own sustainability leadership journey. It is in their power to execute a vision that not only shifts the direction of the company but has the power to change an entire industry—and even, in some modest way, the world.

This book is rich with cases and examples, provided by respected Swedish business leaders from leading large industrial companies to startups, who have generously shared their stories, opened up their toolboxes to reveal their best strategies, and shared their personal motivations for why sustainability is a main driver of their business leadership. Further insights are provided by a range of experts and thought leaders who shared their views with us: investors, economists, next-generation innovators, and sustainability advocates. We have found it to be an inspiring journey and hope you will, too.

In the Conclusion, "No Time to Lose," we leave readers with a call to action. Don't settle for incremental improvement. We don't have all the answers, but the urgency of rising to the challenges of a more sustainable world is greater than ever. It's time to step up and use your leadership platform to make a difference.

The world is counting on us.

Expönentiality Cheat Sheet

These key terms and definitions are unique to this book, and represent our interpretation of these words. As you'll notice with the creative spelling, there's a Swedish flair!

The Sustainability Leadership Model: An original model developed by Elaine Weidman Grunewald and Henrik Henriksson, summarizing three phases of sustainability leadership. These are The Foundation, 1.0; The Core, 2.0, and The Leap, 3.0 which together can lead to exponential sustainability impacts. They are interdependent and the end goal of exponential impacts cannot be achieved without the first two.

Planetary Lens: A way to view and understand a company's impact on the environment and the planet.

Societal Lens: A way to view and understand a company's impact on people, communities, and society more broadly.

Society as a Stakeholder: An approach that looks beyond traditional stakeholders to include society as a key stakeholder and assume responsibility for maximizing the positive impacts and minimizing the negative ones.

Societal Ecosystem: A business ecosystem that applies a planetary and societal lens to understand the science and impacts on people and planet while engaging with other actors, and finding new value chains.

Expönentiality: A company journey to achieve exponential sustainability impact that is based on purpose-driven leadership, a strong integration with your core business, and finding your X-Factor level of ambition.

Expönentiality Formula: The roadmap that links each phase of our model together to achieve Expönentiality.

The X-Factor: A set of leverage points—unique tools and accelerators that enable you to amplify your ambition and achieve greater impact. There could be many others, but we've chosen to highlight societal ecosystem, unconventional partnerships, digital technologies, and your own personal influencing platform.

Digital Pollution: When the use of data or data-driven technologies has harmful or negative unintended consequences on people, planet, or society, as a result of unattended risks, or poor data management.

Notes

1. Decade of Action, UN Sustainable Development Goals, accessed Nov 10, 2019, https://www.un.org/sustainabledevelopment/decade-of-action/.
2. Goal 1: End poverty, UN Sustainable Development Goals, accessed Nov 10, 2019, https://www.un.org/sustainabledevelopment/poverty/.
3. Global Humanitarian Review 2019, UN Office for the Coordination of Humanitarian Affairs (OCHA) accessed Nov 10, 2019, https://www.unocha.org/sites/unocha/files/GHO2019.pdf.
4. Tracking transport, International Energy Agency, May 2019, accessed Nov 29, 2019, https://www.iea.org/reports/tracking-transport-2019.
5. PWC, Global Top 100 companies by market capitalisation, July 2019. https://www.pwc.com/gx/en/audit-services/publications/assets/global-top-100-companies-2019.pdf; Top 100 Companies by Market Capitalization, http://fortboise.org/top100mktcap.html.

2

The Northern Lights Shine Bright

Ask someone to describe Sweden and you're likely to get a couple of predictable responses. "Yeah, I've heard of Sweden, they make great chocolate and clocks." No, that's Switzerland, but try telling that to the New York Stock Exchange, which infamously raised the Swiss flag on the day that one of Sweden's hottest companies, Spotify, went public.[1] Confusing Sweden with Switzerland is one thing, but a more perplexing portrayal for Swedes is having their country described as socialist. "Isn't it like living behind the Iron Curtain?" goes a common refrain. Swedes will take pains to outline the distinction between their social democracy and Communist-style socialism: Sweden embraces capitalism pretty much as much as the US does, albeit through its own "middle way," as we'll describe shortly.

Let's bust that myth of socialism here and now, and instead share some facts about Sweden. When Swedish business leaders talk about what makes them tick, a number of special national qualities surface time and time again. Qualities like balance, equality, and a healthy dose of humility; an outward-facing focus and strong global market mindset; an unwavering emphasis on efficiency, functionality, and continuous improvement; and the ability to think long term and see the big picture. Such traits help in a country the size of California but with a fraction of its population, where people work hard through long, dark winters, keeping the faith that if they persevere, the sun will eventually shine on them during the endless Swedish summer days.

In this prologue, and throughout this book, we explore how Swedish companies are intrinsically connected to their heritage: the culture, the values, the particular model of social democracy, the government's prominent role as a champion of sustainability, and, not least, a national affinity for nature and

© The Author(s) 2020

H. Henriksson, E. Weidman Grunewald, *Sustainability Leadership*,

https://doi.org/10.1007/978-3-030-42291-2_2

respect for the environment that almost verges on religious zeal. We think there's an intriguing story to be told about what it means for a company to be born with the inherent sustainability advantages that derive from the "Swedish brand," and how this can inspire global business leaders.

Among the Scandinavian CEOs featured in this book, some gloss over their heritage while others are quite conscious of how it shapes their decisions and corporate purpose. Pin them down in a conversation—perhaps over that revered cultural institution of *fika*, the Swedish coffee break, and Swedes will (eventually) acknowledge there *is* something special about Swedish leadership that is worth exploring. *Fika* itself is a case in point. These twice-daily breaks in the workday occur universally, from cafes to kitchen tables to conference rooms and C-suites. But unlike the hurried water-cooler office chats that American workers might be accustomed to, these are sit-down, take-your-time sessions—a fair and equal place for an exchange of ideas. And what could be more Swedish than that?

Getting to the Bottom of Brand Sweden

As long-time leaders in iconic Swedish companies, we know it's impossible to separate the culture and values and heritage of Sweden from the factory floor, the offices, and the boardrooms. There may be different ingredients to Sweden's success—a combination of the right policies, geography, luck, or circumstances—but Sweden today has an enviable place among nations, judging from the many top spots it holds in international rankings across the areas of sustainability, human development, social progress, innovation, and transparency.

That leadership is reflected in the corporate world, too. This is not to say that Sweden and Swedish companies are perfect or better than their peers in other countries. On the contrary, as we will show throughout this book, scandals, challenges, and dilemmas have affected Swedish companies just as much as others.

No company or country has come close yet to solving climate change or the host of other global sustainable challenges we face. With its population of ten million, Sweden is pursuing unsustainable levels of consumption like most of the developed world. While below that of many other industrialized countries, Sweden's carbon footprint remains significant and its C-suites and boardrooms, despite notable progress, still have a long way to go in terms of gender equality and other measures of diversity. Clearly, there is a lot more to be done.

It is also just as impossible for the captains of Swedish industry or any responsible corporate citizen around the world to feel self-satisfied in the face of a global climate movement that has been galvanized by a 17-year-old Swedish girl, Greta Thunberg, named *Time* magazine Person of the Year in 2019.[2] Greta's fight began with lonely school strikes outside the House of Parliament in Stockholm in late 2018, sparking the youth protest #FridaysForFuture[3] and eventually inspiring a global movement. On September 20, 2019, Greta led the biggest climate protest in world history, where roughly four million people from some 185 countries took to the streets to demand urgent and decisive action against the climate crisis.[4] In December 2019, an estimated 500,000 people took part in a rally in Madrid to bring that same message to governments and decision-makers at the COP25 climate negotiations.[5]

The world Greta and her generation will inherit is making them, along with other protests and climate movements, like the Extinction Rebellion,[6] angry and worried. Elaine recalls Greta's words at Brilliant Minds in Stockholm 2019,[7] an elite global gathering of politicians, business leaders, entrepreneurs, and artists: "I know you are not acting like this because you are stupid … I know that almost every one of you is simply uninformed, just like the rest of the world's population."[8]

We are equally tired of inaction, as are the business leaders featured in this book. While Greta and other activists are helping to fan a new spark of urgency, the foundations for corporate sustainability in Sweden and elsewhere were started long ago. We recognize that big challenges demand big-picture thinking and bold solutions—they require exponential outcomes.

In the earnest nature of Swedes, they are set on figuring out a better way. In the following pages we offer a *smörgåsbord*[9] of themes to showcase the Swedish approach to corporate sustainability that we believe can offer some inspiration to other leaders.

Small but Mighty

Sweden may be relatively small, compared to the much larger economies of the world, but its influence has been significant. As a small but well-respected player on the global scene, the country and its business leaders are accustomed to forming alliances to leverage change—a useful attribute when it comes to tackling complex challenges.

Because Sweden's prosperity is highly dependent on exports, Swedes are generally outward-looking. The reliance on exports means Swedish companies need to be flexible and adaptable, and yet competitive enough to command a global footprint, to be relevant and survive, especially alongside much larger nations like the US, Germany, China, and Japan.

The Wallenberg family is a leading Swedish business family with investments in most of the country's blue-chip companies. Jacob Wallenberg, the chair of Investor AB, the industrial holding company arm of the family, has reflected on what makes Swedish companies leaders despite the small size of their motherland:

> It is interesting to look at Swedish companies; broadly speaking, we have a disproportionate number of large companies in this country. These companies have one thing in common. They are highly focused, and they are world leaders. The point is that you focus on a few things and make sure that you are really, really good at those things. Then you can survive, and you can become a world leader. How do you continuously develop a company? If you connect that to coming from a small country and being totally dependent on international trade, we are subject to the most severe competition you can think of as you enter the rest of the world. You have no defense other than being as good as possible. You have to focus on excellence and being a world leader.

Considering that Swedes represent just 0.13 percent of the global population, the Nordic nation has a disproportionate amount of influence on global innovation. Sweden tops several indices when it comes to innovation. It is typically in the top five in Bloomberg's "Innovation Index," ranking the 60 most innovative economies worldwide (fifth place in 2020).[10] Further, Sweden is the EU's Innovation Leader 2019 according to the Innovation Union Scoreboard, an index published by the European Commission.[11] It earned the number two spot among 126 economies in the 2019 Global Innovation Index from the World Intellectual Property Organization.[12] Sweden invests more than 3 percent of the country's GDP in R&D, more than many other countries, particularly in the fields of sustainable technology and life sciences.

In support of that creativity, entrepreneurship is enshrined in Swedish law. For the past two decades, full-time workers with permanent jobs have enjoyed the right to take a six-month leave of absence to launch a company (or alternatively, to study or to look after a relative). Their employers can reject the request only if there are crucial operational reasons that they can't manage without a staff member, or if the new business is viewed as direct competition. After the leave period, employees are expected to be able to return to their previous positions.[13]

So, it is perhaps no coincidence that Stockholm has earned the reputation of the startup capital of the world, particularly in ICT and tech. With global successes like Skype, Spotify, MineCraft, Candy Crush, iZettle, and Klarna, Stockholm boasts the largest number of billion-dollar startups in Europe. After Silicon Valley, the Swedish capital is the most prolific tech hub in the world on a per capita basis.[14]

In the areas of peace and security, sustainability, and human development, Sweden also punches above its weight. One of the early architects of the United Nations was Swedish diplomat Dag Hammarskjöld, who became the second Secretary-General of the UN in 1953, the only Nobel Peace Prize Laureate to have been awarded the distinction posthumously.[15] Former Secretary-General Kofi Annan said of Hammarskjöld that he had "done more to shape public expectations of the office" of Secretary General and the UN than any other person in its history.[16] In another world first, the inaugural UN Conference on the Human Environment was held in Stockholm in 1972 and the Swedish government has been a key supporter of the UN Global Compact, the world's largest corporate sustainability initiative, since it was launched in 2000.

Over and above its ongoing commitment to the UN, Sweden has long been committed to doing its share (some would say even more than its share) to address poverty and development. In terms of Official Development Assistance (ODA), Sweden is the largest donor in proportion to the size of its economy; in absolute terms, it is the sixth largest donor country, maintaining a long-term commitment to spend at least 1 percent of its gross national income on ODA since 2008.[17] And in terms of contributions to science, the arts, and letters, the Nobel Prize is widely considered the world's most prestigious award and has become synonymous with Sweden's respect for scholarship, innovation, entrepreneurship, and world-changing contributions to humankind.[18]

What's in a Word?

That a culture which promotes innovation, entrepreneurship, diplomacy, equality, diversity, inclusion, privacy, and respect for the individual also turns out to be a fertile platform for corporate sustainability leadership should perhaps come as no surprise. It's even embedded in the language.

The Swedish term for business is *näringsliv*, which directly translates to "nurturing life." Göran Gennvi is an executive strategic consultant and founder of Nature Academy Learning Lab, where relevant leadership development is held in the form of Nature Quests. Göran often reminds Swedes of the power of their language. One example is *hushålla med knappa resurser*, literally, to run your household economy on limited resources. Göran says when he mentions the term to finance managers or executives, "they get it. They understand that all resources—financial, human and natural—have to be used efficiently and in combination to create the possibility for a sustainable business and planet."

One word in particular captures both an admirable and a challenging trait: *lagom*. Pronounced LAH-gum, the term translates to "not too little, not too much" or "just right." It can be variously translated as "in moderation," or "in balance." With its emphasis on "just enough," the phrase can be interpreted as embracing a middle ground in life. The Swedish proverb *Lagom är bäst* literally means "The right amount is best." In Sweden people joke about a clothing size called "extra medium," which is supposed to fit the entire nation.[19]

Global Strategist at Omnicom Group Mark Boutros, while American-born, is a long-time observer and citizen of Sweden. For Mark, *lagom* is a double-edged sword. "Swedes are so shy to talk about their sustainability or corporate social responsibility attributes, afraid of someone saying 'You are not doing it good enough,' or 'You have made this mistake,' or they are reticent to talk about their accomplishments in sustainability in a way that an American competitor might talk about more aggressively. It's hard to be lagom in a Lady Gaga world." But *lagom* is a fundamental value that infuses how Swedes approach most things.

A Model for Inclusive Growth

Nothing could be more *lagom* than the Swedish model. Described as a strategy for inclusive growth, Sweden's middle way with its social democracy objective is to increase prosperity for the benefit of all, while safeguarding the autonomy and independence of citizens. It consists of three fundamental pillars: a labor market that that facilitates adjustment to change, a universal welfare policy, and an economic policy that promotes openness and stability.[20]

According to Jeffrey Sachs, University Professor and Director of the Center for Sustainable Development at Columbia University and Director of the UN Sustainable Development Solutions Network:

Sweden's social democratic ethos said, "We want to invent a better social model." It was a rather deliberate idea of social engineering in the right way. The goal originally was not environmental, rather it was social inclusion, social justice, and industrial peace. But that meant that Sweden began experimenting and inventing a system that nobody else had, but in a very moderate way. From the 1930s through the 1960s, the economic model alone was innovative and very normative, in the sense of saying "We're not leaving things to the market, we're trying to achieve certain objectives, a fair society, socially inclusive, developing technology, being internationally competitive."

By most accounts, that model has been successful. By international comparison, Sweden is a prosperous country whose wealth is evenly distributed. A sense of a responsibility to do your share extends to the country's generous immigration policies, although these have been tested in recent years with record-breaking numbers of asylum seekers arriving in 2015.[21]

As a "third way between savage capitalism and unrealistic socialism,"[22] the Swedish Model could be exactly what the world needs, according to Sue Reid, Principal Advisor—Finance at Mission2020, a global campaign convened by global climate change leader Christina Figueres.

> In the U.S. and some other countries, Sweden is seen as having a government system that is not American and socialist. That's a barrier that needs to be broken through to translate Swedish sustainability leadership, which is quite real and quite impressive, to correct these misperceptions and beliefs, so that Sweden's leadership gets broader traction as a role model for long-term viability, economically and otherwise. Sweden is one of the few countries that's kind of figured it out in terms of how to exert leadership on sustainability, fully taking into account the equitable equation and how people are situated in society. Together, these qualities build real resilience.

Part of how Sweden has figured it out is a social welfare model that has at its core free education and healthcare for all its citizens. What Swedes may take for granted is not a given in many other countries and it sets the foundation for success in so many other areas: for skilled employment, innovation, and entrepreneurship to sustainability and thriving communities. Because work-life balance is considered important, Swedes have among the world's most generous annual paid leave allowance at 25 days per year[23] (and often more, depending on union membership), stemming from a long history of respecting the rights of workers.

Sweden also leads in its parental leave policy, the most generous in the world, with parents entitled to share 480 days—or around 16 months—paid leave following the birth or adoption of a child.[24] Some 80 percent of Swedes are employed, the highest employment rate in the European Union,[25] and among all OECD countries, Sweden is near the very top when it comes to female labor force participation relative to males.[26] Tax-financed child care has been critical to achieving this high number of women in the workforce.[27] Today Sweden has closed 82.2 percent of its overall gender gap, according to the World Economic Forum's Gender Gap Index.[28] It is fitting, then, that Sweden has the first feminist government in the world, "as a human right and a matter of democracy and justice."[29]

Sustainability at Top of the Agenda

Championing sustainability is something almost all Swedes will tell you is part of their DNA. Sweden has long shown leadership across the fields of environment, sustainability, and human rights. Since the mid-1990s, Sweden has been one of the few industrialized countries to achieve the absolute decoupling of economic growth and greenhouse gas (GHG) emissions: a rising economy paired with falling emission levels. Sweden's GHG emissions are among the lowest in the EU and OECD, whether calculated per capita or as a proportion of GDP.[30] In 1995, Sweden became one of the first countries to introduce a carbon tax,[31] and nearly all energy in Sweden is carbon-free, with 54 percent renewable, the highest percentage in the EU.[32] Sweden has set a goal to become one of the first fossil-free nations, with a zero-emissions vision for 2045.[33] It also scores well in other aspects of sustainable living, such as low air-pollution, high consumption of eco-labeled food and second-hand items, and high recycling rates.[34]

Sustainability advocate Jeffrey Sachs puts it this way:

> Sweden has really been the pioneer of sustainable development from the start. The Swedish model is fair, inclusive, clean, and technologically sophisticated. Sweden brings the technological approaches to these questions, and that's what we really need. We need basically to deploy technologies. I'm not a huge fan of the degrowth agenda, although it depends on how all these terms are defined and so forth. But I take growth to mean progress in quality of life and living standards, which I think can be accomplished, through technological improvements and a social inclusion framework. And this is basically the social democratic approach of Sweden.

The results speak for themselves. From environmental health to competitiveness, Sweden is near the top of innumerable sustainability international rankings:

- First place in the following: top national green economy plan among 20 nations from the Green Economy Coalition launched at the World Economic Forum 2020;[35] the Global Sustainable Competitiveness Index 2019 for the fourth consecutive year; the world's Most Reputable Country in 2018, which examines the 55 largest countries on ethics, perception of corruption, aesthetic-beauty, and that "feel-good" factor;[36] among OECD countries in the 2019 Sustainable Development Index for its implementation of the SDGs;[37] and the RobecoSAM Country Sustainability Ranking (2018 and 2019).[38]
- Third out of 180 countries in the Corruption Perception Index 2019.[39]
- Fourth in the Good Country Index, which ranked it four of 162 on everything from living standards to environmental sustainability,[40] and in the Rule of Law Index 2019.[41]
- Seventh of 189 countries in the Human Development Index 2018.[42]

Denmark, Norway, and Finland can also routinely be found at the top of these lists. That the Nordic countries share so many leadership traits makes perfect sense to Jeffrey Sachs. "The neighborhood is friendly that way," he observes.

> Denmark, Norway, and Finland all have a shared perspective on this, so there's a lot of interchange, and a shared framework and we just hear a lot of good ideas coming from the Nordic region. It makes a very big difference. All of the Nordic countries are making longer-term plans. That's also a core feature of Scandinavian or Nordic politics, that the region is stable enough to have a long-term view, which is not the case for many countries. I think in Sweden you couldn't find— as far I know—a climate-denying company, or you couldn't find a lobby that would say "slow down!" Everybody wants to solve problems in a practical way. Maybe everyone's just scared of Greta, but whatever it is, we don't want to be scolded!

Respect for Nature

Whether it is really a fear of being scolded, or rather the desire to do the right thing, Swedes by and large share a fundamental respect for the planet, tied to their basic affinity for nature, something that runs deep in the Swedish soul— and contained in yet a few more essential Swedish terms. More than 80 percent of Swedes lives within five kilometers of a national park, nature reserve, or other nature conservation area.[43] The idea of *friluftsliv* (nature-based outdoor recreation) is a movement with its roots in the late nineteenth century.[44] Sweden is also unique in its concept of *allemansrätten*, or "universal access laws,"[45] which tosses out the concept of trespassing on private property so that anyone can enjoy the right to be anywhere in nature provided they show consideration to animals and nature. Some see this right as a symbol of what is typically Swedish and a national symbol of equality.[46]

According to executive coach Göran Gennvi: "Thanks partly to *allemansrätten* and to our traditions, we have created this platform for how we relate, act and understand the world. Many decision-makers, it could be politicians or CEOs, people of power, they spend time at their summer houses in the archipelago or they go skiing or hiking in the mountains, they go hunting in the woods, fishing by the streams. They take time to be in nature" (Fig. 2.1).

Whether it's expressed in their fervent support of conservation or the way they enjoy the wide, open spaces and the forests that cover more than half of the country's total land area, Swedes are proud of their country's leadership in sustainability. Almost 80 percent of Swedish citizens believe that it is important that Sweden is a pioneer and leading country in environmental and climate work.[47] At the same time, Swedes think deeply about the impact of their lifestyles on the environment. Research from Nordic ecolabel showed that 40

Fig. 2.1 Göran Gennvi in water (© Göran Gennvi). Executive coach Göran Gennvi, who leads business leaders on nature quests, takes the Swedes' love of nature to a new extreme to highlight the dramatic consequences of climate change in a normal workday

percent of Swedes often think about sustainability when they make choices in their everyday lives, and two out of three said they are highly worried about the climate crisis (jumping to 77 percent of those under the age of 29).[48] Swedes also expect their companies to be part of the solution; one in two recognizes an increase in sustainability at their workplace, and two-thirds see the company's sustainability engagement and work as crucial when they choose an employer.[49]

All of this adds up to a decided "brand advantage" for Swedish companies but naturally, they're reluctant to make that claim as it would be committing that cardinal sin of "bragging" about Swedish values and accomplishments. There's a Swedish word for that, too: *jantelagen*. More like a moral code, *jantelagen* dictates that you should not think you are better than anyone else and Swedes are quick to call out anyone who breaks this norm. The origin of Jantelagen—or The Law of Jante in English—is from a rule-abiding town called Jante, featured in a novel by Norwegian-Danish author Aksel Sandemose in 1933. But academic Stephen Trotter writes that it is essentially a mechanism for social control—not pretending to know more than you do or acting above your station—and that includes talking about your wealth.[50]

Not bragging or being too flashy keeps everyone grounded and removes the discomfort people might feel in group settings. It's a society where politicians travel by subway, bus, or train like everyone else and a CEO or prime minister are as likely as anyone else to wash up the coffee cups in the break room. In keeping with this, Swedish executives also like to keep things down to earth. Their employees call them by their first names. They're more likely to dress casually and leave the suits at home; they don't admire arrogance and don't generally put on airs. A Swedish luxury is typically a sailboat for cruising the Stockholm archipelago or a country house. Other values generally matter more than high salaries. Total pay for top executives in Sweden and Denmark is about 75 percent of the European average, and lower again in Norway and Finland, according to data from management consultancy Hay Group (Fig. 2.2).[51]

The adherence to *jantelagen* runs deep in the Swedish soul. As Henrik reflects,

> Part of our culture is that we're very wary of what other people think of us. I think there's something in Swedish behavior that makes us sensitive to what others think about us. We want to be the best pupil in the class, maybe because we are small country and the only way for us to stay relevant is that we are really good at what we do. We place a big judgement on ourselves. We don't want someone to point fingers at us and say, "You haven't done your homework or

Fig. 2.2 Osvald Bjelland, founder and CEO of advisory firm Xynteo, and his brother Sveinung Bjelland at their sheep farm in Bjelland, Norway (©Osvald Bjelland). They take a long-term perspective: "Most of us from the Nordic countries come from a history of hard work and survival, and that's not long ago. I am an active sheep farmer today and I love it. We have lived there with our neighbors for hundreds of years. And they are likely to be there for another few hundred years"

your part, you should be ashamed." On the other hand, you don't want to come across as a bully or someone who is overconfident, because one day you may not be so successful or might make a mistake. It's a little bit looked down on if you are bragging too much; that's not seen as something positive.

In fact, at this point in our Prologue, Henrik already thinks we are boasting too much about Sweden. But Elaine, an American who has spent close to 20 years living in her adopted country, thinks we still haven't done true justice to describing the Swedish commitment to sustainability.

A Responsibility to Lead

Swedes acknowledge that the benefits of a safe, peaceful, and stable democracy, which provides every citizen with the basic needs for what they need not only to survive but to thrive, give the country an enviable launch pad for leading in sustainability.

"I think honestly we probably should avoid pounding our own chest too much, but I think there are a couple of things that are relevant and the one that is most important, and the one we shouldn't forget, is the Maslow Needs Hierarchy," Jonas Samuelsson, CEO of Electrolux, explains. According to Maslow's hierarchy of needs (1943), once a society has met its basic physiological needs (food, water, warmth, rest) and safety needs (security, safety) and psychological needs (belonginess and love, self-esteem, and self-actualization), it is in a better position to lead in other areas.[52] "Once you cover your material needs, then the emotional and maybe the societal needs become more important," Jonas says. "As societies progress up that staircase, things like the environment become more important. Sweden, Scandinavia and Northern Europe in general have reached further on that journey than many others. So just by that alone, we have to be leaders, I think."

This resonates with the younger Swedes we interviewed, and whom you'll meet in these pages, like Elsa Bernadotte, Co-founder and President of food waste startup Karma, and Niklas Adalberth, founder of the successful e-commerce firm Klarna and now a leading tech investor in social impact in the Nordics at Norrsken Foundation. Neither categorizes privilege as simply financial wealth, as other cultures might. For them, privilege is defined as the safety and security that they grew up with, and the access to free health and education which afforded them a healthy, productive start in life and helped lead to their eventual success (Fig. 2.3).

Can't We All Agree?

The recognition that we all have to get along if we're going to save the planet is a natural manifestation of the Swedish tendency toward cooperation rather than competition and a dislike of conflict. It is true for the Swedish management style as well: consensus is as much the Scania way as the Swedish way, Henrik says.

Fig. 2.3 A love of nature is something that runs deep in the Swedish soul, and it starts at a young age (photograph by Henrik Henrikkson). Henrik's children explore the beauty of one of the country's iconic, wide-open spaces: the golden yellow of a rape-seed field in spring

There is something in our culture at Scania where you deeply respect people's knowledge and you are comfortable delegating responsibility. There is a belief at Scania that management *doesn't* know best. We listen to the experts and to the people that are the most knowledgeable. I don't assume I know everything. In many cases, if you delegate an issue upwards, you delegate to someone who knows less on the subject.

Henrik has observed both benefits and drawbacks to the consensus-style approach.

The potential weakness I see with consensus is that when we need to make a big change in direction or priorities, there are a lot of people you need to convince. It is not enough that you, at the top, simply tell people, "Let's go right" or "let's go left." There will be slow progress. People want to understand why. So, you invest your time to explain and answer why—many times. But the payoff is that the engagement becomes more long term, because you've taken your time to get them to really understand the situation or decision at hand. And then implementation goes fast, it's unstoppable, like a snowball.

In Elaine's words:

You get the involvement of everyone, with consensus-driven approach. In a consensus-driven culture, if someone doesn't feel they own something, they're not really feeling responsible for it and nothing happens. It's not without frustration and it was hard for me in the beginning as an American. But I learned that while it often takes longer to reach a decision, once a decision is taken, it is usually well-anchored across all stakeholder groups, and implementation happens swiftly. Compare that to a more hierarchical company culture, where a decision could be more like an order, and you might spend a lot more time dealing with discontent or people not following the decision after the fact.

Perhaps one of the things which most strikes outsiders about the Swedish corporate culture is a management style that is non-hierarchical, with a comparatively flat structure. And while there are many cultural differences around the world and theories for how to successfully run a company, the Swedish model with its decentralized approach has been quite effective, rendering leaders more accessible and fostering practices that are in the main more transparent.

"Part of that is the willingness and the openness to change and I think the Nordic culture facilitates that," argues Christian Sinding, a Norwegian who is the CEO of global investment organization and private equity firm EQT, based in Sweden. "We have this very open and transparent society where if there is an issue, you can put it on the table and speak about it and people will debate it. I think that's quite healthy and since it happens in society it also happens in companies."

The idea of cooperative advantage is enshrined in the Scandinavian culture, according to Robert Strand, Assistant Professor of Leadership and Sustainability with the Copenhagen Business School and a visiting scholar with the Center for Responsible Business at the University of California-Berkeley Haas School of Business. Strand has written extensively about the deep-seated traditions of stakeholder engagement across Scandinavia, asserting that the concept of "creating shared value" has Scandinavian origins.

"If Scandinavian companies have long practiced shared value strategies with considerable success, why has nobody noticed?" Strand asks. "The short answer is that Scandinavian companies demonstrate a tendency toward 'walking the walk' before 'talking the talk.' "[53]

With a final nod to that famous Swedish modesty, we introduce you to the leaders and the companies who have walked the walk and who will be sharing their sustainability journeys with you in the course of this book. As we say in Swedish, *välkommen*! Which, of course, means Welcome!

Notes

1. Anita Balakrishnan, "NYSE says it briefly flew a Swiss flag to honor Spotify—which is a Swedish company," April 3, 2018, CNBC, https://www.cnbc.com/2018/04/03/spotify-ipo-nyse-flies-swiss-flag%2D%2Dthe-wrong-country.html.
2. Time 2019 Person of the Year, Greta Thunberg, *Time Magazine*, accessed Dec 1, 2019, https://time.com/person-of-the-year-2019-greta-thunberg/.
3. Fridays For Future, Greta Thunberg:—Everybody is welcome, everybody is needed!, accessed July 17. 2019
    https://www.fridaysforfuture.org/.
4. Sandra Laville and Jonathan Watts, "Across the globe, millions join biggest climate protest ever," *The Guardian*, Sept 20, 2019, https://www.theguardian.com/environment/2019/sep/21/across-the-globe-millions-join-biggest-climate-protest-ever.
5. "COP25: Protesters call for action at Madrid climate rally," DW, accessed March 22, 2020, https://www.dw.com/en/cop25-protesters-call-for-action-at-madrid-climate-rally/a-51565278.
6. Extinction Rebellion, Act Now, accessed 17 July, 2019, https://rebellion.earth/act-now/.
7. Brilliant Minds, https://brilliantminds.co.
8. Charlie Smith, "Swedish teenager Greta Thunberg urges wealthy people to stop stealing others' carbon budgets," Straight Talk, Vancouver Free Press, June 23, 2019, https://www.straight.com/news/1258421/video-swedish-teenager-greta-thunberg-urges-wealthy-people-stop-stealing-others-carbon.
9. *Smörgåsbord* is a type of Scandinavian meal, originating in Sweden, served buffet-style with multiple hot and cold dishes of various foods on a table. In the global lexicon, it has also come to refer to a number of different things that are combined together as a whole.
10. Iman Ghosh, "Ranked: The Most Innovative Economies in the World," Visual Capitalist, Feb 28, 2020, https://www.visualcapitalist.com/world-most-innovative-economies/.
11. European Innovation Scorecard 2019, European Commission, accessed April 13, 2020, https://ec.europa.eu/growth/sites/growth/files/infographic-innovation-scoreboard-2019-leaders-full-size.jpg.
12. Innovation in Sweden, the Swedish Institute, accessed March 8, 2020, https://sweden.se/business/innovation-in-sweden/.
13. Maddy Savage, "Sweden's surprising rule for time off," BBC Worklife, Feb 6, 2019, https://www.bbc.com/worklife/article/20190206-swedens-surprising-rule-for-time-off?hmsr=hackcv.com.

14. ICT and tech opportunities in Sweden, Business Sweden, The Swedish Trade and Invest Council, accessed August 10, 2019, https://www.business-sweden.se/en/invest/industries/ict.

15. Dag Hammarskjöld, The Nobel Prize, accessed January 15, 2020, https://www.nobelprize.org/prizes/peace/1961/hammarskjold/facts/.

16. Lecture by Kofi Annan on Dag Hammarskjöld and the 21st Century, United Nations Secretary General, Sept 6, 2001, accessed January 5, 2020, https://www.un.org/sg/en/content/sg/speeches/2001-09-06/lecture-kofi-annan-dag-hammarskjöld-and-21st-century.

17. Donor Tracker, accessed January 5, 2020, https://donortracker.org/country/sweden.

18. A Short Guide to The Nobel Prize, Swedish Institute, accessed January 5, 2020, https://sweden.se/society/the-nobel-prize/.

19. Altman, W. "Leadership the Sven-Goran Eriksson Way [engineering Management]." *Engineering Management Journal* 12, footnote 38.

20. The Swedish Model, Government Offices of Sweden, Ministry of Finance, accessed June 20, 2019 https://www.government.se/information-material/2017/06/the-swedish-model/.

21. Admir Skodo, "Sweden: By Turns Welcoming and Restrictive in its Immigration Policy," Migration Policy Institute, Dec 6, 2018, https://www.migrationpolicy.org/article/sweden-turns-welcoming-and-restrictive-its-immigration-policy.

22. Huw Pill, Ingrid Vogel, Petter Johnsson, and Ola Nordquist, "Welfare State and its Impact on Business Competitiveness: Sweden Inc. for Sale?" *Harvard Business Review*, 2002, https://hbr.org/product/welfare-state-and-its-impact-on-business-competitiveness-sweden-inc-for-sale/703019-PDF-ENG.

23. Annual Leave Act (1977:480), government.se, accessed June 20, 2019, https://www.government.se/4a80ac/contentassets/eaf3467d4f484c9fb7274a067484c759/1977_480-annual-leave-act.pdf.

24. World economic forum, These 4 Nordic countries hold the secret to gender equality, 2018, accessed June 20, 2019. https://www.weforum.org/agenda/2018/12/nordic-countries-women-equality-gender-pay-gap-2018.

25. Kollega, Sverige har högst sysselsättning i EU (Sweden has highest employment in the EU), accessed September, 2, 2019 https://www.kollega.se/sverige-har-hogst-sysselsattning-i-eu.

26. Labour force participate rate, by sex and age group, OECD.stat, accessed October 12, 2019, https://stats.oecd.org/index.aspx?queryid=54741.

27. "10 Things That Make Sweden Family-Friendly," The Swedish Institute, accessed October 12, 2019, https://sweden.se/society/10-things-that-make-sweden-family-friendly/.

28. World Economic Forum, The Global Gender Gap Report 2018, accessed July 8, 2019, http://www3.weforum.org/docs/WEF_GGGR_2018.pdf.

29. A Feminist Government, Government Offices of Sweden, accessed July 8, 2019, https://www.government.se/government-policy/a-feminist-government/.
30. "Sweden tackles climate change," The Swedish Institute, accessed July 8, 2019, https://sweden.se/nature/sweden-tackles-climate-change/.
31. Ben Wilde, How Sweden became the world's most sustainable country, top 5 reasons, accessed July 4, 2019, https://info.esg.adec-innovations.com/blog/how-sweden-became-the-worlds-most-sustainable-country-top-5-reasons.
32. Eurostat, Renewable energy statistics 2017, accessed July 8, 2019, https://ec.europa.eu/eurostat/statistics-explained/index.php/Renewable_energy_statistics.
33. SOU 2016:21 Ett klimatpolitiskt ramverk för Sverige (A climate framework for Sweden), Delbetänkande av Miljömålsberedningen (Partial report by the Environmental Goals Committee), accessed July 4, 2019, http://www.sou.gov.se/wp-content/uploads/2016/03/SOU_2016_21_webb.pdf.
34. How Sweden lays the foundation for sustainable manufacturing, Business Sweden, accessed 4 July 2019 https://www.business-sweden.se/en/Invest/industries/Manufacturing/sustainability/.
35. Green Economy Tracker, January 2020, accessed February 5, 2020, https://greeneconomytracker.org/policies/national-green-economy-plan.
36. Reputation Institute, 2018, accessed Nov 15, 2019, https://www.traveller.com.au/most-reputable-country-rankings-2018-reputation-institutes-list-h11t91.
37. Sachs, J., Schmidt-Traub, G., Kroll, C., Lafortune, G., Fuller, G.: *Sustainable Development Report 2019. New York: Bertelsmann Stiftung and Sustainable Development Solutions Network (SDSN).* 2019.
38. RobecoSAM, Country Sustainability Ranking Update—June 2019, accessed August 7, 2019, https://www.robecosam.com/media/5/0/1/501ef5d870cb3ce805fa16fa490e0654_20190627-robecosam-country-sustainability-ranking_tcm1011-20021.pdf; RobecoSAM, Country Sustainability Ranking Update, November 2018 Available at: https://www.robecosam.com/media/9/7/2/97240b9afc893d103d558ce50f066bc5_2018-11-robecosam-country-sustainability-ranking-en_tcm1011-16188.pdf.
39. Corruption Perceptions Index 2018, Transparency International, accessed August 7, 2019, https://www.transparency.org/cpi2018.
40. Rule of Law Index 2019, World Justice Project, accessed August 7, 2019 https://worldjusticeproject.org/sites/default/files/documents/ROLI-2019-Reduced.pdf.
41. Good Country Index, accessed August 7, 2019, https://www.goodcountry.org/index/results.

42. United Nations Development Programme, Human Development Indices and Indicators 2018 Statistical Update. 2018, accessed August 7, 2019, http://hdr.undp.org/sites/default/files/2018_summary_human_development_statistical_update_en.pdf.
43. Sweden, Swedes Loves Nature, Accessed 11 July 2019, https://sweden.se/nature/swedes-love-nature/.
44. Thomas H. Beery. Nordic in nature: friluftsliv and environmental connectedness, Environmental Education Research, (2012) 19:1, 94–117. https://doi.org/10.1080/13504622.2012.688799.
45. Naturvårdsverket, allemansrätten, accessed July 5, 2019, https://www.naturvardsverket.se/allemansratten.
46. Dahl, G. Wildflowers, Nationalism and the Swedish law of commons. Worldviews: Environment, culture, religion 2 (p. 281). 1998. Cambridge: The White Horse Press.
47. Regeringen, Uppdrag Framtid: Omställning till hållbarhet och konkurrenskraft. (Government: Future Assignment: Revision for Sustainability and Competitiveness), accessed July 5, 2019, https://www.regeringen.se/497fe3/contentassets/035bacd87b9f4ab887c5120bffede83d/slut_rapport_sammanfattning_omstallninghallbarhetkonkurrenskraft-tillg.pdf.
48. Expressen, Stor mätning: Det tycker svenskarna om klimatet, (Big measurement: This is what Swedes think about the climate), accessed August 6, 2019, https://www.expressen.se/nyheter/qs/stor-matning-det-tycker-svenskarna-om-klimatet/.
49. Nordic Ecolabel, Strategies for sustainable business development—The Report. 2019, accessed August 6, 2019, https://www.svanen.se/siteassets/rapporter%2D%2Dundersokningar/the-report/rapport_a4_svanen_190628.pdf.
50. Maddy Savage, "Jantelagen: Why Swedes won't talk about wealth," BBC Worklife, Oct 9, 2019, https://www.bbc.com/worklife/article/20191008-jantelagen-why-swedes-wont-talk-about-wealth.
51. Lower CEO Pay and Better Results in Europe?, CNBC, accessed September 2, 2019, https://www.cnbc.com/id/100540655.
52. Saul McLeod, "Maslow's Hierarcy of Needs," updated 2018, *Simply Psychology*, accessed September 2019, https://www.simplypsychology.org/maslow.html.
53. Robert Strand, "Scandinavia can be an inspiration for creating shared value," *The Financial Times*, April 25, 2014, https://www.ft.com/content/84bbd770-b34d-11e3-b09d-00144feabdc0.

Part I

Sustainability Leadership Model 1.0: The Foundation

As you embark on your sustainability journey, we recommend having a few fundamental building blocks in place. These basic building blocks comprise 1.0, the Foundation of the Sustainability Leadership Model, and set the stage for everything that follows.

Clarifying and setting a company's purpose, and aligning it with culture and values, is the first step. It establishes the "why" and determines the direction of travel. We also set the basic expectations for sustainability leadership, such as knowing the company's footprint and what matters to stakeholders in order to set the right priorities. Last but not least, we argue that successful, purpose-driven businesses are built on trust and transparency. And trust starts with personal leadership.

The companies and organizations that feature in this section of the book are: Karma, Scania, Electrolux, SAS, Telia Company, Volkswagen, Ericsson, Verizon, Houdini, Northvolt, Xynteo, and Norrsken Foundation.

3

Purpose-driven Leadership

Up Close: Elsa Bernadotte, CEO of Food Waste Startup Karma on Finding Purpose

They were about to see their brand-new startup go off the cliff. Elsa Bernadotte and her three partners, all young Swedish entrepreneurs, had to admit that their online deals platform (think crowd-sourced Groupon) was not thriving. The platform had become so diluted it was tricky to navigate. They had three weeks to find a way to save their company before they ran out of money. When they looked hard at their data, the answer was right under their noses: the most popular deals on the platform were discounted offers on food from supermarkets and restaurants that would otherwise go to waste. They dug a little deeper and were astounded to discover a third of all food worldwide is wasted, resulting in 1.3 billion tons of waste worldwide. That amounted to $1 trillion in losses annually, with 30 percent of the food waste coming directly from retailers like restaurants and cafes. As far as they could see, no one was solving this problem on a global basis. And so, the Karma app was born, connecting restaurants, cafés, and grocery stores with users eager to purchase unsold food at a lower price. "That's when we realized our true purpose as a company: to become The First Zero Food Waste Generation," Elsa, Karma's President and Chief Operating Officer, says. "With the deals platform, we saw a huge potential but then, we asked ourselves, 'What problem are we solving? Does it matter if it exists or not?' Once we saw the potential with food waste, it felt like we had found what we were meant to do, and everything clicked."

For Elsa and the other founders, Hjalmar Ståhlberg Nordegren, Ludvig Berling, and Mattis Larsson, their calling came in the nick of time. While the financial circumstances demanded they act, they are part of a generation driven by a search for purpose—and tackling food waste fulfilled that vision.

© The Author(s) 2020
H. Henriksson, E. Weidman Grunewald, *Sustainability Leadership*,
https://doi.org/10.1007/978-3-030-42291-2_3

"It was in 2016 when we made that pivot and we had no funding left. We went back to our existing investors who were excited by the idea. We were able to raise a new small seed round." Those investors included Norrsken Foundation and Sweden-based investment company Kinnevik, bringing the total amount raised by Karma to date to $18 million. It was a purpose that resonated not only with investors but with customers, too. Since launching, Karma has attracted 1.2 million app users in 225 cities in Sweden, the UK, and France, working with 6700 retailers. As of April 2020, Karma said it had saved over two million meals, diverted over 1000 tons of edible food from landfill, and reduced CO_2 levels caused by food waste by 1500 tons[1] (Fig. 3.1).

But don't make the mistake of confusing Karma with a social impact venture, even if its vision is to eliminate food waste in the whole food value chain. Elsa, with a hint of the impatience that comes from her youthful energy to make change happen *fast*, explains:

> When you talk about sustainability and you are working with social impact, people ask, "So you are a nonprofit, then?" and when we say, "No, we're a

Fig. 3.1 A customer picking up a Karma purchase (© Karma). For Swedish food waste startup Karma, the purpose is clear: to become The First Zero Food Waste Generation. The Karma app connects restaurants, cafés, and grocery stores with users eager to purchase unsold food at a lower price, rescuing food that would otherwise be thrown away

for-profit company," they ask "How are you going to make a profit?" And we reply, "Why wouldn't we make a profit? It's a massive problem, a trillion-dollar opportunity, and we have found a way to solve it and the solution is good for everyone involved." People think if you want to be impact driven it has to be a nonprofit but that's not the case anymore. We make sustainability profitable. If we want to have impact on a global scale, we have to be a profitable company.

A Generation Searching for Meaning

By 2025 millennials (born between 1980 and 2000) will represent 75 percent of the workforce[2] and many studies show that, for this generation, having a clear purpose is no longer a nice-to-have or feel-good perk, but an essential element of their career path. A PwC study found that millennials who have a strong connection to the purpose of their organization are 5.3 times more likely to stay.[3]

Growing up in a world of globalization, disruption, the threat of climate change, and lack of trust in traditional institutions, millennials want to be part of something bigger and are seeking meaning, rallying around important causes and looking for authenticity.[4] Their top purchasing drivers include the products they buy being made by a company they trust, being environmentally friendly and demonstrating commitment to social values.[5]

Even more than millennials, the generation that follows, Gen Z (born between 1996 and 2010) could be called "The Purpose Generation," according to a survey that found meaningful work and pride in their organization to be among their key work values.[6] This is a sizeable population with a lot of influence; Gen Z is nearly 65-million-strong in the US alone and represent 40 percent of total US consumers.[7] Of course, it's not just younger generations who care about company values: according to Deloitte, nearly three-quarters (73 percent) of employees who work for a purpose-driven organization are engaged, compared to less than a quarter (23 percent) of employees at organizations not driven by purpose.[8]

Given the values and buying power of younger generations, it is no coincidence that so many next-generation companies in Sweden have sustainability in their DNA and at the core of their operations. Walk into Karma's offices in Stockholm, tucked just beyond the entrance to the city's main train terminal, Central Station, and the first thing you'll notice is a huge sign emblazoned with the slogan "The Zero Food Waste Generation." It's a purpose that has helped the company grow quickly, attracting like-minded, mostly younger, people (many of them millennials like the founders) to work for Karma (Fig. 3.2).

For Elsa Bernadotte, having a purpose at work comes so naturally that she has to pause to think about where that motivation comes from. "In Sweden, there is a big focus on the collective rather than the individual, compared to the US, for instance and that is perhaps a driver for us, as purpose-driven companies—looking at social issues we can solve," she reflects.

She is well aware of the privilege of her upbringing, in a country that has been at peace for over 200 years, with a strong social safety net and a well-ordered and well-functioning society.

I never had to grow up fearing for my life because of the risk of war. I am part of a generation that has grown up with a safe environment and so you have room to look and think outside your own safety net. That could be why we are seeing more of the younger generation in Sweden starting companies with a social mission, as you have the time to think about it.

Fig. 3.2 The Karma team (© Karma). With its millennial founders, the Karma team are part of a generation driven by a search for purpose. That influences where they work, what they buy, and whom they trust

In fact, as we described in the Prologue, Elsa echoes a number of Swedes of both younger and older generations who recognize their high standing in Maslow's Hierarchy of Needs and are therefore in a better position to lead in other areas.

Niklas Adalberth, founder of the successful e-commerce startup Klarna who left to start the Norrsken Foundation, an incubator for social impact entrepreneurs, shares a similar perspective (for more on Niklas' journey from Burger King employee to tech billionaire, see Chap. 11). As he says: "I was born in one of the best countries in the world, with lovely parents, a free education, the employees I hired benefit from free education and free healthcare. I've worked long and hard for this success, but I've also been lucky."

It's not just the younger generations who expect to see companies demonstrating a purpose beyond profit. Consumers are increasingly making purchase decisions based on a brand's purpose. According to a survey by Accenture, 62 percent of customers want companies to take a stand on issues like sustainability, transparency, and fair employment practices.[9] This is also true for employees. The same study showed that two-thirds of workers considered that a company talking about purpose but not living it would have a negative impact on their work by causing distrust in leaders and reducing productivity. Almost half said the perceived hypocrisy makes them want to leave their company.

Finding True Purpose

So, what is it that purpose-driven individuals, across all generations, share in common and what does it mean to be a purpose-driven company?

Here is how we define purpose: *Purpose is the one thing that a company can do better than anyone else that brings value to society; it is a cause greater than profit.* A purpose is strong when it feels true, reflects the culture of the organization, and builds on the company's core existence. When the purpose also has a clear focus on how the company can contribute to society, then it has the potential to transform a company—in whatever direction it chooses to take.

Earning a profit is a definition of a company but not its purpose. Purpose-driven leaders evangelize the cause that resonates with their business and make it their passion. They ensure that the purpose guides decision-making, and permeates core business operations, at all levels. A purpose-driven CEO sets the tone at the top and engages his or her organization in the cause itself. In our view for a sustainability ambition to truly take off, it must be reflected and articulated in the company purpose, culture, and values.

Distinguishing between a purpose that is authentic versus just another branding exercise has been the subject of much analysis. As more companies adopt purpose statements and leaders opportunistically pepper their conversations with "purpose" catchphrases, they run the risk of mere "purpose washing" and missing the real power that purpose can bring to an organization.

For many companies, the purpose journey starts with the corporate culture, where deeply embedded founding values around engagement, accountability, innovation, and corporate heritage can help to anchor purpose. In other cases, such as for startups like Karma, it is the purpose that shapes the culture. This is backed up by recent research published in *The Harvard Business Review* which showed that purpose is as strong a driver in high-growth companies as creating new markets and serving broader stakeholder needs. Two distinct strategies for developing purpose emerged from the research: retrospective or prospective.[10]

The retrospective approach:

- Builds on firm's existing reason for being
- Requires you look back, understand the organizational culture, makes sense of firm's past
- Focus of the process is internal and historical
- You might ask questions like: Where did we come from? What makes us unique to stakeholders? In what ways does our DNA open up future opportunities?

The prospective approach:

- Reshapes reason for being
- Focus of process is external and forward-looking
- Requires you to "take stock of the broader ecosystem in which you want to work, and assess your potential for impact in it"
- Making sense of the future
- Might ask questions like: What can we do? Which trends affect our business? What new needs, opportunities, risks can we foresee? What can we do to open up opportunities that we believe in?
- Can be especially useful for new CEOs

Either avenue can be effective. A CEO can lead a purpose journey by looking forward and defining a new direction, or by reflecting back on the original, historical purpose within the company. The optimum approach will depend on company context. Combining both approaches provides an opportunity to think about what the organization is today, and what it could be. A strong purpose-driven culture is the starting point to shift from a linear or incremental sustainability approach to a transformative one.

Done well, purpose can truly transform corporate culture. If a purpose is authentic, it shines a light on inconsistencies, weaknesses, and gaps in corporate culture, making it stronger and helping the organization to pull together in the same direction. This starts with the CEO being purpose-driven and demonstrating consistently and authentically that sustainability is a priority for the company. That purpose-driven leadership starts at the top is one of our most simply stated and fundamental pieces of advice for a successful sustainability leadership journey. Our experience points to three key elements of authentic corporate sustainability leadership—culture, values, and purpose. These are inseparable, reinforce each other, and are a precondition for bringing an organization's sustainability commitment to life. That is as true for a startup like Karma as it is for companies with 100-year legacies like Scania, Electrolux, and Ericsson that can draw on a long history and heritage of purpose in society.

Successful purpose-driven leaders are trusted, credible in their belief in their purpose, and unwavering in their commitment to ethics and transparency. They need to empower their leaders in turn, and make it clear that engagement is expected. If the CEO commitment to sustainability is genuine and engagement with stakeholders is consistent and powerful, the likelihood of success and transformation is great. Many studies point to the importance of commitment and engagement from the CEO as a driving force in a company's sustainability work.[11]

It is worth investing the time and effort to get purpose "right." Several studies show that purpose-driven companies are more successful across multiple dimensions, and are more attractive to customers, to employees and to investors. For example, an analysis of "purposeful" companies by the Corporate Board/EY Global Leadership Forecast found that purposeful companies outperform the stock market by 42 percent while companies without a sense of purpose within their vision or mission underperform the market by 40 percent. The comparison evaluated companies that simply have a purpose statement and which deliver average performance against those which embed purpose in everything they do.[12]

The opposite is also true: purpose can backfire if a leader is not authentic, or purpose is not well grounded in the organization. "What ultimately kills purpose is when the core business—the activities from which it actually makes money—does not fit with the purpose," according to Osvald Bjelland, founder of Xynteo, an Oslo-based advisory firm that specializes in empowering leaders and businesses for transformation. He adds: "No team will reorient its culture to support a particular purpose if they are being measured daily against Key Performance Indicators (KPIs) that contravene that purpose."

Being Honest About Challenges

For successful sustainability leaders, transparency is king. Speaking openly about the challenges (as well as the triumphs) is key to building credibility. We have found that many company leaders are all too happy to talk about the opportunities and great things their people do but keep their challenges under a tight lid. The risk is that the challenges get out anyway or that this leadership style gets passed on to subordinates who won't dare speak up when they notice something wrong because they fear the consequences—losing their job or even litigation. Willingness to confront challenges is essential to any sustainability transformation, according to Georg Kell, founder and former Executive Director of the UN Global Compact:

> My experience has been that in any sustainability transformation, it is actually about the real leadership behind it. It is based on the committed leader who is driving very hard. I know there are many change agents who make it through to the leadership ultimately, but the fastest and best way is if the leadership has the understanding of the challenges and is willing to make the journey. Because if you don't have it, you can bang your head against the wall for a long time. Maybe you make progress here and there, maybe you make it up to change, but the fastest way is clearly leadership. It is also the ability to see the world in its full beauty and complexity.

When a situation does arise that calls into question a company's values and sustainability commitment, it's vital to face the consequences and be ready to take the costs. That may mean turning down certain business deals that don't reflect the company's culture or values or firing people who don't behave in accordance with company rules. Ultimately, it's about accountability and taking responsibility for the issues that are within a leader's power to change.

According to Osvald Bjelland: "I personally believe an organization can never go beyond the capacity or the spirit of its CEO, so if you have a locked-up, unevolved leader, there is a very strict limit to what that organization can do." As he describes it, the theory of change in an organization therefore has to occur in three steps:

First, you can only change a system if the CEO is open-minded and open to that. Second, once you are blessed with such a leader, you can unlock change in his or her organization. Third, when you have an organization that is purpose-driven and you have your foundation, you can start to change your industry and society and the system of which you are a part. That is why it is so important with that whole leadership foundation, to have leaders who see a purpose in doing something beyond themselves. So, in essence, you need to have the evolving leader, the evolving organization and the evolving industry or system or society. But only if you are able to do the first two steps can you get to number three. This is what I have learned over a lifetime and that is why it is so critical who you spend time with. For me, I spend all my time at Xynteo finding people who I believe have the capacity to do something.

Moving from Vision to Action

A sustainability-leading CEO needs to inspire the organization with a clear vision for the company; otherwise, it simply won't stick. With transformational and disruptive times ahead, having a strong purpose at the core of a company's journey, and its business strategy, is the best way to navigate future challenges.

Environmental and social responsibility had been part of the Scania approach for several years, but Henrik felt a sense of urgency to take it further. He wasn't alone: for several years prior to becoming CEO, when he was head of Sales and Marketing, Henrik and a few other senior executives in the company including Erik Ljungberg, at the time Head of Communications at Scania, had been trying to link the higher purpose of the company to sustainability. Even if not every member of Scania's top management team shared an equally fierce passion for sustainability, they could all agree on the rationale for focusing on energy efficiency—which creates great customer value (since energy/fuel is often the biggest cost). For instance, investing considerable resources into creating a platform for renewable fuels was one of the quickest ways to do something bigger and better and that got the entire team on board. As CEO, Henrik reformulated the sustainability agenda to build it into the structure of the company and accelerate the transformation journey. In the short term this was not an obvious strategy for creating customer value, but over time it created a solution that generated value for both the customer and for society.

Henrik's experience of engaging his management team (Scania's Executive Board) on sustainability is an instructive example of how to engage key individuals internally on a purpose journey. In Henrik's case, it took two years of intensive discussions and debates before the entire Executive Board was fully onboard with the idea that going forward, all of Scania's activities would be under the umbrella of sustainability—that in fact to address the greatest challenges humankind is facing, sustainability had to be at the heart of the company. In the initial discussions, it seemed the entire team shared that position. But as day-to-day decisions played out, optimizing short-term profits or conflicts with internal targets took precedence over the new company purpose.

For the next six months, Henrik worked with his team to better understand why the engagement wasn't there. It became clear that while several of his top managers shared Henrik's sense of urgency, not everyone had the same passion or personal beliefs about climate change and sustainability as the biggest driver for the company. What they could all agree on, however, was that if Scania didn't transform as a company to be more sustainable, it would sooner or later hit a tipping point where sustainability became the norm. And if Scania did not embark on a sustainability transformation journey across every aspect of the company including its products, services, and operations, it would no longer be relevant as a company. No one would buy its products or services, no one would invest in the company, and no one would want to work for Scania. And on that point, the entire Executive Board was in agreement: everyone could stand behind the notion of the need for transformation.

Scania has been able to change, evolve, and become a sustainability leader in the transport sector because its values are closely entwined with its history—and at the same time, an affirmation of the company's future direction. Transforming an existing company with a 129-year history can be a challenge; such a journey is perhaps easier with a new or younger company. But in Scania's case, as Henrik described it, it was figuring out how to transform a dinosaur.

Fortunately, the "dinosaur" had those ancient Scandinavian bones of respect, consensus, and sufficiency that lend themselves well to sustainability. That included, at the time, three core values, which just about any Scania employee will agree, are "for real": Customer first, respect for the individual, and elimination of waste. Later, determination, team spirit, and integrity were added to the core values. These are not just empty words on company pamphlets but are part of the spirit of the company. The values have been anchored in Scania's operations for generations, a way of thinking about the world, relating to others, and taking responsibility for one's actions.

With the foundation of those values and the culture, Henrik created a strong link to a new purpose—To Drive the Shift towards a Sustainable

Transport System. When people in the organization could hear and feel the connection of the purpose to Scania's long-standing core values, they recognized themselves. Sustainability then felt like a natural fit for Scania because it has everything to do with the company values and principles, and it showed where the company wanted to go. To Drive the Shift was anchored.

Henrik takes every opportunity to talk about sustainability within the organization, repeating the messages over and over again as he describes it, "like a tireless preacher." There is a risk that leaders get sick and tired of hearing their own voice when they know their team has heard this message a dozen times before, but they still do it. It might be the fourth or tenth time that the messages start to trigger thoughts and connect the sustainability journey to a specific situation or challenge in the organization that someone is wrestling with.

Make the Journey Inclusive

For Jonas Samuelsson, CEO of Electrolux, defining the purpose of leading global appliances company Electrolux—to Shape Living for the Better—was a natural continuation of the company's long sustainability journey. The process of arriving at the company purpose, which expresses both more sustainable and enjoyable living, took about four years and a great deal of engagement across all levels of the organization.

"We've been focused on sustainable solutions for more than 25 years and that is something we've been able to focus the organization on and which makes business sense in many ways," he says. "What we call our Green Spirit of more efficient and sustainable operations fit very well with the engineering soul and spirit of Electrolux of continuously improving."

He continues:

> But a very important part of our purpose is rooted in our history. We are all deeply aware and proud of the fact that Electrolux has been part of an enormous transformation in how people live their lives over the past 100 years. The liberation of women, the freeing up of enormous amounts of time from daily household chores which was hard and unhealthy in many ways. We had been proud of that heritage but had not really formulated what that meant to us a company until we began defining our purpose.

The purpose-defining journey began in 2014 with Jonas having conversations with Henrik Sundström, Vice President for Group Sustainability Affairs, to formulate the sustainability work into three distinct areas: Better Solutions, Better Operations, and Better Society. Extensive work followed involving interviews across the Group including Group Management to find alignment on the three areas and nine initiatives supporting those areas. "We spent a fair amount of time making it come to life, creating objectives as well as the words and visuals around it."

The communication part was important, he emphasized. "I think it is important to solidify and to express sustainability in simple, compelling, memorable and engaging language." The sustainability work coincided with the company's desire to express its role as a company more clearly through the purpose. The engagement and dialogue led to the purpose: "To Shape Living for the Better." The intention all along, Jonas explained, was to make the process as inclusive as possible.

> When we were done, we thought "That wasn't that hard." But actually, it was a very long process to get there. But that is why it has been so powerful, particularly internally. Wherever I go in the organization, our purpose is about the people in the company who are very proud of our purpose and feel committed to it. It has helped to focus our work and our strategy, so it's been a very powerful experience from a business perspective, too.

Other companies agree on the importance of connecting the dots for everyone. As Rickard Gustafson, CEO of SAS, sees it, getting an organization to rally around sustainability is essentially about change management.

> How do you get an organization really geared up around this? How do you rethink your purpose and your brand promise, to make this the starting point and embrace it? If sustainability does not connect to your business culture and values, it won't work. You need to start there before you can push the agenda. Initially, I think we missed this. We started, many years ago, in different directions by doing a little bit here and a little bit there, but we did not connect the sustainability dots all the way up to our purpose and brand promise. As a result, the sustainability agenda didn't really stick in our organization. It lacked trustworthiness and was confusing for our people and customers. Today, sustainability is clearly an integrated part of our purpose and our employees are engaged and proud that we demonstrate industry leadership in this important transformation. They now understand the direction that we are we going and how it all hangs together with our broader brand promise. As a consequence, our customers also recognize our efforts and start to view it as a competitive advantage for SAS.

Build a Coalition of the Willing

The likelihood of success is far higher when company sustainability initiatives are a good fit for the company culture. Scania and the organizations described above demonstrate how organizational engagement can grow when people are supported to deliver on a shared purpose. It's about building a coalition of the willing. Once internal advocates for sustainability are suitably empowered, they are more likely to take ownership. Ideally, it creates a movement—perhaps starting with only a few and then spreading throughout the organization. Not everyone will be a supporter of the sustainability agenda. Rather than spend energy to try to convert the skeptics, it can be wise to find those who are willing and passionate to create a tidal wave of change.

C-suite team members can become evangelists for sustainability when they feel aligned to the purpose. Elaine recalls how "Technology for Good" was that kind of galvanizing platform at Ericsson, where the purpose had meaning and deep commitment. It became a platform to educate and inspire 24,000 R&D personnel, frame employee engagement and volunteering, and steer use of the company's products. Technology for Good implied an intention and a direction: talking about technology for good implicitly meant working to actively prevent the bad. At the time, Elaine saw her team's primary role as providing colleagues with the fact-based sustainability information they needed to carry the message forward, and this helped amplify and ultimately drive positive sustainability ambitions at Ericsson.

Through this process, former Chief Technology Officer for Ericsson, Ulf Ewaldsson, now Senior Vice President of Technology Transformation at T-Mobile, became one of the top company evangelists for sustainability at Ericsson. He recognized the crucial role of broadband in building more sustainable societies. Rather than grounding dialogue with governments, regulators, customers, and other stakeholders on technical aspects alone, such as radio spectrum, Ulf saw how sustainability and connection to society could create other types of value. For example, broadband was a clear driver for the SDGs, in delivering services such as improving access to education, health, and other vital aspects of a nation's sustainable development. He saw the power of the platform and was excited and engaged by it. Ulf had strong internal and external networks and getting the message out via his channels was incredibly impactful.

"The promise of everything being connected in a world of 5G also comes with completely new and much more sustainable ways of solving old problems in novel ways," Ulf explains. "That leads in a direction where technology itself becomes a much more sustainable way of solving issues for every industry in ways that were never possible before. That is what 5G and the networked society is all about. That is why we invented the slogan of 'everything that can be connected will be connected'. Mobile systems and wireless just makes that possible in an economic and very fast way."

From Elaine's perspective, having a CTO embrace and talk about sustainability in that way is a surefire sign that it is impacting the core business. While the power of Ericsson's purpose in action to deliver Technology for Good may have been most evident in markets like Sri Lanka or Rwanda or South Sudan, evidence of its true success is when it's reflected all the way through the organization. Ericsson had customers from all over the world that preferred doing business with the company due to its Swedish heritage and commitment to caring for society. In the markets where Ericsson was present, it was a long-term commitment; people were hired locally, and the company contributed to the development of those societies. With this strong foundation, the SDGs naturally became a global platform Ericsson could speak from with a credibility and authenticity that the company's competitors could never copy. Even if those competitors gave away network equipment for free, they could not duplicate that inherent, hard-earned Swedish brand advantage.

The Most Important Business Asset

If done right, the benefits of a well-defined purpose are numerous: increased customer loyalty, reputational value, investor attractiveness, and employee retention and engagement, especially for the more sustainability-minded younger generation. A commitment to a greater cause than just money can be the ultimate motivation for any individual or group confronted with a complex problem. To build a great company culture, that purpose needs to be phrased in a clear and compelling way that resonates with employees.

For Michael Treschow, former chairman of Unilever who served as CEO of Electrolux as well as CEO of other leading Swedish companies, this sense of purpose is connected to the Swedish or Nordic values and heritage of sustainability, as we explored in the Prologue. Michael points out: "You can never underestimate or overestimate purpose, people and passion. Those three together become the driver. I believe it is easier probably from a Nordic perspective to find the purpose; that it is not only profit, profit, profit."

Sustainability has been shown to create more engagement because it affects all of us, establishes a connection to individuals' personal core values and priorities (e.g., protecting the environment, or creating a fair and more equitable society), and engenders emotional engagement about doing the right thing. It also invites collaboration, as system thinking is at the heart of sustainability and resilience, because the most sustainable companies are the ones responsive and agile enough to adapt to a changing world (Fig. 3.3).

A strong sustainability commitment forces a company to be honest with itself and its stakeholders: to be transparent, to measure and disclose performance and communicate openly on how it is confronting challenges and risks. It is a journey with which outdoor wear company and sustainability leader Houdini is intimately familiar. Being authentic has been essential to the success of the brand, asserts CEO Eva Karlsson:

> The magnetism and trust that we experience as a brand comes from being honest, which means having values that you actually live by: our company's values of "doing good, playing hard, pushing boundaries and having fun" form keel and rudder. We simply do not compromise. Not with product performance, quality or aesthetics, nor with the world around us environmentally, socially or ethically. I believe this has been business-critical for us—never accepting trade-offs in any direction. This is what attracts the best talent to our company, this is how we achieve great things (being unwilling to compromise) and this is what exceeding product expectations is all about to us.

Fig. 3.3 Outdoor wear company and sustainability leader Houdini's values of "doing good, playing hard, pushing boundaries and having fun" form keel and rudder of their brand (© Houdini). CEO Eva Karlsson says: "We simply do not compromise"

A company not living up to its purpose can quickly become obvious, sometimes resulting in serious breaches of trust, as we explore in Chap. 5. In fact, research from Accenture shows that having a meaningful purpose can mitigate the damage from a trust event on customer relationships—and therefore sales—"by giving consumers another reason to believe in the companies with which they do business." At the very least, a meaningful, relevant, and authentic purpose, twinned with transparency and honesty, increases the likelihood that customers will give a company a second chance following a trust incident.[13]

But while a strong sense of purpose provides a constant North Star for business, that does not mean remaining static. As executive coach and founder of Nature Academy Learning Lab, Göran Gennvi, points out, "Leadership is like surfing at the edge of chaos. It is about adaptivity, you never know what you have to deal with. You have to make plans but if you lean into them too much, there will be unpredictable changes all the time." To lead the world on the kind of sustainability journey needed to meet global challenges and make the leap to more transformative, systemic thinking, we need both the large companies with over 100-year-old histories and values that have withstood the test of time, and startups which have leapfrogged directly to sustainability as their birthright. Sustainability leaders across generations can agree on this: start with a clearly defined purpose and stay true to it, but be agile when it comes to implementation.

With a company purpose in place, the next chapter looks at how to put a firm stake in the ground and get the organization onboard.

Key Takeaways

1. A purpose authentically defines what you do better than anyone else that brings value to society; it is a cause greater than profit.
2. Connect the dots between values, culture, and purpose to reflect your ambition and make purpose part of your company's DNA.
3. Be inclusive and involve people across the organization in the purpose journey, from the C-suite to the factory floor, to build a coalition of the willing. Empower them to take ownership.
4. Encourage your leaders to seize every opportunity to reinforce the purpose to make it come alive and hold yourself and your team accountable for this.
5. A strong purpose will attract and retain talent, inspire your customers, and lay the foundation for a sustainability transformation.

Notes

1. Karma website, accessed March 26, 2020, https://karma.life/.
2. "How Millennials Could Upend Wall Street and Corporate America," The Brookings Institution, May 28, 2014, https://www.brookings.edu/research/how-millennials-could-upend-wall-street-and-corporate-america/.
3. "Putting Purpose to Work: A study of purpose in the workplace," PwC, June 2016, https://www.pwc.com/us/en/about-us/corporate-responsibility/assets/pwc-putting-purpose-to-work-purpose-survey-report.pdf.
4. Daniel Fisher, "The Millennial Consumer: A Driving Force For Corporate Sustainability," Ecosphere+, Jan 22, 2018. https://ecosphere.plus/blog/millennial-consumer-driving-force-corporate-sustainability/.
5. Nielsen, "Green Generation: Millennials say Sustainability is a shopping priority," Nov 5, 2015. https://www.nielsen.com/eg/en/insights/article/2015/green-generation-millennials-say-sustainability-is-a-shopping-priority/.
6. The Change Generation Report, 2017 The Lovell Corporation, https://www.lovellcorporation.com/the-change-generation-report/.
7. "Dollars & Change: Young People Tap Brands as Agents of Social Change," Do Something Strategic, 2018, retrieved from https://medium.com/dosomethingstrategic/dollars-change-young-people-tap-brands-as-agents-of-social-change-2612b717e5f7.
8. "Culture of purpose—Building business confidence; driving growth 2014 core beliefs and culture survey," Deloitte, 2014, accessed August 10, 2019, https://www2.deloitte.com/content/dam/Deloitte/us/Documents/about-deloitte/us-leadership-2014-core-beliefs-culture-survey-040414.pdf, 10.
9. "From me to we: the rise of the purpose-led brand," Accenture, accessed August 10, 2019, https://www.accenture.com/_acnmedia/thought-leadership-assets/pdf/accenture-competitiveagility-gcpr-pov.pdf#zoom=50, 2.
10. Thomas W. Malnight, Ivy Buche, and Charles Dhanaraj, "Put Purpose at the Core of Your Strategy," *Harvard Business Review,* September–October 2019.
11. Anamaria Vargas, and Antonio Negro Pietro, "Driving organisational culture change for sustainability. Employee engagement as means to fully embed sustainability into organisations" (2019). http://muep.mau.se/bitstream/handle/2043/29227/OL646E-1201-MASTERTHESIS-EXAMINATION1-NEGROVARGAS.pdf?sequence=1&isAllowed=y.
12. Global Leadership Forecast 2018: 25 Research Insights to Fuel Your People Strategy, The Conference Board, EY, accessed August 10, 2019 https://www.thegeniusworks.com/wp-content/uploads/2019/10/global-leadership-forecast-2018_ddi_tr.pdf.
13. "From me to we: the rise of the purpose-led brand," Accenture, accessed August 10, 2019, https://www.accenture.com/_acnmedia/thought-leadership-assets/pdf/accenture-competitiveagility-gcpr-pov.pdf#zoom=50,d.

4

A Stake in the Ground

Up Close: Henrik Henriksson, CEO of Scania, On Why He Nearly Called for a Strike on Scania Climate Day

You wouldn't expect a CEO to call on his own employees to strike. But that was the original impetus for the Scania Climate Day on September 20, 2019. Henrik was inspired by the millions of people around the world expected to take part in the Global Climate Strike, and he wanted to do something, too. Scania's lawyers quashed the idea of a strike—obviously, a strike can only be called for by employees. Instead, Henrik took an even more bold and impactful action and decided to temporarily close down Scania's global operations simultaneously for a Scania Climate Day.

Henrik's management team was completely on board with the decision, intended to create internal momentum and ensure the climate change message was reaching all of Scania's 52,000 employees. In preparation for the day, Head of Sustainability Andreas Follér with his team ensured that more than 2500 managers were trained to facilitate sessions with their teams about climate change, with material translated into 33 languages. Meeting in small groups, employees were asked to share ideas about how they could make a difference in their daily work. The initiative was designed to have an ongoing impact and created a new level of awareness and action both at work and at home. Local teams were challenged to come up with short-, medium- and long-term actions to reduce climate impacts within their operations, to be followed up as part of Scania's continuous improvement process work.

"This is a manifestation of our purpose—our purpose to drive the shift to a more sustainable transport system," Henrik told employees. "This purpose comes from the heritage and the culture and the values at Scania, and that's why I hope you recognize it. But it's also a manifestation and a purpose that

© The Author(s) 2020
H. Henriksson, E. Weidman Grunewald, *Sustainability Leadership*,
https://doi.org/10.1007/978-3-030-42291-2_4

fits well with one of the biggest challenges that mankind is facing: global warming."

To close down operations, even temporarily, is not a decision that many CEOs would undertake lightly, if at all. For Henrik, it was about creating a sense of urgency. It also made good business sense, since he sees Scania's future profitability directly tied to how well it lives up to its purpose. With its focus on sustainable solutions for the heavy vehicle sector, Henrik believes Scania is uniquely placed to drive the shift in its industry (as we explore in depth in Chap. 10). Getting the entire organization behind him is the only way to realize that ambition.

In fact, as Henrik spent Scania Climate Day meeting with mechanics at a Scania dealership, workers on the truck assembly line, and a local purchasing team in charge of plastic components, people came up to him and said, "We do recognize ourselves. This is us." For Henrik, it was exactly what he had in mind: to make people proud and get each and every employee to understand that they counted in this fight. As he puts it: "There has to be this pride, that the coolest thing you can do in the company is to work with sustainability. And if you get people truly engaged with that, it will be unstoppable. Even if we couldn't strike, we could do something more impactful, proactive and lasting" (Fig. 4.1).

Laying the Foundation

That story sets the stage for this chapter, which is about purpose in action. Scania's expression of purpose didn't start with the Climate Day and it won't end there. Yet daring to take that action, to do something bold, something unexpected, was a clear signal from Henrik that he really wanted to get people on board and undertake measures to make it stick. That Scania employees recognized themselves in that call to action is a sign of a company having done the hard work of getting certain fundamentals in place. Getting real traction on sustainability begins with having a clear purpose and leaders willing to publicly commit and put a stake in the ground. This is the first step. But no matter how inspiring a purpose might be, it must be supported by a few basics, like knowing the company's impacts, embedding sustainability across every function of the organization, being clear on priorities, understanding what matters to stakeholders, and reporting on progress, which should be continuously improving over time.

In setting the level of ambition and commitment, business leaders should consider their role in creating a more sustainable world, and the

Fig. 4.1 Henrik speaks to a group of Scania workshop technicians on Scania Climate Day (photograph by Andreas Foller). Henrik discussed why he decided to temporarily close down operations to share knowledge and to reinforce the urgency of every employee taking action around climate change

commitments the company is willing to make to accelerate positive impacts and minimize negative ones. A purpose-driven leader takes a good, hard look at the company's greatest sustainability challenges and opportunities, and sets priorities accordingly, closely aligning with business and stakeholder priorities. For business leaders, this should become as straightforward over time as knowing the income statement and balance sheet.

A few searching questions can help leaders chart their course. What is your moonshot? What goals will help you achieve it? What are the best opportunities to use your personal platform to reshape your industry and influence the market? And how does sustainability relate to your brand promise?

There are many ways to define an ambition level but once that is done, a basic next step would be to ensure a supporting policy commitment that lets stakeholders know what a company is committed to, and what it stands for. Of course, drawing on those quintessential Swedish qualities of inclusion and consensus, stakeholders should be consulted and engaged on the formation of those policies, and that engagement is a core part of this chapter. The next step is to move on to strategies and work out how sustainability integrates with the business strategy. The final element is to distribute responsibilities across different functions in the organization in order to embed them. This cross-functional approach is most effective when it includes specific targets set for a specified time period and describes the steps the organization needs to take to achieve those goals. As input to that goal setting activity, Table 4.1 highlights some examples of cross-functional integration challenges, and suggestions for how to address those challenges.

Table 4.1 A cross-functional approach to integrating sustainability

Business function	Potential challenges	Possible actions
Strategy	Sustainability and business strategies not integrated, causing friction and inefficiency because organization is pulling in different directions, or just lack of traction on sustainability.	Ensure a single, business strategy that integrates sustainability. Consider macro trends, competitor and customer analysis, as well as impacts on society and the planet.
Regulatory Affairs	Reactive policy stance and hidden or unclear lobbying.	Transparently define positions on key industry challenges and how you might influence them. Keep abreast of regulatory developments. Explore cross-sector alliances where you could have common interests.
Human resources	Sustainability not embedded in culture, values, or tone from the top. Younger generation doesn't see a clear purpose connection.	Roll out company-wide training in core values, ethics, responsible business, and other relevant topics to support commitments. Consider specific employee engagement programs around sustainability. Ensure a strong and clear purpose is visible to the organization. Tie employee/executive incentives to sustainability outcomes.
Performance management	Lack of metrics and weak targets lead to poor performance	Make CEO and C-suite support for sustainability leadership explicit, underpin ambitious goals with fact- and science-based targets, and use performance incentives. Treat sustainability goals the same way you treat other company goals, that is, the C-suite signs off.

(continued)

Table 4.1 (continued)

Business function	Potential challenges	Possible actions
Marketing and Comms	Risk of green- or SDG-washing through unsubstantiated claims.	Integrate sustainability and purpose with brand. Ensure that all claims are backed by facts and figures. Be transparent and balanced; that is, don't paint an overly optimistic case. Consider third-party certification or validation to demonstrate product credentials.
Investor Relations	Increasing stakeholder requirements for non-financial data and reporting. Ensuring robustness of data.	Prioritize non-financial and KPIs and ensure reporting routines are integrated with financial reporting routines to ensure high-quality information.
Design and product development	Negative environmental impacts during production or high energy consumption during product use.	Adopt circular economy approach including Design-for-Environment requirements or best-in-class specifications that improve product performance. Consider banning or restricting harmful substances and set limits on energy consumption, and/or explore use of renewables. Encourage integration of features to optimize sustainability, in partnership with customers.
Supply	Poor choice of materials in terms of, for example, recyclability, or lack of transparency in supplier materials selection.	Set requirements for materials selection and resource use, and be sure to have knowledge of what is in your products.
Sourcing	Reputational risks arising from use of suppliers in high-risk geographies or industries.	Ensure a supplier code of conduct is in place. Adopt a program to audit and build capacity/train high-risk suppliers. Re-use the quality management process also for sustainability.
Transport and logistics	Significant carbon footprint.	Shift to fossil-free transport and leverage digital logistical solutions.

(continued)

Table 4.1 (continued)

Business function	Potential challenges	Possible actions
Sales	No measurement of value created through sustainability-related sales.	Involve your customers and include sustainability criteria in the sales funnel, and when tracking sales leads. Educate salesforce and incentivize them to sell sustainable solutions.
After-sales service / disposal	Regulator/consumer demands for extended producer responsibility.	Introduce closed loop product take-back scheme or clear waste minimization plans.

Know Your Footprint

Once a leader is clear on the direction to take, the next step is to get the facts together. Just like a chef selecting the precise ingredients for a signature dish, leadership starts with knowing the company's full range of sustainability impacts and how to address them. Good data, like good-quality ingredients, is key to success. This also helps to establish the baseline; set targets, objectives, and plans for improvement; and measure progress toward these.

Taking a lifecycle approach is a useful way to understand the company's footprint. Capturing the full range of social and environmental impacts means knowing what is in a company's products, how they are used, and how they are disposed of. In other words, the pursuit of a circular economy approach rather than a linear approach. While knowing the company's footprint is a fundamental baseline expectation, continuously measuring and understanding how this links to profitability is equally important, which we explore in Chap. 8.

Map What Is Most Material

To carry out a meaningful analysis of key challenges, leadership opportunities, and business benefits in an organization, it must be anchored in an understanding of the issues most important, or material, to a company's stakeholders. Materiality assessments help to define and prioritize an organization's key sustainability issues, and how those issues map to key stakeholders' expectations. It can illustrate to stakeholders that a company has adequately analyzed, understood, and prioritized the key social and environmental issues that present risks or create opportunities to the company and society. Done well, they inform both risk management and strategy. Investors are increasingly looking for a robust materiality assessment to ensure a company is addressing the things that actually matter. The objective is not to show that a company is perfect—or can create spectacular charts—but rather that it can identify important challenges and develop credible and effective means of addressing them.

Understand Stakeholders' Priorities

Any commitment to sustainability has to be rooted in knowing what is important to a company's key stakeholders. That requires thorough knowledge of a company's key stakeholders and an appreciation of what matters to them.

To ensure consistency in understanding stakeholders' expectations and engaging with them effectively, it can be useful to monitor changes over time. Elaine instituted this practice at Ericsson to take the temperature, so to speak, of how stakeholders were thinking. She and her team annually convened a group of responsible business investors as well as civil society and NGOs. For example, in the spring in advance of the Annual General Meeting, or tied to annual sustainability reporting, or at investor roadshows, she and her team regularly met stakeholders to explain what they were reporting on, and to invite feedback on whether or not they thought that Ericsson was doing a good job. Elaine included a number of executives at Ericsson in this process, so stakeholders could see how deeply rooted the issues were across the company. This engagement provided direct feedback on the quality of Ericsson's reporting and where the company should expand its analysis or strategy.

In the next few pages, we take a closer look at individual stakeholder groups, and share some examples of how to effectively engage them.

Remember: Customer Is King

In the world of sustainability, there is no single more important success factor than getting customers to purchase a company's products and services offering because of its sustainability attributes. In some instances, customers might impose clear requirements on a supplier in order to win the business. In other cases, companies incorporate sustainability into their product and service portfolio, sales, and marketing, and proactively take an integrated offering to their customers.

Whatever the approach, the vision must be clearly articulated and understood, and the customer engaged. It's important to know if and why they buy into the value proposition, how they view the company's sustainability efforts, and their recommendations to make the approach more relevant to them. It would be a missed opportunity to simply wait for customers to issue sustainability requirements rather than seize the chance to be proactive and test new ideas and offerings. Ultimately, if customers don't see value in the offering, then a company may well be on the wrong track.

Encourage Employees to Lead the Way

The talent an organization represents is a key capital asset and source of value creation. As mentioned earlier, employees live and breathe the culture and values and purpose and play a huge part in supporting a company brand and reputation that centers on sustainability. Engaged in the right way, they are a leader's strongest champions and best source of intelligence and innovation. Sustainability efforts can lead to greater employee productivity and enhanced ability to attract, retain, and motivate employees. When people are truly engaged with sustainability, it has a snowball effect and becomes unstoppable.

The greatest impact lies in fostering a commitment to sustainability among all employees. That's a challenge, of course, but engagement drives personal responsibility and ownership. When people are thinking about how their role and department can contribute to achieving the company's sustainability goals, the commitment is gaining traction, as illustrated by the Scania Climate Day at the start of this chapter. It's also important to regularly take the pulse of employee sentiment to gauge their views on the company's sustainability efforts. A systematic approach should be in place to harness employees' ideas and innovations and give them the opportunity to play a role in the company's success. In addition to broad employee engagement, some ideas for engaging specific functions in sustainability are included in Table 4.1.

Get Boards and Owners Onboard

A critical element of anchoring and validating sustainability is to ensure that the Board of Directors and owners support the sustainability agenda. It is vital for governance but also if you want to take big bets. A proactive approach can help bring Boards and owners along on the journey, especially if the ambition and agenda are aimed at transformation.

We recommend an approach to engaging the Board and owners that is fact-based and upfront about the business issues and risks related to sustainability. The best approach is to focus on opportunities for long-term value creation alongside governance and compliance issues.

Other ways to engage the Board include providing sustainability Board training, especially for new Board members. You should also educate the Board on the business and financial implications of sustainability risks. The Board can be the CEO's best ally (or not) in a sustainability transformation, and how they are engaged on the issues can be crucial to your success.

It is also critical to keep abreast of new governmental mandates and corporate governance requirements. For example, in Europe and in Sweden, Board engagement is becoming a non-negotiable element of setting up the basics of sustainability. Many governments are starting to require that companies disclose non-financial data that can give a more complete assessment of risks. The EU Directive on Disclosure of Non-financial information, adopted in October 2014, requires that large undertakings with more than 500 employees must prepare an annual non-financial statement.[1] Sweden is leading in this evolving view of fiduciary duty. The Swedish reporting requirement went above and beyond the EU directive. It applies to all undertakings that have more than 250 employees—half the EU minimum requirement.[2] It also applies to all types of companies, not just publicly traded companies or certain financial institutions.

Revisions to the Swedish Corporate Governance Code effective from January 1, 2020 state that the Board of Directors has responsibility for identifying how sustainability issues impact risks to and business opportunities for the company.[3] At least in part, this directive puts sustainability on the Board agenda. Because of this, Swedish companies are accustomed to governance and accountability, with the engagement of Boards and owners leading to well-anchored support for sustainability positions.

Make the Case to Investors

Today most companies are receiving a growing number of inquiries about sustainability from their investors. Getting investors to understand a company's sustainability ambition is another part of building the foundation for leadership. Many investors focus solely on the risk side of the equation, but we think it is also important to communicate the company or leader's vision and expected business opportunities. Fortunately, while approaches have evolved over time, today more investors and shareholders are recognizing the value of companies that put a sustainability stake in the ground. In the 1990s, the movement was centered on Socially Responsible Investing (SRI), an investing approach in which companies were selected for investment portfolios based on a wide range of social and environmental criteria. Today a form of SRI 2.0 has emerged, also known as Environmental, Social and Governance (ESG) investing and which includes impact investing (investments made with the intention to generate positive, measurable social and environmental impact alongside a financial return), with sustainable investments reaching assets of around USD 30 trillion.[4]

"Today responsible investing has gone totally mainstream. Ten years ago, very few investors focused on this, other than socially responsible investors focused on climate-related risks and climate solutions opportunities," notes Sue Reid, formerly Vice President of Climate and Energy for the sustainability nonprofit Ceres that works with investors and companies to build leadership and drive solutions, and today Principal Advisor—Finance at the global collaborative platform for climate action, Mission2020. "Now all flavors of investors, including big asset owners and asset managers, are focusing to varying degrees. There's a gradient, but we see investors focusing on climate-related risk in particular and climate solutions opportunities."

This trend is being propelled by the industry-led Task Force on Climate-Related Disclosure (TCFD), established in 2016 by the G20 Financial Stability Board to develop recommendations for more effective and standardized disclosure of financially material climate-related risks and opportunities.[5] Sue explains:

> The TCFD came out with recommendations two years ago for companies across sectors, including investors and insurers, which control an estimated $30 trillion in assets globally. They're often overlooked as investors, but they have huge pools of capital. The TCFD really pointed out the risk exposures for the sectors and brought new attention to the need to take stock of exposure to climate-related risks and revise business and investment plans accordingly. And that's gotten a lot of traction.

Georg Kell, Founder and former Executive Director of the UN Global Compact and Chairman of Arabesque Partners which works in ESG investing, welcomes what he calls the "wake-up call" among investors:

> The fact that finance is waking up to sustainability means increasingly investors will be prepared to give a premium for good performance. Already today most companies are receiving a growing number of inquiries about sustainability

from their investors. We can argue there's been a massive relocation of assets with more capital allocated to more sustainable companies. For the frontrunners, that means premiums are down, cost of capital is down, and the valuation is higher. It accelerates the race towards the top. That's the systemic impact of ESG investing.

In November 2018, the Swedish parliament approved major reforms requiring the four main national pension funds to become "exemplary" in the field of sustainable investment.[6] Sweden was also the first country in the world in 2007 to make it mandatory for state-owned companies to report on ESG matters based on the Global Reporting Initiative (GRI) guidelines.[7]

By setting up those relationships well, if a company experiences a sustainability-related issue, such as a major social or environmental breach that hits the media, you are in a better position to be proactive, to reach out to investors directly and explain what actions you are taking to address the situation. As they will be getting questions from their shareholders, they need straight answers to address those concerns. Another useful tactic is to brief the investor community about key issues, risks, and opportunities before the publication of a sustainability report or the Annual General Meeting. Since many investors are risk-focused, those need to be addressed in detail. But remember to put the business opportunities forward as well—ultimately that is where the opening for sustainable value-creation lies.

While standardized approaches help to streamline, it is also important to stay close to your main investors as many have started to develop their own criteria and evaluation models for both reporting and scoring. Henrik found this to be the case in recent interactions with investors and pension funds in Sweden, where there is a trend toward developing tailor-made approaches to be more precise in evaluating sustainability performance, and where companies can gain a competitive advantage rather than being assigned a generic average.

Reach Out to NGOs and Civil Society

There are many ways in which companies can engage non-governmental organizations (NGOs) and civil society organizations. One strategy is to map the influential and knowledgeable organizations to specific topics, for example, environment, or human rights. Under Elaine's leadership, for example, Ericsson worked closely with the NGO Shift, the leading center of expertise on the UN Guiding Principles on Business and Human Rights (UNGP),[8] to carry out Human Rights Impact Assessments (HRIA) and better understand Ericsson's impact on human rights across its operations. To live up to one of the requirements under the UNGP around stakeholder engagement, it was important for Ericsson to address its impact on stakeholders potentially affected by its business operations. Engaging with NGOs and other civil society stakeholders as early as possible to understand their perspectives and make sure their interests were represented at early stages of the process was an important part of the equation, and engagement with Shift and their Business Learning program helped Ericsson to identify risks, mitigate them, and learn from best practice.

Integrate Across the Organization

To get traction internally, it is important to integrate sustainability across all functions, as opposed to designating one function to be ultimately responsible, as described in Table 4.1. One mistake many companies make is to appoint a person responsible for sustainability because they want to get started with the basics, but they fail to integrate that function with other business roles, which means responsibilities don't get distributed.

Table 4.1 maps a few examples of the kinds of challenges different functions across the organization could face in implementing sustainability, and how they could address those challenges. This is by no means comprehensive—there are many more topics that any one function might take on or want to address, and of course every company will have its own organizational structure. But the examples illustrate the kind of mindset needed to adopt an integrated approach to sustainability.

Reporting on Performance

Putting a stake in the ground and taking an inclusive approach to stakeholder engagement are ultimately about being accountable. The final element of the basics is getting the word out: reporting on performance. A sustainability report is essentially a static snapshot in time. But the reporting process is a continuous one: a good sustainability report is only as good as the data being collected on performance and activities throughout the year, with supporting metrics, as we address in Chap. 8. It is essential to make sure that robust programs are in place before a company begins the exercise of reporting.

When it comes to reporting frameworks, there are a number of options. The Global Reporting Initiative, the most widely accepted global standards for sustainability reporting, provides a useful framework.[9] As a reflection of the growing trend to move to integrated annual reports that include social, environmental, and financial/economic performance in a single report, the International Integrated Reporting Council (IIRC) is a global multi-stakeholder coalition that has developed an "Integrated Reporting" framework to accelerate adoption of integrated reporting around the world.[10]

A mistake companies frequently make is to see sustainability reporting as a one-off exercise, but continuous engagement and communication on topics and issues should occur throughout the year. Similarly, don't make the mistake of sharing only the good side of a company's sustainability story: credible sustainability programs, initiatives, and reporting on performance, address both risks and opportunities, upsides and downsides. It is important to be transparent about challenges, and how they are being tackled. No company is perfect and putting a stake in the ground is about showing continuous improvement over time and partnering on wicked problems. That is what will resonate with stakeholders. If everything appears too perfect, it will be hard to build trust.

Trust is at the center of the next chapter, where Johan Dennelind, former CEO of Telia Company, takes us through the journey of how the company managed to turn itself around from one of the largest corporate corruption scandals, building its foundation again from scratch. Telia Company is certainly not alone in facing that challenge, and the next chapter will shine a light on how to instill a culture of integrity as the best protection against a company allowing its basic foundation to crumble and losing its way.

Key Takeaways

1. There is no perfect time to start a sustainability leadership journey, so just start!
2. Put a stake in the ground to set the level of ambition and commitment and be realistic so that you can back it up.
3. Know your footprint, prioritize what is most material to the company's sustainability impact and ambition, and be sure to collect relevant data and facts.
4. Understand and address what matters to stakeholders, take their pulse regularly, and find ways to actively engage them.
5. Engage cross-functionally to integrate sustainability in the relevant line functions—delegate to them and encourage everyone to be a teacher.
6. Be accountable by measuring and reporting regularly and transparently on performance. Treat sustainability performance like any other business performance.

Notes

1. Non-financial reporting, European Union, accessed March 20, 2020, https://ec.europa.eu/info/business-economy-euro/company-reporting-and-auditing/company-reporting/non-financial-reporting_en.
2. Swedish Legislation on Sustainability Reporting—what is it about and how to approach it, Worldfavor, accessed March 20, 2020, https://blog.worldfavor.com/swedish-legislation-on-sustainability-reporting-what-it-is-about-and-how-to-approach-it.
3. The Swedish Corporate Governance Code, Swedish Corporate Governance Board, 2019, available at: http://www.bolagsstyrning.se/news/a-revised-corporate-governance-code-1-ja__3906, 17.
4. Michael Holder, "Global sustainable investing assets surged to $30 trillion in 2018," GreenBiz, April 8, 2019. https://www.greenbiz.com/article/global-sustainable-investing-assets-surged-30-trillion-2018.
5. Task Force on Climate-Related Financial Disclosures, accessed April 4, 2020, https://www.fsb-tcfd.org/.
6. Robert G. Eccles and Svetlana Klimenko, "The Investor Revolution," *Harvard Business Review*, May-June 2019. https://hbr.org/2019/05/the-investor-revolution.
7. GRI, Sweden and Denmark lead the way in Sustainability Reporting, Oct 6, 2010. https://www.globalreporting.org/information/news-and-press-center/Pages/Sweden-and-Denmark-lead-the-way-in-Sustainability-Reporting.aspx.
8. Shift, shiftproject.org, https://www.shiftproject.org.
9. Global Reporting Initiative, accessed March 22, 2020, https://www.globalreporting.org/Pages/default.aspx.
10. International Integrated Reporting Framework, accessed March 22, 2020, https://integratedreporting.org/resource/international-ir-framework/.

5

How to Earn Trust

Up Close: Former Telia Company CEO Johan Dennelind on Rebuilding Trust After a Corruption Scandal

In 2013, when Johan Dennelind took on the job of Chief Executive Officer (CEO) of Telia Company, the largest Nordic telecoms operator and fifth largest in Europe, most telecoms executives would have turned it down. The company was embroiled in a massive criminal corporate bribery and corruption case, its former CEO Lars Nyberg and other senior executives had left or been fired, and six of eight members of the Board of Directors were replaced.[1] Employee morale was at an all-time low. People were so ashamed, Johan recalls, they avoided telling family and friends where they worked. Customers threatened to cancel contracts, investors were edgy, and business was hurting.

Yet Johan, an experienced telecoms industry veteran, stepped up and stayed for six years, guiding the company on a new course that placed sustainability at the center of the company's culture, values, and business strategy. First, though, he says he had to "clean house."

The scandal broke in 2012 when an investigative reporting team with SVT, the Swedish national public television broadcaster, reported that between 2007 and 2010, Telia Sonera (now Telia Company) admitted to paying more than $331 million in bribes to an Uzbek government official in order to do business in the country.[2] In 2017, Telia Company reached a settlement with US and Dutch authorities amounting to $965 million, one of the largest criminal corporate bribery and corruption resolutions ever.[3] At the time, the company was partly government-owned and among the largest publicly owned entities in Sweden. In a nation with relatively low corruption,[4] Telia's Swedish employees were not used to this kind of reputational fallout and employee morale was at an all-time low.

© The Author(s) 2020
H. Henriksson, E. Weidman Grunewald, *Sustainability Leadership*,
https://doi.org/10.1007/978-3-030-42291-2_5

Johan and the new Board Chairwoman Marie Ehrling quickly realized that the problem didn't stop at Uzbekistan. As Johan noted:

> It was a systemic problem exemplified by one country, where we'd ended up in big trouble. Even more problematic for the culture and the company long term was the way it was set up to deal with risk and the regions where we operated and to deal with dilemmas. We realized that sustainability had long been a very under-invested area. There was no clear ethical compass from the top and no policies, procedures, compliance or formal framework in place. If you don't have that, you're destined to end up in trouble.

A number of corporate scandals and ethical lapses have led to an erosion of trust, with often costly consequences. A breach in trust has a hefty price tag that can include a hit to stock prices, customers walking away, and low employee morale. It can also damage a company's competitiveness. According to Accenture Strategy, the direct impact on future revenue losses due to trust events conservatively totaled US$180 billion for more than 7000 companies analyzed. That comes to approximately US$4 billion for a US$30 billion company.[5] Telia hopes that others can learn from its experience and take the necessary steps to avoid a situation of weak business ethics developing in the first place.

Yet handled right, trust can also create a powerful business premium. In this chapter we look at both sides of that coin, but we start first with establishing the importance of responsible business practices as part of any company's sustainability foundation.

Responsible Business Matters

What is responsible business and why does it matter? Fundamentally, it comes down to behavior both as a company and as a leader. It's about the values demonstrated through actions; it's about whether there is accountability for those actions and the role of governance in the company. What inspires trust? We define it as when a company or its leader acts fairly, when words and actions are aligned and in tune with society's expectations, and ethical, responsible behavior is held up consistently as the model for the organization, with people held accountable for unethical, irresponsible conduct. These are leadership qualities that fit well with the natural Swedish tendency toward humility. The trustworthy leader openly admits when things have gone wrong and works with genuine commitment and humility to fix it.

Trust can provide a tremendous business advantage. A trusted company is a preferred supplier, a valued customer, and a favored employer. As we have already pointed out, millennials in particular determine what they buy and where they work based on how trustworthy they perceive companies to be—a trend increasingly mirrored by investors when determining where to place their investments.

The 2020 Edelman Trust Barometer found that business is the most trusted institution (58 percent), taking the lead in global governance. In the survey of more than 34,000 respondents across 28 markets, CEOs are expected to take the lead. Some 92 percent of employees say CEOs should speak out on issues of the day, including the ethical use of technology and income inequality. Three-quarters of the general population believe CEOs should take the lead on change rather than wait for governments to impose it.[6]

While trust can be easily eroded, developing a robust platform for responsible business can be an important insurance in the event of an incident that breaches trust, which is likely to happen for most companies at some point. With a strong framework in place, if something does happen, a leader is prepared to swiftly and credibly acknowledge, address, and rectify the situation.

This opens up a key opportunity for employers to lead by example. More than half (58 percent) of people surveyed by Edelman did not believe that corporate initiatives to address societal issues were sincere unless the company's CEO is personally involved.[7] While this in and of itself isn't reason to act, it presents a clear invitation to business leaders to step up on responsible business by embedding robust practices, demonstrating tone and commitment from the top, and proactively engaging stakeholders and managing risks. The good news is that the company will be better managed, too.

Three Building Blocks of Responsible Business

We have already underlined the importance of having a clear purpose and strong core values. Responsible business is where the rubber hits the road—it is about how well a company delivers on that purpose and how actively it lives by its stated values. When purpose and values are properly embedded and sustained—and in tune with societal needs and expectations—the result is a culture of integrity. There is a world of difference between complying with the law and building a responsible business culture. For responsible business practitioners, legal compliance is a baseline expectation and we take it for granted that leaders have that under control. If you don't, our advice is to put this book down and consult a lawyer!

Here are what we consider to be the three essential building blocks of responsible business that are covered in this chapter:

1. Clear boundaries for appropriate behavior and ethical conduct which are firmly embedded in culture and values.
2. A consistent tone from the top, built on a solid governance foundation with a strong control framework and consequence management.
3. A proactive approach to defining and mitigating risks, taking a holistic, 360-degree view that includes broad stakeholder engagement.

Creating a responsible business culture starts by defining the rules for acceptable and non-acceptable behavior, typically in the form of a Code of Conduct or Code of Ethics. A strong code, together with a robust governance framework and clear accountability, is no guarantee that a company will avoid controversy, but building, strengthening, and evolving the foundation makes an organization more resilient to weather those challenges when they arise.

Through a number of illustrative examples from Telia, Volkswagen, Electrolux, and Ericsson, we look at how leaders have recognized, sometimes too late, how essential it is to integrate a responsible business approach into every aspect of the business. From product development (knowing what's in products) to the supply chain (responsible sourcing) to operations (how facilities are managed, employees are treated, and how business is conducted globally, even in markets that pose cultural or political challenges to doing business responsibly) to sales (beyond legal compliance, understanding what constitutes ethical business behavior), we explore where things can and have gone wrong. These hard-earned lessons are intended to show how different companies have successfully overcome difficult dilemmas, and hopefully serve as a source of learning for others to avoid the pitfalls and risks that inevitably arise when the house is not in order.

Building Block 1: Embedding Ethical Conduct in Culture and Values

As discussed in Chap. 3, purpose-driven leadership is an important element of building a strong responsible business culture. A purpose-driven and committed leader must consider how to realize the company's responsible business commitments and ensure that company values are lived. Several steps are involved, from implementing clear policies and guidelines, to educating and training employees, having clear accountability when things go wrong, to setting up processes that ensure compliance. This includes audits and checks, continuous reviews, and improvement plans. Last but not least is setting the right tone from the top, as we will explore in more detail below. In our view, leaders must be held to higher standards, as the CEO is the ultimate role model for the type of behavior he or she wants to see reflected.

We can also draw some interesting reflections on how Swedish companies approach the question of culture. The Swedish business environment, typically non-hierarchal and rooted in openness and transparency, can lay the groundwork for a strong business ethics culture. On the other hand, the decentralized approach common to Swedish companies which emphasizes local autonomy can present a risk without a strong tone from the top and adequate oversight that company-wide business ethics requirements are being met.

At Scania, the company's core values and principles have been foundational in creating a strong culture. These core values are rooted in the LEAN journey that Scania embarked on in the late 1980s and have been tied to the company Code of Conduct for many years. The initial focus was on building a stronger production system to ensure quality and efficiency. The Scania production system then evolved into a whole-of-company management system: the Scania House. The foundation of the house is Scania's core values, and the walls and roof represent the principles (Fig. 5.1).

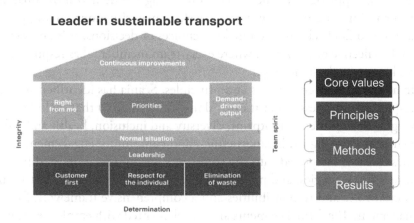

Fig. 5.1 The Scania House. This represents the company's core values, main principles, and the management system (a common way of working) together with the thinking model (a common way of thinking). Together they form the basis of Scania's corporate culture—"The Scania Way." By using this approach, Scania has been able to create a strong and united culture

To make sure these values and principles are lived every day at Scania, a simple yet comprehensive training program is continuously rolled out. Each rollout starts with the CEO training the Executive Board, then cascades throughout the organization, with every cycle taking up to two to three years to ensure traction. The training starts by defining what "customer first" means to the team and to each individual, including the immediate customer as well as others along the customer chain. For Scania's core value "respect for the individual," the training focuses on the impact an individual's behavior has on team members, as well as in terms of respect for the world we live in. The teams debate each of the core values and principles, and every individual's voice and opinion is respected.

To support use of the values and principles in daily work at Scania, time is allocated for "improvement work" and diagnosis and resolution of "deviations" across all disciplines, teams, and functions within the company. When a team member is not getting the desired results, Scania's "thinking model" (a common way of thinking) guides them to review their working method to understand how this could be changed to provide the right result. Specifically, employees are encouraged to ask themselves "why" at least five times, to understand the root cause, the details, and the context of the problem. If addressing the method does not solve the issue, the team member is encouraged to question the principles. Never in question, however, are the core values.

By using this approach, Scania has been able to create a strong and united culture. The approach has succeeded in fostering the desired individual and team behaviors in day-to-day work as well as new situations, giving people solid tools to fall back on when making choices or decisions. It is an example of a self-reflective organization where every team member takes responsibility by seeking to understand *why*.

In addition to its core values and principles, Scania has identified six areas of responsible business (what it calls "doing things right") that include minimizing its environmental footprint, diversity and inclusion, health and safety, human and labor rights, business ethics, and community engagement. Each of these areas is integrated into the company's operations, supported by relevant policies, strategies, and processes. There is a strong governance structure with clear roles and responsibilities and a comprehensive framework for risk management. The formal elements are complemented with employee training and guidance around how to deal with ethical dilemmas. But even a strongly embedded values-based culture is no guarantee against a lapse in business ethics—issues can and will arise even in the most responsible companies; the question is how a business leader deals with it.

Scania faced such a case in India, linked to responsible business practices in its sales operations. In 2013, Scania established a bus business in India including a bus manufacturing plant. It became evident after just a few years of operation that there was a lack of adherence to Scania's Code of Conduct and other policies and procedures, and an unacceptable culture had emerged in the local company. Repeated failure to adhere to these policies and expectations led to dismissal of the local management and sales representatives in the India bus business structure and prompted a number of investigations and audits. Efforts to turn the culture around and implement the right behavior failed, leading ultimately to Scania pulling its bus business out of the India market completely and closing the bus business it had established four years earlier. At the core of the problem was that the behavior in the market was not anchored in the Code of Conduct and the core values.

In general, the decentralized culture often favored by Swedish companies can spur innovation and empower employees. At the same time, it gives a large degree of autonomy to local offices and affiliates. The trick is to find the balance. Too much trust and delegated responsibility can result in ethical drift. Paradoxically, the more trust and independence within an organization, the better the controls need to be to ensure that the same standards and policies are followed everywhere the company does business. A strong culture and values are a great foundation. But as companies grow in size and complexity, clear boundaries, training, and accountability mechanisms are needed to reinforce that foundation. For some functions, such as finance, sales, or procurement, that are more exposed to responsible business risks than other areas, specialized training is a wise course of action.

What happens when ethical conduct is not embedded? Swedish telecom giant Telia Company has some valuable lessons to share.

Telia Company's Wake-up Call: Coming Back from a Corruption Scandal

Telia Company (hereafter referred to as Telia) is a great example for understanding what can go wrong when responsible business is not a deeply integrated part of a company's sales approach and what can happen when ethics and governance are not firmly embedded or monitored. For Telia, the wake-up call of the Uzbekistan scandal was a result of all three building blocks presented in this chapter not being in place. This posed an enormous challenge to win back trust. And in a typically Swedish way, humility was a big part of it—an acknowledgment that when things go wrong, which they will, strong leaders accept the consequences.

A cornerstone of good leadership is honesty and transparency. As Johan explains:

> We had to lay the foundation first, because we had no legitimacy to talk about all the good things we can do as a company and an industry around digital impact and sustainability if we didn't have our own house in order. Once you have a crisis, once you're stamped as a crook, you need to show that you're serious and that takes time, a lot of communication and engagement and meetings. Through it all, I was very upfront and proactive, to honestly say to all our stakeholders, "We will most likely go wrong again, but when we do, we will know what to do." You always have to balance an ambitious approach with humility, acknowledge that you are not perfect. But you want to be better and you want to improve. If you can get that drive into people, you will learn as you go along and hopefully minimize the big mistakes.

Although Johan left his position at Telia in September 2019, he left feeling that those rough years of deep, sometimes uncomfortable, cultural change within the organization Telia had managed to turn things around—not perfectly, but profoundly enough to continue its transformation journey:

> We had reached a point where we felt we had control, we were doing the right things, we had rebuilt our reputation. Then, when we had that credibility, we could start talking to a new set of stakeholders about the opportunities for us to make a positive societal impact. When you see that investors come back, customers come back, and employees come back, when you see you've regained the trust and pride of employees, you realize, "Okay, we *are* back, and we are now way beyond where we were before."

From the beginning, it was clear that compliance alone would never be a winning strategy. The company had a Code of Conduct, but in name only, Johan admits, so one of the first steps was to strengthen the Code.

> It was not adhered to, there was ambiguity around it, about how to apply it. This was a wake-up call for many people, that we had lacked these codes and policies and frameworks in the past and the training to make sure it was understood. But we said, "We're one company and we have one policy that applies everywhere." And it can't be a tick-the-box on the participation rate for training. Because then you don't have ownership, it will never become part of the DNA

of the company. You have to build the brand around it. It's not a compliance thing, it's about values and culture.

For Johan, this meant, as CEO, constantly communicating with employees, customers, and investors about Telia's work to steer the company in the right direction. "I didn't lose an opportunity to talk about our responsible business initiatives," he says. He didn't relish spending the majority of his hour-long calls with investors in the months after the scandal talking mainly about the corruption case rather than the company's business prospects, he says, "but we had to speak about the problems first."

That people didn't dare to speak up prior to the Uzbekistan corruption case was an endemic problem for Telia, according to Johan, so a whistleblower hotline was set up. "Because we really didn't have a clear framework for people to relate to, people could do wrong without people really noticing or caring. People didn't speak up; we didn't have a speakup line. We had a hotline that went into the IT department that was looked at by Legal once in a while. It wasn't really used, there were zero cases. Now we have hundreds of cases reported in through our speak-up line and there's good and bad with that but at least people dare to speak up now." Telia Company launched a new set of values: Dare, Care and Simplify. It was no coincidence that one of the three new values that Telia adopted under Johan's leadership was "dare." As he explained, "That came a lot from, 'Dare to speak your mind', when you see something wrong, you have to dare to tell us, to speak openly," Johan explains. "But it's also dare to innovate, dare to challenge. A lot of the thinking around dare came from the fact that people had been quiet when they saw a problem."

In addition, Telia set up a robust framework for anti-bribery and corruption (ABC) requirements, including effective reporting, investigation, and remediation of misconduct and corrupt practices, and the Board of Directors set up a separate sustainability and ethics committee. There was regular ABC training for employees and third parties in roles with high corruption risk exposure, and comprehensive, dilemmas-based ethics training for all employees with annual refresh and responsible business training became part of onboarding new employees. A Governance, Risk, Ethics and Compliance Forum (GREC) was created, in which management meets at least quarterly to update, discuss, decide, and follow up on ongoing activities and initiatives within the different risk areas and sustainability focus areas. Among the responsibilities for GREC was carrying out regular risk reviews, monitoring of progress, and closing of gaps. All management teams in all countries and functions at Telia Company have a GREC day about every three months for a deep dive to stay on top of the issues. As part of the comprehensive changes made in the aftermath of the bribery scandal, during 2018, Telia divested its companies in Azerbaijan, Georgia, Kazakhstan, and Uzbekistan.[8]

The support of the company's new Board of Directors and its chair at the time, Marie Ehrling, was also critical. As Johan acknowledged: "In the first two years I was CEO, these topics were a regular part of the Board agenda and having the Board's support was paramount. If I hadn't had that, I would have been too alone on this journey. Marie's and the Board's one hundred percent commitment was an absolute prerequisite."

If Johan were to sum up the qualities that he thinks a CEO needs to confront a similar challenge, it would be the following:

- Stick to your beliefs.
- Get your people onboard.
- Be clear on your expectations.
- Be ambitious but also listen and be present.
- Own the commitment to responsible business.
- Be open and transparent.
- Encourage a relaxed and informal workplace but demand the best of people.

For Telia, it was a costly and time-consuming exercise. In fact, a lack of trust from shareholders persisted for the first three to four years on the company's new journey, as measured by the company's metric for Total Shareholder Return. Telia's example shows how lack of a culture of speaking up can lead to serious problems, and points to three broader questions responsible companies should ask themselves to help ensure that ethical conduct is properly embedded:

1. Who is responsible when something goes wrong?
2. Does everyone understand the implications of wrongdoing, the severity of the risks, and the consequences?
3. Do employees know what to do when they suspect wrongdoing?

Telia's journey also illustrates the importance of good leadership and tone from the top to get the culture right. We look at this next.

Building Block 2: Governance and Tone

There is nothing more important in establishing a culture of ethical conduct than for a leader to live up to it. Responsible business conduct is every employee's responsibility but as a role model a CEO is held to even higher standards than everyone else. Senior leadership on ethics is non-negotiable, according to the authors of *Creating a Culture of Integrity: Business Ethics for the 21st Century:*

> It's a cliché, but when it comes to ethical culture, tone from the top—or how the most senior people in your organization act—it really does count. Leaders set the example. They determine direction, goals and priorities. They make important decisions and choose who and what to reward. And when things go wrong, they determine the consequences. Getting the role models and authority figures in your company to walk the talk may be the single most important thing you can do to build your culture of integrity.[9]

As well as a sustainability-inspired mission and values that fortify company culture, responsible business leadership requires a strong moral compass and dedication. As a CEO, it is important to continuously and constantly communicate about upholding the values of the company, walking the talk, and making ethical behavior part of the everyday conversation. Good leadership means drawing a line in the sand about what is and is not acceptable behavior, and confronting dilemmas, especially in "gray areas," as a tool for continuous improvement.

In addition to consistent tone from the top, a robust responsible business approach must be supported by a strong governance framework—and governance is of growing importance on the CEO's report card. In *Harvard Business Review's* annual ranking of The Best-Performing CEOs in the World, ESG (Environmental, Social and Governance) factors count for 20 percent of the overall score.[10]

Being aware of the potential risks and impacts across a company's operations enables a leader to put the right governance and risk management measures in place where they can have the greatest effect. It also helps to determine which principles and commitments the company stands for in the areas most important to the company and its stakeholders—from anti-bribery and corruption, ethics and anti-discrimination, to deforestation and conflict minerals. These principles can be captured and articulated in a formal corporate code of conduct. A strong code of conduct demonstrates a level of commitment, but if it is not tied to values, or enforced, a company can be exposed to compliance breaches, and any progress that might have been made will flounder.

Fortunately, a number of tools and frameworks are available to guide companies, from the UN Global Compact's ten principles in the areas of human rights, labor, anti-corruption, and environment, to the World Economic Forum's Partnership Against Corruption Initiative. Specifically in the area of human rights, the UN Guiding Principles for Business and Human Rights (UNGP) are a recognized global benchmark, establishing that companies should prioritize and respect human rights across their operations and supply chains or face potentially enormous business risks.[11]

As well as investing in prevention, the tone that business leaders set and their timely response when something goes wrong are critical in minimizing reputational fallout, containing problems, and ensuring that the organization seizes the opportunity to learn from its mistakes. To illustrate the importance of strong ethical leadership and good governance when trust has been breached, we share some lessons from Volkswagen, the main owner of Scania.

After Dieselgate: "Crisis Is an Opportunity"

In 2016, Georg Kell, former founding Executive Director of the UN Global Compact with a long record of experience in corporate responsibility, took on a special assignment at automotive giant Volkswagen in the wake of its so-called "Dieselgate" emissions cheating scandal. Asked to lead Volkswagen's newly formed International Sustainability Advisory Board, Georg saw it as an opportunity to think deeply about crisis management and the lessons that can be learned following a loss of trust.

In September 2015, the US Environmental Protection Agency (EPA) revealed that the diesel-powered engines of many Volkswagen cars sold in the US contained a "defeat device" to artificially, deliberately lower nitrogen oxides (NOx) only while being tested by regulators[12]—in other words, to cheat emissions testing. The engines emitted NOx pollutants up to 40 times what is permitted in the US, a violation of the Clean Air Act.[13] The EPA's findings covered 482,000 cars just in the US,[14] but Volkswagen admitted the device may have been fitted to as many as 11 million of its vehicles worldwide. An analysis by *The Guardian* showed that the device caused nearly one million tons of extra pollution.[15]

The fallout was swift. Then-CEO Martin Winterkorn said the company had "broken the trust of our customers and the public" and resigned under pressure, and the head of Volkswagen in the US Michael Horn, acknowledged, "We've totally screwed up."[16] The week after EPA's announce-ment, the Volkswagen share price dropped over 35 percent, its market cap contracted by more than $25 billion,[17] and the company posted its first annual loss in 20 years, of 4.1bn euros.[18] Other countries initiated investigations into the company's practices. In October 2016 a US judge approved a $14.7 bil-lion deal with Volkswagen, one of the biggest corporate settlements on record. Volkswagen agreed to spend over $10 billion on the buybacks of polluting cars and owner compensation and $4.7 billion on programs to offset excess emissions and boost clean-vehicle projects.[19]

For Georg Kell, the crisis was not just a threat but an opportunity: "The question is, how do we deal with it? Because everyone panics and everyone is willing to abandon old mindsets, they're willing to consider all the options on the table. There's a beautiful opening up which would be very hard to get otherwise, a possibility to rethink your own DNA."

The nine-member Sustainability Advisory Board was charged with working in three areas: a technology shift, a policy shift, and a cultural shift, and Volkswagen pledged €20m to the Council for the first two years for the pro-posal and funding of projects. The council included experts from business, politics, science, and society including Professor Dr. Ottmar Edenhofer, Deputy Director of the Potsdam Institute for Climate Impact Research, Director of the Mercator Research Institute on Global Commons and Climate Change; Connie Hedegaard—former EU Commissioner for Climate Action; and Margo T. Oge, former Director of Transportation Air Quality, US EPA.[20]

According to Georg, the Sustainability Council was explicit in its three demands to Volkswagen management and to the Board:

1. A technology shift: "The only credible long-term response to the diesel crisis was electrification (in addition, naturally, to the company settling its liabilities in the short term)."
2. A push for decarbonization: "We said, 'If you're serious you have to com-mit to decarbonizing all your activities.' "
3. A cultural shift: "This was an area where the council deliberately did not get involved due to the ongoing work of the monitor appointed by the U.S. Department of Justice to work with Volkswagen on a corporate gov-ernance framework."

"I think we have been quite successful in our three demands," Georg reflects. While acknowledging the journey is still ongoing, he adds, "We have helped to give the company courage to move with speed on these changes."[21]

Volkswagen, with current CEO Herbert Diess at the helm, is now in the forefront among established major car manufacturers challenging the position of electric vehicle pioneer Tesla.[22] As Tesla cofounder and CEO Elon Musk put it in a tweet, "Herbert Diess is doing more than any big carmaker to go electric."[23]

Georg Kell's Three Lessons in Crisis Management

Georg says his work over the years advising companies experiencing crisis comes down to three essential lessons:

1. *Timing matters*: The sooner you act, the better. It's very costly to wait. Because then the disease spreads, with the negativity and brand damage that come with that.
2. *Tackle the root cause directly*: Face it head-on. Don't look away, even if it's ugly. Then come up with a remedy that fits the root cause.
3. *Translate what you've learned into the organization's strengths*: Make sure future operations actually benefit from the learning. This is the most difficult piece—for example, on the anti-corruption front, when you learn the lessons and embrace transparency and integrity, how do you turn this into a competitive advantage?

A powerful example of how to manage a crisis by acting swiftly and decisively in line with core values comes from Swedish global appliance company Electrolux.

When Action Counts: Echoes of Bhopal for Electrolux

A basic responsible business expectation is that a company knows precisely what is in their products so it can avoid potential harm to people or the environment. So what happens when a business leader becomes aware of a serious environmental problem of which they had no knowledge? One response would be to keep the issue quiet, hidden from the public, and conduct an internal investigation before taking any action or admitting any culpability.

But that is not the way it went down in 1998, when Michael Treschow, then president and CEO of Electrolux, got word that Swedish reporters had discovered that the company's ovens were releasing toxic gas upon first use.

The gas was methyl isocyanate (MIC), the same gas that killed 3323 people in Bhopal, India, in 1984.[24] While the emissions were measurable only in millionths of a gram, Michael and Per Grunewald, a clean tech investor and then Senior Vice President of Group Environmental Affairs, jumped into action.

Production of the faulty ovens was immediately stopped. All ovens already delivered were serviced by local sales representatives to fix the problem and render them harmless and instructions were sent to purchasers. Electrolux took full responsibility, even though the gas was coming from oven insulation made by supplier companies. The company set up a crisis group to communicate with the media on a 24-hour basis. The toxic insulation material was replaced and a general inspection order went out to check other substances and chemicals in white goods production. While the Electrolux share price took a dive when the news first broke, it regained immediately when the company admitted fault. The proactive stance meant local media stopped pursuing the story. Lost production and realignment costs amounted to almost $4 million. More extensive studies might have shown no harmful effects from the insulation material, avoiding the need to replace it, but the calculation made by Michael and Per was that the company's brand name and reputation as a responsible business were at stake.[25]

There was no discussion of whether the company had enough evidence to act, whether it should wait, or that taking action might be costly. "For me there was only one thing to do and that was to stop everything, all production," Michael says.

> Later, we did discover that the insulation material in the ovens did in fact have MIC but it was such a minimal amount that it could not have caused any harm. But when faced with a crisis situation, right or wrong, you just stop the whole thing. It is about coming back to your values and to the heritage of your company. If something happens, stop what you're doing. Don't try to hide, don't try to hedge by saying, "We need to know more before we act."

Taking a precautionary approach, as Electrolux did, being transparent, and putting human safety and wellbeing (or environmental protection for that matter) before the short-term bottom line builds long-term trust and stakeholder engagement. Many companies make the mistake of glossing over or denying their risks and challenges, which ultimately comes across as greenwashing or purpose-washing at best, or at worst a deliberate and cynical attempt to dodge responsibility. A company that doesn't acknowledge its challenges will never be a credible sustainability leader. Which brings us to the importance of good risk management—a vital tool for responsible leadership.

Building Block 3: Proactive Risk Management

It's impossible to manage what a leader doesn't know, so responsible business leaders always seek to understand their business better and identify new risks and opportunities that may arise. That means taking a holistic, 360-degree view to gauge where in the operations and wider value chain issues are most likely to occur. The right measures can then be put in place where they will be most effective to mitigate the risk and drive appropriate actions and improvement, then continuously monitor and report on performance over time.

Classic risk management in companies tends to focus on aspects such as business continuity, currency fluctuations, supply constraints, and compliance, but we consider these issues to be a bare minimum. Contemporary responsible business risk management encompasses a far broader, more complex risk landscape that extends upstream and downstream in a company's operations, spanning the full universe of risks associated with its products or services. It is also critical to be sharply aware of the changing landscape, as the nature of sustainability risks affecting companies is always evolving. In the late 1980s and early 1990s, risks focused on environmental spills, quality, and safety. And it was only a few years ago that safety KPIs for mining were linked with financial performance.[26] Today business leaders face a host of new and emerging issues. Now, through the work of the Taskforce on Climate-related Financial Disclosures (TCFD) carbon risk is becoming similarly linked with financial performance. In the future, with increasing digitalization, we expect privacy intrusion and possible misuse or overuse of data to become new risk frontiers, tightly connected with human rights (see box below).

Examples of Key Sustainability Risks

The following are examples of sustainability risks we believe are important to consider as part of the normal risk management processes. Their relevance and significance will of course vary by industry.
- Health and safety (own operations as well as supply chain)
- Regulatory (e.g., failure to live up to the EU General Data Protection Regulation (GDPR)
- Environmental pollution (e.g., emissions, use of harmful substances)
- Fraud, bribery, and corruption
- Human rights violations (e.g., modern slavery, privacy)
- Discrimination, diversity, and inclusion (e.g., sexual harassment)
- Child or forced labor in supply chain (e.g., poor labor or environmental conditions)
- Non-compliance with ethical codes (e.g., responsible sales practice.)

(continued)

(continued)
- Waste (e.g., hazardous materials, improper disposal)
- Climate-related risks (e.g., lack of adaptation and mitigation, stranded assets)
- Product performance (e.g., developing a product that will not meet emissions or safety standards)
- Geopolitical, market, or cultural risks (e.g., certain countries do not share the same values)
- Data-driven risks from new uses of technology and digitalization (see Chap. 12)

In our view, proactive risk identification and mitigation is a non-negotiable part of any sustainability program. We recommend that companies conduct a thorough assessment of sustainability-related risks encompassing its entire value chain and make sustainability-related risks part of normal risk handling and procedures. Of course, as illustrated in the box above, the list of possible risks can be broad, so a robust materiality process can help companies to prioritize. Managed well, sustainability risks can become opportunities to gain competitive advantage and build a responsible brand. However, if not actively managed in a credible way—or underpinned with meaningful action and initiatives—such risks can become business-critical issues.

Human rights is an example of how a company can respond to evolving responsible business risks. The UN Guiding Principles for Business and Human Rights (UNGP) have provided an invaluable tool for helping companies understand how their operations impact and enable human rights, and today, human rights risks are becoming part of every company's integrated risk management. Legislation such as the 2015 UK Modern Slavery Act now also requires businesses over a certain size to disclose annually what actions they have taken to ensure no incidents of modern slavery occur in their business and supply chains,[27] making it untenable to claim ignorance as a defense. In Chap. 8, we touch in more detail on how a company can account for its human rights impacts as a key indicator of responsible business performance (Fig. 5.2).

For Elaine, the need to create better governance in the area of human rights and sales compliance became patently clear in 2011, when shortly after the start of the Syrian conflict and uprising against Syrian President Bashar el-Assad's regime, a group of Syrian protesters gathered in front of Ericsson's headquarters in Stockholm. Business human rights risks tend to be thought of as an upstream supply chain challenge such as poor labor conditions—but in this case the risk had emerged downstream in the sales process, with Ericsson

Fig. 5.2 A refugee settlement in South Sudan (Photograph by Elaine Weidman Grunewald). How a company responds to evolving responsible business risks, including human rights impacts, is a key indicator of responsible business performance. In her work for Ericsson, Elaine visited a number of places, such as this refugee settlement in South Sudan, that vividly illustrated how a company through its core business has an opportunity—and a responsibility—to find solutions to help address the needs of vulnerable populations

accused of supporting repressive regimes through its sale of surveillance technology. That story quickly spread in the media.

What had been sold to Syrian telecom companies was standard GSM/3G telecom equipment, but the specific technology in question was lawful interception, a functionality that is a global requirement for all mobile networks. All governments have detailed processes around how this information can be accessed, when and by whom, and due processes should exist to protect individual rights. Lawful interception allows authorities to identify the location of a phone in order to fight crime and respond in emergencies. While the potential for misuse of the technology did raise privacy concerns, industry, regulators, and law enforcement had agreed that there needed to be exceptions to privacy for the purposes of law enforcement and safety. But despite its intended use, lawful interception can be misused, for example, by authoritarian regimes to track dissidents.

To manage this human rights risk, the first step was to re-purpose Ericsson's existing Trade Compliance Board to a Sales Compliance Board with broad company representation.[28] The board oversaw the Sales Compliance Process, which applied to all 180 countries where Ericsson operates and was aimed at reducing the risk of misuse of the company's technology. Today called the Sensitive Business Board, human rights due diligence in the sales process is a key part of Ericsson's approach. When a high-risk sales opportunity is identified by the sensitive business automated tool, the Market Area submits an approval request in accordance with the sensitive business process. Submissions are evaluated according to the sensitive-business risk methodology and may be rejected, approved, or approved with conditions, with all decisions documented in the Ericsson Annual Report.[29] Conditional approvals include technical and/or contractual mitigations to prevent unintended use of sensitive functionality.

The dilemma around whether to leave or stay in a country and do business where human rights are at risk, or bribery and corruption are rampant, is one that many companies confront—and which can have significant financial implications. According to the UN, the cost of corruption amounts to as much as 5 percent of global GDP, costing at least $2.6 trillion each year.[30] According to Transparency International's Corruption Perceptions Index, the best-scoring region was Western Europe and the European Union while the lowest-scoring was sub-Saharan Africa.[31] Yet major sustainable development gains can ensue from remaining in a market and doing business—responsibly—if that risk can be mitigated.

A recent lawsuit against several US tech giants tells a cautionary tale about how lack of supply chain transparency in high-risk geographies can lead to companies being accused of lack of respect for human rights. In 2019, International Rights Advocates, a human rights legal organization, representing unnamed victims, filed a civil lawsuit against Apple, Google's parent company Alphabet, Microsoft, Tesla, and Dell, alleging that their outsized profits are being generated off the labor of children in the Democratic Republic of Congo, or DRC, toiling in what the complaint described as "Stone Age conditions," sometimes paying with their lives.[32] When *Fortune* ventured into the cobalt sector to investigate the methods used to dig the mineral found in lithium-ion batteries—used in every smartphone and electric vehicle—children were working 12-hour days, some for as little as $2 a day, digging and hauling sacks of cobalt-rich rocks, a hugely valuable commodity. Nearly two-thirds of the world's current cobalt supply originates from a tiny part of southern DRC, a war-torn country marked by deep corruption and crippling poverty.[33]

Swedish-based sustainable battery cell and systems supplier Northvolt has carefully considered this conflict. Given concerns around being able to protect human rights in connection with mining in the DRC, Northvolt does not source any minerals from the DRC but is actively working to find a way to source from DRC in the future that would help foster a sustainable and safe value chain in the country. This approach follows the guidance for companies from organizations such as Amnesty International.[34] Through its due diligence and traceability strategy, according to CEO Peter Carlsson, "We know exactly where our material comes from, the exact mine and refinery. We source from all over the world. We're also investing in a European refinery to bring a sustainable supply chain for our critical materials to Europe." The aim is to assure a value chain free of conflict, child labor, and human rights abuses. In short, today's leaders need to look not only at their own organization, but be aware of the wider impacts they inadvertently have on others, and put a robust system in place to forecast and mitigate those risks before they occur. Taking a "rights-based" approach by focusing on those people or communities who are affected—that is, a stakeholder or societal perspective—is the approach advocated by the UN Guiding Principles on Business and Human Rights. This marks a departure from the traditional, company-centric approach most businesses use to consider how risks affect *them*.

Whatever the risk, it is important to assess the likelihood that it will occur, the severity of the impact if it does, and measure how successfully a business leader will manage the risk by setting meaningful and credible targets (for more on how to do this, see Chap. 8). In a business operating environment that has moved from a "trust me" and "tell me" to a "show me" world, stakeholders expect companies to report transparently on the issues.

It is worth pointing out, however, that even with good systems and processes in place, responsible business lapses can—and will—still occur from time to time, reinforcing the need for continuous vigilance, reinforcement, and improvement of sustainability integration in all organizations. A case in point is the recent settlement between Ericsson and the US Securities and Exchange Commission and US Department of Justice, in which Ericsson has said it will pay $1 billion to resolve investigations into bribery and corruption breaches in five countries, China, Djibouti, Indonesia, Kuwait, and Indonesia.[35] Even with the company's zero-tolerance stance on corruption, without strong accountability and internal controls, bad eggs can pop up and challenging markets can test the system, at significant cost to the company.

We believe the answer lies in embedding sustainability at the core, so it is not a bolt-on or an afterthought, but the company's very reason for being in business. When it is fully integrated, the friction between doing business and doing business responsibly disappears. This is what we talk about in the next stage of our model, 2.0 The Core.

Key Takeaways

1. Embed ethical conduct in the culture and values of your organization.
2. Don't make the mistake of neglecting challenges in favor of accentuating the "good news" stories.
3. Identify and mitigate sustainability risks as you would other business risks, and integrate these into your governance, risk, and consequence management and control frameworks.
4. Establish clear rules of behavior, and ensure clear lines of accountability if something goes wrong. Make sure that the tone from the top does not leave room for doubt.
5. Invest in adequate education for all employees, with specialized education for key functions that may be more exposed to certain ethical or sustainability issues. Be sure to include dilemma-based discussions as part of the company toolbox.
6. Keep your Board of Directors and owners informed about issues and performance, and ensure they are trained on these issues (including onboarding for new Board members).

Notes

1. Salomon Bekele, Telia 2013–2018: A Story about Dealing with a Dual Challenge, Telia Company, 2019, https://www.teliacompany.com/globalassets/telia-company/documents/investors/other-information/telia-2013-to-2018%2D%2D-a-story-about-dealing-with-a-dual-challenge.pdf.
2. Jessica Dye, "Telia to pay $965m to settle Uzbek bribery claims," *The Financial Times*, Sept 21, 2017, https://www.ft.com/content/93a4d8c2-0eb8-33a3-ad63-5ade9df23704.
3. Dye, "Telia to pay $965m to settle Uzbek bribery claims."
4. Ola Westerberg, "The TeliaSonera Scandals: A Swedish Trauma," OCCRP, 2015, https://www.occrp.org/en/corruptistan/azerbaijan/azerbaijan-telecom/the-teliasonera-scandals-a-swedish-trauma.
5. From Me to We: The Rise of the Purpose-led Brand," Accenture Strategy Global Consumer Pulse Research, December 5, 2018, https://newsroom.accenture.com/news/majority-of-consumers-buying-from-companies-that-take-a-stand-on-issues-they-care-about-and-ditching-those-that-dont-accenture-study-finds.htm.
6. 2020 Edelman Trust Barometer Reveals Growing Sense of Inequality is Undermining Trust in Institutions, Edelman, Jan 19, 2020, https://www.edelman.com/news-awards/2020-edelman-trust-barometer.
7. Ibid.

8. Telia Annual and Sustainability Report 2018, accessed December 10, 2019, https://annualreports.teliacompany.com/globalassets/pdf-till-download-center/engelsk-pdf/telia-company%2D%2Dannual-and-sustainability-report-2018.pdf.

9. Andrea Spencer-Cooke and Fran van Dijk, *Creating a Culture of Integrity: Business Ethics for the 21st Century*, Routledge, 2015.

10. "The Best-Performing CEOs in the World 2018," Harvard Business Review Staff, November–December 2018 issue, accessed Oct 2, 2019, https://hbr.org/2018/11/the-best-performing-ceos-in-the-world-2018.

11. The UN Guiding Principles on Business and Human Rights, Business and Human Rights Resource Centre, https://www.business-humanrights.org/en/un-guiding-principles, accessed September 20, 2019.

12. Russell Hotten, "Volkswagen: The scandal explained," BBC News, 2015, https://www.bbc.com/news/business-34324772; Christopher Painter and Jorge Tiago Martins, "Organisational communication management during the Volkswagen diesel emissions scandal. A hermeneutic study in attribution, crisis management, and information orientation," Knowledge Process Management, (2017) 24:204.

13. Lauren Hepler, "Volkswagen and the dark side of corporate sustainability," GreenBiz, 2015, https://www.greenbiz.com/article/volkswagen-and-dark-side-corporate-sustainability.

14. Hepler, "Volkswagen and the dark side of corporate sustainability."

15. Karl Mathiesen and Arthur Neslen, "VW scandal caused nearly 1m tonnes of extra pollution, analysis shows," *The Guardian*, September 23, 2015, https://www.theguardian.com/business/2015/sep/22/vw-scandal-caused-nearly-1m-tonnes-of-extra-pollution-analysis-shows.

16. Hotten, "Volkswagen: The scandal explained."

17. Hepler, "Volkswagen and the dark side of corporate sustainability."

18. Painter and Martins, "Organisational communication management during the Volkswagen diesel emissions scandal: A hermeneutic study in attribution, crisis management, and information orientation," 204.

19. "U.S. Judge Approves $14.7 billion Settlement in VW Diesel Scandal," Reuters, October 26, 2019, *Fortune*, October 26, 2016, https://fortune.com/2016/10/26/settlement-vw-diesel-scandal/.

20. Volkswagen Group Sustainability Council, accessed Oct 2, 2019, https://www.volkswagenag.com/en/sustainability/sustainability-council.html.

21. A big investment in electrification is emerging under the leadership of current CEO Herbert Diess. Volkswagen plans to spend up to 70 billion euros ($84 billion USD) to bring 300 electric vehicle models to market by 2030 across all its brands (Alexandra Micu, "Volkswagen is investing 70 billion Euros into electric vehicles, ZME Science, May 30, 2018, www.Zmescience.com/science/vw-electric-vehicles.

22. Christopher Rauwald and Francine Lacqua, "Volkswagen CEO Confident He Can Catch Tesla in E-Car Race," Bloomberg, January 24, 2020, https://www.bloomberg.com/news/articles/2020-01-24/volkswagen-ceo-confident-he-can-catch-tesla-in-electric-car-race.

23. Elon Musk, Twitter, Sept 24, 2019, https://twitter.com/elonmusk/status/1176552859229310976.

24. "A crisis in the Oven," Electrolux Environmental Report 1998, p. 4, accessed November 15, 2019, https://www.electroluxgroup.com/en/wp-content/uploads/sites/2/2010/03/Electrolux-Environmental-Report-1998-English.pdf, 4.

25. "A crisis in the Oven," Electrolux Environmental Report 1998.

26. "Big Investors Looking for Better Safety Outcomes," Australasian Mine Safety Journal, accessed December 5, 2019, https://www.amsj.com.au/big-investors-looking-for-better-safety-outcomes/.

27. Modern Slavery Act 2015, published June 10, 2014, last updated July 30, 2018, https://www.gov.uk/government/collections/modern-slavery-bill, accessed September 20, 2019.

28. Ericsson Sustainability and Corporate Responsibility Report 2011, p. 32, https://www.slideshare.net/EricssonFrance/2011-sustainability-and-corporate-responsibility-report-ericsson.

29. Ericsson Annual Report 2018, "Respect for human rights," accessed November 8, 2019, https://www.ericsson.com/en/press-releases/2019/3/ericsson-annual-report-2018-published.

30. "Pervasive corruption costs $2.6 trillion; disproportionately affects 'poor and vulnerable,' says UN chief" UN News, Sept 10, 2018, https://news.un.org/en/story/2018/09/1018892.

31. Corruption Perceptions Index, Transparency International, January 29, 2019, https://www.transparency.org/news/feature/cpi_2018_global_analysis.

32. Vivienne Walt, "Apple, Microsoft, Tesla, Alphabet and Dell Sued for Allegedly Profiting off Child Labor," Fortune, Dec 16, 2019, https://fortune.com/2019/12/16/child-labor-case-apple-google-alphabet-tesla-microsoft-dell-human-rights-big-tech/.

33. Vivienne Walt, "Apple, Microsoft, Tesla, Alphabet and Dell Sued for Allegedly Profiting off Child Labor."

34. Digging for Transparency, Amnesty International, 2015, accessed November 25, 2019, https://www.amnesty.org/en/documents/amr51/1499/2015/en/.

35. "Ericsson reaches resolution on U.S. FCPA investigations," Dec 7, 2019, https://www.ericsson.com/4ae314/assets/local/investors/documents/2019/191106-phase-2_press-release_revb.pdf.

Part II

Sustainability Leadership Model 2.0: The Core

With the basics in place, it is time to move on to 2.0 of the Sustainability Leadership Model, the Core. In this phase, sustainability is integrated into the business model, day-to-day operations, R&D, product portfolios and sales, and across the value chain. We make the case for why there's no such thing as a sustainability strategy, only a business strategy. We highlight the importance of sales, because if you're not getting customer traction, you probably won't get much traction at all. In measuring impact, we discuss why profit is not the only measure of success and why using non-financial metrics and reporting credibly, transparently, and scientifically on corporate performance matters. Your commitment as a leader in this phase is instrumental—be a teacher.

The companies featured in this section are Northvolt, Scania, Axel Johnson, Ericsson, EQT, Houdini, Telia Company, and Electrolux.

6

Embedding Sustainability in the Core

Up Close: Green Battery Cells and Systems Supplier Northvolt CEO Peter Carlsson on the Key to Sustainability Integration

When your ambition is to build the world's greenest lithium-ion battery, sustainability simply has to be at the heart of everything you do. That has been the vision of Peter Carlsson, CEO of Northvolt, a Swedish-based European supplier of sustainable, high-quality battery cells and systems. The company is on a mission to build the batteries that will power a massive transition to renewable energy and electrification. It is building Europe's largest lithium-ion battery factory with potential annual production of 40 GwH—enough to power more than 600,000 electric vehicles. Central to that vision are clean energy, recycling, and sustainable processes—all geared to ensure that the gigafactory can help deliver on Northvolt's ambition.

For Northvolt, talking about sustainability *is* business-as-usual; because it is so firmly embedded into the core business it is just how things are done. Some companies may start out with a sustainable vision that is deepened and developed, as in Northvolt's case. Others work to pivot and embed sustainability within an existing business. While Northvolt is a clear example of a company that has put sustainability at the core of its business, that doesn't mean there aren't challenges. As Peter Carlsson explains it:

> The starting point of Northvolt was to build a profitable company. But just as importantly the starting point was to solve a big problem, to address the problem of the need for energy storage and batteries in order to drive the transformation away from oil and gas dependency. As part of our vision and mindset, that was a strong driving force. We are changing the rules of the game by building a significantly greener product than what is currently available. Unlike traditional battery companies that means we have a different cost structure. The cost and

© The Author(s) 2020
H. Henriksson, E. Weidman Grunewald, *Sustainability Leadership*,
https://doi.org/10.1007/978-3-030-42291-2_6

sustainability of energy becomes a prime factor, versus just looking at labor costs. The complexity of this project can be a huge challenge. It's super hard to build.

That doesn't deter Peter, who brings with him world-class industry experience from Tesla, where he was head of sourcing and supply chain, before starting Northvolt in 2016 with another former Tesla executive, Paolo Cerruti. In June 2019 Northvolt announced a $1 billion equity capital raise for its first gigafactory in Sweden, expected to start large-scale production in 2021, as well as a planned 50/50 joint venture with Volkswagen on another gigafactory in Germany.[1] Henrik and Peter have been working closely to realize a sustainable vision since 2018, when Scania and Northvolt entered a partnership to develop and commercialize battery cell technology for heavy commercial vehicles, with a EUR 10 million investment from Scania[2] (Fig. 6.1).

Being smart about using scarce resources is fundamental to Northvolt's approach to green batteries. To make the company's value chain as green as possible, sustainability and recycling are built into the business model. Powered by 100 percent renewable hydropower from Sweden's north, Northvolt's large-scale manufacturing process will produce close to zero atmospheric carbon dioxide emissions. It is also supporting its customers with electrified solutions to replace diesel trucks for mining operations and logistics.

Fig. 6.1 The Northvolt factory (© Northvolt). Northvolt, a sustainable battery-cell and systems manufacturer, is building Europe's largest lithium-ion battery factory in Skellefteå in northern Sweden. When completed, it will have potential annual production of 40 GwH—enough to power more than 600,000 electric vehicles

Another aspect is its commitment to a circular economy. Each battery cell will find its way back to the production line in one way or the other. Northvolt will dismantle and recycle raw materials, take care of the resources, and make sure they are prepared to the quality level of refined material and safe to reintroduce in the production line,[3] with the goal of reaching 50 percent recycled material in new cells by 2030.[4]

This approach has required enormous creativity from the team. In one example, Northvolt was faced the issue of what to do with the salt that is a byproduct of graphite manufacturing and which could contaminate waterways if released during manufacturing. Emma Nehrenheim, Chief Environmental Officer at Northvolt, figured that instead of treating the salt as a waste product, the company could invest a bit more in the processing so that the salt could be sold to the food and cosmetics industry. "When you have that solutions-oriented mindset, there are so many things you can do," Peter says.

Northvolt's approach has important implications for the way it manages its value chain. It is disrupting the status quo for battery production to achieve scale. It is establishing a manufacturing platform that provides a lower processing cost than Northvolt's competition—in essence, combining sustainability with a lower cost of production, a lower cost of manufacturing, and energy efficiency. That means it can offer quality, product, cost, and capacity, while still building the world's greenest batteries and, in so doing, gain a competitive advantage. As Peter explains,

> We will see a situation, and I hope I'm right, where in ten to fifteen years, sustainability becomes quality. Competition will just have to adhere if they want to play in the game. Certainly, it's a challenge to have a lot of partners, a lot of supply chains and putting ourselves out there with high ambitions. There will always be a way to find something that is not perfect and it's hard to anticipate what challenges we might encounter. We are working with different kinds of suppliers from all over the world, so for example, a risk is that some supplier is not living up to our responsible business standards. But if we succeed, that is why we'll be the choice over other competitors. It will drive everyone else in the industry to adhere to the same set of standards.

Northvolt distinctly illustrates how a company integrates sustainability into the core of their business. For other companies it is not always that straightforward, especially if the company has been established for some time. In this chapter, we make the case that for sustainability to take root, and have a meaningful impact, it needs to be embedded in the core business elements including business models, value propositions, value chains, portfolio integration, R&D, and empowered organizations.

Value Propositions and Business Models

The journey begins with company purpose, as we set out in Chap. 3, where we advocate that leaders should ask themselves: what is the single most important thing my company can do for society, better than anyone else, and how can you make that as sustainable as possible?

Many successful companies have a well-defined value proposition, but we suggest it be revisited from a sustainability and purpose perspective. A successful business model describes the underlying rationale of how an organization creates, delivers, and captures value. How can sustainability enhance the value proposition, grow the benefits that a company's products and services deliver to its customers, and how can it help differentiate the value of the product or service from similar offerings?

Scania's approach to integrating sustainability with its business model underlines the point. At Scania, the business model is defined as (1) the value proposition and (2) how Scania charges for that value. Here is how sustainability is captured throughout this model:

The *value proposition* is the total solution offered to customers—selling a vehicle or services that are as sustainable as possible while making the customers more profitable. The solution comprises both products and services. For example, it could include a truck, connectivity services, and a four-year lease that includes a repair and service contract for the duration of the lease. Such a total solution is designed to mitigate the risk and hurdles while also incentivizing customers to move from an existing solution to a more sustainable one.

Scania *charges for this value* by offering customers a better total operating economy that helps them become more profitable. That often makes the vehicles more expensive upfront, but over the lifetime use of the product, customers benefit from lower operating cost and higher income. So, instead of selling a truck or a bus as a normal asset sale—for a price tag, for example, $100,000— the solution is sold based on the function that is delivered, similar to "software as a service" (SAAS). Most of Scania's sales today comprise a solution which is charged as a cost per kilometer, like a monthly mobile phone bill. This way of charging for the value reduces the hurdle for customers to choose a more sustainable alternative fuel solution over a fossil fuel powered vehicle.

When sustainability is central to a company's value proposition, and resonates with the market, it sends the right signals to the organization engaging at multiple functions and levels. Getting internal buy-in for a strong sustainability value proposition is as vital as receiving it from your customers.

Everyone from the R&D team to manufacturing to sales will be more engaged in developing the next generation of sustainable products when they see a strong market demand for it.

The goal is to reach the point where the sustainability-profitability link is clear. And that means a company has demonstrated the ability to improve profits by creating superior products and services that customers are willing to pay for and that are also sustainable—for example, more energy efficient or less resource intensive.

As part of a multi-year sustainability integration journey, Scania has developed a business model in which it gains a return for its sustainability investments. This is not to say that sustainable products are more profitable than others, but they are equally profitable. If business leaders have made the necessary changes to become a more sustainable company, transforming the company's footprint, products, and services, and it is still not making a profit, then the risk is that it has been done in the wrong way—an unsustainable way. It's a simple rule: if a company is not profitable, it is not sustainable. It might be that the transition was too rapid; a company bet everything on one technology or product line and didn't have its customers on board. In the worst-case scenario, a company might make a big mistake, and suffer huge losses and even lose the business, which is also not sustainable. To be truly sustainable, a business model has to work; otherwise, it is simply an interesting experiment that will never gain traction or scale.

Of course, there will always be some customers for whom a strong sustainability value proposition is not persuasive. Focusing on this segment runs the risk of missed opportunities as a growing number of customers (not to mention investors) choose to work with suppliers and business partners who share their commitment to sustainability. Provided the value proposition is strong, it is up to the company's leadership, and its sales team, to work out how best to emphasize sustainability with individual customers.

There Is Only One Strategy

There's no such thing as a sustainability strategy; there is only a business strategy that is—or isn't—sustainable in the long term. Too many companies approach sustainability as a separate strategy or a campaign. That can be useful in generating interest for a period of time, but has no real sticking power in the long run, and won't sustain the necessary momentum. Having a separate sustainability strategy will rarely build organizational support and commitment for sustainability, especially if there are high ambitions. To successfully embark on the journey of scaling sustainability impact, sustainability should not be separate from the business model. The greatest benefit comes from dovetailing and interweaving sustainability with other key strategic elements. These include, for example, competitive analysis, customer priorities, growth plans, cost improvements, performance targets, technology roadmaps, macro trends, risk identification and management, and geopolitical analysis. In other words, treat sustainability as a cohesive part of these fundamental business activities, not separate from them.

At Scania, there is no separate sustainability strategy, only one company-wide sustainable business strategy. This single strategy includes functional and cross-functional targets, plans, and activities, covering four main company processes: demand to cash, product development, service development, and the sales process. A signature feature of Scania's approach is that the detail of these plans is developed through a bottom-up process by the people in the organization who are experts in their fields and understand best how to integrate sustainability into their specific areas of expertise.

Whether the approach is top down or bottom up, driving change is ultimately about getting people to accept and embrace sustainability as part of their own agenda, complete with appropriate target-setting and performance measurement. It's a cliché but it's true that "what gets measured matters." Success will remain elusive without a clear strategy, targets, and measurements. Strategy and target integration is one of the most fundamental ways to get sustainability fully embedded into the core of an organization. Fostering a sense of individual ownership is also crucial.

Create an Empowered Organization

If the first step toward sustainability leadership is to embrace sustainability in the purpose, another critical step on the journey is to make sustainability a living, breathing reality for every employee. For Henrik, that starts with making sure he personally stands for the company's purpose. It was a conscious decision of the Scania Executive Board that responsibility for sustainability lies with him because, as CEO, he wants to ensure that the prioritization is clear. Making the sustainability agenda an Executive Board issue, along with engaging his top executives, also ensures that sustainability stays top-of-mind and gets it into the blood of an organization, even if associated tasks are delegated to various functions or teams.

Toward this goal, and early on in his role as CEO, Henrik developed an approach for encouraging ownership of sustainability throughout the organization. To support sustainability integration and coordination at Scania, a cross-functional Sustainability Advisory Board was created, comprised of senior executives that report to the CEO and Executive Board. As well as being an accelerator for company-wide initiatives and innovation, the Advisory Board has the mandate to take investment decisions in all major functions.

For the CEO to personally conduct training is one of the best ways to become genuinely knowledgeable in a subject. As noted in Chap. 5, to ensure the sustainability commitment is well anchored at Scania, Henrik trains his own Executive Board, which then cascades the training to their teams, with Henrik participating in that next level of training applying the grandparent principle. The team training led by Henrik kicked off with a straightforward set of questions: what does the purpose of *Driving the Shift* mean to you? How can we be guided by our purpose and core values in our daily work and decisions? Are the principles that guide us in our work supporting sustainability? Do we need to change any of our principles or methods to reach our targets and plans? With each relevant manager or team leader facilitating these talks—with CEO support—the resulting interactive team dialogue cascaded from the top down and out to all teams across the organization. At Scania, Henrik has found this to be an effective method for building sustainability into the core of the organization, with each functional head taking sustainability on as part of their responsibility. In addition, since 2015, more than 150 people across the organization, from Purchasing to R&D to Production and Sales, now have the word "sustainability" in their job title.

For Swedish industrial group Axel Johnson, four out of six identified business-critical target areas for monitoring company performance within the Group are directly entwined with sustainability. The six focus areas are valuable customer offering; resource-efficient, eco-friendly, and high-quality operations; innovation; digital transformation; sustainable and efficient production, and values-based employeeship and leadership. Each of the companies within the group, which span retail to food to fashion, reports on sustainability KPIs monthly as part of monitoring performance. Axel Johnson's approach is to always offer a sustainable choice to customers.

Each one of the Axel Johnson companies has embedded sustainability into the core business strategy, although CEO Mia Brunell Livfors acknowledges that the industrial companies may be lagging behind the consumer-facing businesses in that regard, as a consequence of how developed the respective sectors are in this aspect. In terms of organizational structure, while Axel Johnson has sustainability managers, it expects that every business manager should have sustainability as their responsibility. According to Mia: "I want the responsibility for sustainability to be under every business manager, not someone on the side being responsible for sustainability."

These examples from Northvolt, Scania, and Axel Johnson illustrate that there are many different pathways to embed sustainability in an organizational structure. No single blueprint will fit every organization: each company needs to decide on its own where to anchor the role. Some companies choose to position sustainability within Human Resources to link to purpose and values, while others opt to place the sustainability function in the marketing or communications department. In our view, these types of placements can make it harder to anchor sustainability within the core business and runs the risk that sustainability is perceived merely as a brand or public relations exercise.

But however a business leader chooses to do it, one thing is non-negotiable: the CEO must make sure the organization knows that sustainability is an integrated part of how the company does business.

Integrate Sustainability into the Portfolio

True product and portfolio integration is achieved when sustainability criteria are applied across the board. Creating a stand-alone green product can help a company learn what works and what doesn't and serve as inspiration, but it's important not to stop there. The guiding aim, even if long term, should be to transform entire product lines and, ultimately, the portfolio, into a sustainable offering.

In the fast-moving consumer goods industry or in the wholesale retail or food and beverages sectors, for example, a company might choose to start with a couple of product lines. Global appliance company Electrolux has been steadily developing its most water- and energy-efficient products and now applies that learning across the board, as we explore further in Chap. 8. As a result, product efficiency and use of recycled materials have become a key part of R&D and innovation across every product category. One example is Electrolux's Powerforce Green vacuum cleaner, made with more than 60 percent recycled plastic, and which uses 60 percent less energy compared to a standard 2100W vacuum cleaner.[5]

In other cases, embedding sustainability across the business may require rethinking one-size-fits-all strategies for products and portfolio. For Ericsson, one challenge involved creating competitive advantage by evolving from a "superior performance" to an "energy performance" telecom strategy. The company's superior performance strategy had been based on delivering large, high-capacity telecom sites, with a focus on performance to ensure the network would run continuously and flawlessly in dense urban environments. However, when it came to building out sites in remote, rural, off-grid areas, Ericsson realized that energy was a key driver of operational expenditure and thus energy efficiency could be a point of differentiation from competitors offering less expensive upfront solutions. Ericsson's approach was to dramatically lower the total cost of ownership by offering new features and functionality designed to reduce power consumption. One example was the ability to put the entire network into "sleep mode" in off-grid areas at night when there were fewer active users or when traffic was lower. Another innovation was new types of batteries for remote sites to enable solar energy to run effectively. These solutions were solving real customer challenges and had sustainability at the core.

In an example from another industry, Sweden-based private equity and global investment organization EQT considers sustainability as an integral part of its business model. EQT, as well as its funds' portfolio companies, aims to identify and capture value-creating opportunities from sustainability while mitigating risks. EQT has established a thematic approach of investing in businesses with positive societal impact, advancing the progress of one or more of the United Nations Sustainable Development Goals (SDG)—which we explore further in Chap. 11. To do this it has created its Sustainability Performance Framework to measure sustainable practices against societal impact.

As EQT CEO Christian Sinding explains, "When we make decisions about companies we are considering investing in, we have a matrix in which one axis shows how sustainable the company is today, and the other axis shows how easy it would be for us to make the company even more sustainable in the future," Christian says. "But if a company has a negative starting point, we won't invest at all, unless there is a clear case for how EQT can help transform that company and its industry into a positive contributor to society. We map this and the kind of questions we ask companies when we're buying them is, how do the industry trends align with the SDGs? How does the company contribute to society?" (Fig. 6.2).

Despite many gains being made in socially responsible investing, or impact investing, it is still somewhat unusual in the mainstream financial markets to think this way. Many investment and private equity firms start impact funds parallel to their other investment funds, but EQT did not take that approach; instead, it integrates the goal of positive sustainability impacts into its core portfolio, that is, all of their investments.

Fig. 6.2 Christian Sinding, CEO of private equity and global investment firm EQT (© EQT). For Christian, sustainability is a way to capture value-creating opportunities while mitigating risks. Unlike many others in their field, EQT evaluates investments based on a company's ability to contribute positively to society

Commit to Research and R&D

While sustainability is increasingly being integrated into functions like sourcing or production processes, relatively few companies have yet to routinely incorporate it into R&D and specific criteria or design principles are often lacking. Yet R&D is a powerful means of exploring new ways of doing things that can enhance competitiveness and meet regulations as well as deliver substantial sustainability gains. Scania's R&D work provides a case in point.

At Scania, product development starts and ends with the customer. Customers shape the demand for future product features that Scania development engineers bring to the R&D lab. Their R&D work is based on well-established design principles as well as an understanding of customers' needs in order to balance and optimize different product properties. Sustainability is a growing demand among Scania's customers but there can still be resistance to change. To that end, Scania also deploys a strategy of both technology push, focusing on breakthrough technologies, and customer pull: driving the adoption of sustainable solutions and the uptake of tailored, here-and-now sustainable solutions. In this way, sustainability is an integral part of the product development just as it is in sales, which we delve into in Chap. 7.

To be a sustainable leader in its industry, Scania invests heavily in constantly trying out new technology and solutions, to find leaps in reducing CO_2 emissions and providing safer vehicles. Customers are introduced to sustainable innovations early in the process to support the vision for driving the shift. One such solution is electrified or e-highways for heavy vehicles. On an e-highway, trucks can connect to electrified overhead catenary lines along a section of road for electric power. This sustainable system solution is essentially building a train system on tarmac. Scania pioneered the technology together with Siemens, as the first truck to drive the world's first e-highway in Sweden in 2016 and now also in Germany.[6] The benefit is that the trucks can run on renewable electricity when on the highway and then use battery power or renewable biofuels when they leave the highway. This can reduce CO_2 emissions by more than 90 percent and still give the flexibility of a normal truck (Fig. 6.3).

The cost of the infrastructure is of course substantial as most countries in the world will need to build new electrical grids along the highways to ensure charging for both passenger cars and heavy commercial vehicles. The additional cost of then building the overhead lines will be marginal. In comparison to static charging, this solution allows commercial vehicles to charge while driving, hence improving the revenue and efficiency of the transport company. This cooperation between Scania and Siemens uses mature technology from both companies to develop a solution that would not have been possible had they not entered a cross-sector partnership. The lesson to be drawn is to stretch beyond integrating sustainability into the core process of R&D, to also challenge silo thinking from a technology point of view, and to seek partnerships that can further anchor R&D activities into the core business.

Matching commitments in sustainability to investments in R&D is fundamental to identifying real solutions and helps create a foundation for a company to take ownership of sustainability in its industry. Swedish sportswear company Houdini is another example of this approach.

Houdini: "Design Is Our Most Important Tool"

When it comes to an authentic commitment to incorporate sustainability into the product portfolio, it's worth taking a look at Houdini (for more, see our deep dive into Houdini's comprehensive approach to sustainability in

Fig. 6.3 An electrically powered Scania truck (© Scania). Showcasing the potential for electrification of heavy-duty vehicles, Scania is part of the German eHighway trial. Scania is supplying 15 hybrid trucks equipped with special pantograph power collectors, developed by Siemens, so they can drive electric on roads with an overhead catenary system. In 2016, a Scania electrically powered truck also made the inaugural journey on the world's first electric highway in Gävle in central Sweden

Chap. 9). Since its launch in 1993, Houdini has set out to create state-of-the-art clothing with minimal impact on the environment. By 2022 it has committed to 100 percent of its product being circular, made from recycled or biodegradable fibers and recyclable or biodegradable at end of life. By 2030, its commitment is that 100 percent of its value chain and entire ecosystem will be circular.[7]

The first Houdini product made from recycled and recyclable fibers came out in 2007; now a majority of its products are circular by design. According to CEO Eva Karlsson, "What was interesting at Houdini was the opportunity to build a company from scratch and do it right from the start, because there were only very few products in the portfolio back then. Building it right meant we could become part of the solution and not the problem. It meant not having a company with huge design flaws built in and then having to change them."

Eva Karlsson continues:

We are a values-driven company but that directly translates into being design driven in our case. This is because more or less everything in our industry needs to be redesigned, from products and value chains to business models and systems. In the field of product design my strong opinion is that corporations use the skill sets and ambitions of their designers poorly. Designers come out of school with the ambition of creating truly amazing products, but then the corporate machinery hits them, where focus is on price rather than value, timeline and margin rather than product excellence, and quantity rather than quality. At Houdini we are aligned with the personal drive of our designers and can accomplish great things.

At the heart of Houdini's design approach is its Designer Checklist.[8] To make sure its product development is headed toward 100 percent circular products by 2022, its designers follow a specific methodology to ensure the product aligns with the company's philosophy:

- Does this product deserve existence?
- Will it last long enough?
- Is it versatile enough?
- Will it age with beauty?
- Nothing added that isn't needed, right?
- Will it be easy to repair?
- Is it durable enough for our rental program?
- Do we have a "next-life" solution?

Eva Karlsson admits that Houdini's business model is unconventional; the company views the natural resources it uses as borrowed from the planet and acts as their custodian, responsible for handing them back to the planet and future generations in good shape. That's why its ambition to go 100 percent circular draws on nature's circular principles as its blueprint, with four core strategies to help the company become a regenerative force: design a circular system, reconnect to nature, set the example, and build a community.

The strategy seems to be working. Eva points out that without any traditional advertising, Houdini is growing its business 20–30 percent per year and at double that speed in its 15–20 export markets. She attributes much of this success to the honest dialogue Houdini has always had with its partners, customers, end-users, and followers, being open about the challenges it faces. This has created trust—along with the fact, she says, that "our products exceed expectations, creating strong ambassadors among our customers and a grassroots movement."

There have been challenges along the way—and some are extremely difficult to solve.

That includes the problem of microfibers, small plastic particles that origi-
nate from products in plastics manufacturing, or as ingredients in skincare,
tires, and toothpaste and other products. Textiles can release these fibers when
being used or thrown away in nature as trash, but also when washed. Through
rivers, streams, and sewages, the plastics in these fibers end up in the ocean,
and, in the long run, in the tissue of certain marine animals.[9] As Eva explains,
microfibers remain a challenge even though they have been working on it
since 2013. "We usually manage to get on the solution-side of things fast but
in this case, we are part of the problem, although a very small part." She put
her design team to work in finding the best-possible solutions. "We made a
priority list of fabrics and products to exclude or redesign. We started working
with academia and innovation hubs and with other apparel industry companies and finally, six years later we are seeing some substantial results of our
efforts, in terms of textile and polymer engineering."

Houdini only uses high-quality fiber and precision manufacturing practices as this minimizes fiber loss and the release of microplastics. It also does
not mix fibers, never using natural and synthetic fiber in the same garment as
it increases microplastic loss and makes recycling difficult. Finally, by encouraging customers to bring back their garments for recycling, Houdini aims to
take full producer responsibility to eliminate synthetics from ending up in
landfill or in nature. More recently, it has developed products in organic,
renewable, and biologically decomposable materials. Similarly, new garment
cutting and construction methods limit fiber loss.

Still, it hasn't entirely eliminated the problem of microfibers and Houdini
is bucking up against its 2030 deadline to have a circular ecosystem in place.
"If we have not solved microplastics by then, we would have to remove all the
synthetics," Eva says. And so, it's back to the drawing board.

The Sustainability and Profitability Nexus

A basic premise of this book is the solid link between sustainability and profitability when sustainability is successfully integrated into the core business. A
growing body of research supports this conviction. Yet whether sustainability
can be profitable remains a fundamental question that many business leaders
grapple with.

A *Harvard Business Review* (HBR) study that looked at companies that
adapt sustainability practices identified a pattern demonstrating competitive

advantage, innovation power, and cost savings, leading to increased financial performance.[10] The HBR study found that companies can also charge higher price premiums based on positive corporate responsibility performance. For example, the HBR noted that companies experience an average internal rate of return of 27–80 percent on their low-carbon investments. And an analysis by research and consulting firm IO Sustainability found that companies integrating sustainability into their business enhanced sales by as much as 20 percent; increased productivity by 13 percent, reduced employee turnover by half; increased the company's share price by up to 6 percent; and created a "reputation dividend" worth up to 11 percent of market capitalization. Further, such companies were able to reduce financial risk, the cost of equity, and the cost of borrowing.[11]

For industry leaders, the dividends can be even higher. Companies that are able to move faster than others or develop practices that are difficult to imitate can achieve a competitive advantage that can lead to increase return on capital and market valuation multiples.[12] But it will be difficult for a company to realize these commercial benefits if it hasn't established the right foundation, with basic sustainability principles and practices in place, and if sustainability hasn't been integrated into the core business.

Telia Company and its Board of Directors have committed to a statement of materiality in their sustainability reporting framework which says in part: "It is Telia Company's firm belief that the best way of ensuring sustainable growth and profitability is integrating sustainable, responsible business practices into all parts of business and strategy, to create long-term shared value for the company, its stakeholders and society."[13] As former CEO Johan Dennelind explains: "Having said that on a piece of paper doesn't mean much, but when you have it fully integrated into what we do, it shows we have come a long way. We show that sustainability *is* profitable, that it *is* a prerequisite for long-term profitability, and we talk about this to investors a lot. It is this connection that makes sustainability core to our strategy and our equity story."

Jonas Samuelsson, CEO of Electrolux, agrees. He "absolutely" sees a definitive link between sustainability and profitability, borne out by the sales of its most water- and energy-efficient products, which outperform the rest of the portfolio (see Chap. 8). Sustainability is also firmly integrated into product R&D; Electrolux spends one-third of its R&D budget on sustainable product innovation, with a particular focus on water and energy efficiency.[14]

Sustainability investments in operations and within product development at Electrolux, Jonas continues, drives a higher level in terms of capital expenditures and requires returning investment in manufacturing technology and new solutions, but also reduces costs over time. He says:

The more energy efficient your manufacturing, the more profitable it is, and the more energy efficient the products are in terms of reducing consumer energy bills, the more consumers are willing to pay for those products. And it helps sell more of these products, because the superior environmental performance is a visible aspect of the product, as most countries now have energy labels on products where the annual energy consumption is rated on the product.

From Core to Market

As exemplified by Northvolt at the start of this chapter, using scarce resources in a smart way, making sustainability part of everything a company does, and adopting a value chain approach are all necessary ingredients in making sustainability part of the core. In Northvolt's case, and for the other companies examined in this chapter, there are a number of key elements in integrating sustainability. These include making it an executive issue, finding the right organizational structure to deliver on the commitments, not relegating sustainability to a separate, add-on strategy, and prioritizing it within R&D, design, and innovation to shape the product portfolio in line with sustainability aims.

The next challenge is to get sustainability product and service offerings to market because the fastest way to really embed sustainability within the company and grow the sustainability impact is to get customers on board. Chapter 7 discusses the importance of linking sustainability to sales, and presents a number of compelling company examples that offer inspiration in this regard.

Key Takeaways

1. There is no sustainability strategy, only a business strategy, that is, or isn't sustainable in the long term.
2. Create (or revisit) the company vision and value proposition to determine how sustainability can be built into the business model.
3. Leadership starts at the top. Drive sustainability as an executive issue but also build from the bottom up: make sustainability everyone's job by empowering people and delegating responsibility. Be a trainer yourself.
4. Integration of sustainability into the product and portfolio perspective can be incremental or can encompass the entire portfolio, as long as the company is headed in the right direction.
5. It's a leader's responsibility to know what is in their company's products and the impacts caused by its business activities. Ignorance could be negligence.
6. When designing and developing future products and services, use design principles and sustainability indicators to enhance R&D. This will put you on the right path to find the sustainability-profitability nexus.

Notes

1. Phil Dzikiy, "Northvolt secures $ billion from VW, others for Gigafactory; joint factory with VW also planned," June 12, 2019, https://electrek. co/2019/06/12/Northvolt-gigafactory-volkswagen-1billion/.
2. "Scania and Northvolt partner for heavy vehicle electrification," Jan 25, 2018, Scania.com, https://www.scania.com/group/en/scania-and-Northvolt-partner-for-heavy-vehicle-electrification/.
3. The Northvolt Loop, Northvolt.com, accessed March 13, 2020, https://Northvolt.com/loop/.
4. The Northvolt Loop, Northvolt.com, https://Northvolt.com/loop/.
5. Electrolux Green Range, accessed March 13, 2020, https://www.electrolux.com.au/green/.
6. "World's first electric road opens in Sweden," June 23, 2016, Scania.com, https://www.scania.com/group/en/worlds-first-electric-road-opens-in-sweden-2/.
7. How we want to change the world, Houdinisportswear.com, accessed April 5, 2020, https://houdinisportswear.com/en-eu/sustainability/how-we-want-to-change-the-world.
8. Design philosophy, Houdinisportswear.com, accessed April 5, 2020, https://houdinisportswear.com/en-no/sustainability/design-philosophy.
9. "The fight against microfibers," Houdinisportswear.com, accessed March 13, 2020, https://houdinisportswear.com/en-eu/sustainability/the-fight-against-microplastics.
10. Tensie Whelan and Carly Fink, "The Comprehensive Business Case for Sustainability," *Harvard Business Review*, Oct 2016, https://hbr.org/2016/10/the-comprehensive-business-case-for-sustainability.
11. Maureen Kline, "How to drive Profits with Corporate Responsibility," Inc., July 24, 2018, https://www.inc.com/maureen-kline/how-to-drive-profits-with-corporate-social-responsibility.html.
12. Ioannis Ioannou and George Serafeim, "Yes, Sustainability Can Be a Strategy," *Harvard Business Review*, Feb 2019, https://hbr.org/2019/02/yes-sustainability-can-be-a-strategy.
13. Telia Company Sustainability Reporting Framework, Telia Company, March 20, 2019, https://www.teliacompany.com/globalassets/telia-company/documents/about-telia-company/sustainability-report/telia-company-sustainability-reporting-framework-2018.pdf.
14. Electrolux Sustainability Brief 2018, accessed April 7, 2020, https://www.electroluxgroup.com/sustainabilityreports/2018/files/elux-2018/SustainabilityinBrief.pdf.

7

It All Comes Down to Sales

Up Close: Åsa Bergman, CEO of Sweco, on Partnering with Customers to Build the Sustainable Communities and Cities of the Future

Sea level rise is one of the most vivid signs of climate change. The Netherlands is among the countries in the world considered ground zero for a more watery and unwelcome future. Today, almost half of the Netherlands' 17 million inhabitants live along its 350-kilometer coast or in regions which are below sea level.[1] The government estimates that if sea level rise overwhelms water defenses, 60 percent of the country could be flooded.[2]

That's an alarming prospect for anyone—and the Netherlands is not alone in being worried about how to be more resilient in the face of climate change. In fact, new research shows that some 150 million people are now living on land that will be below the high-tide line by midcentury. According to C40, a network of the world's megacities, over 90 percent of all urban areas are coastal, putting most cities on earth at risk of flooding from rising sea levels and powerful storms.[3]

Because of this scenario, the Netherlands was searching for viable solutions to help their cities and communities persevere and thrive in a climate-constrained future, and they found that in Sweco. The leading engineering and architecture consultancy in Europe, Sweco is on the frontlines of helping cities and communities cope with the effects of climate change.

Sweco's headquarters may be in Stockholm, and its roots Swedish, but its locally based consultants are spread across Europe, where they gain a deep understanding of the challenges facing clients. Because of that, they can deploy Sweco's competence in a more accessible, attentive, solution-oriented, and result-focused way. That is exactly the intention of Sweco's decentralized model, explains President and CEO Åsa Bergman: to be close to the clients in

© The Author(s) 2020
H. Henriksson, E. Weidman Grunewald, *Sustainability Leadership*,
https://doi.org/10.1007/978-3-030-42291-2_7

all 70 countries where it operates, with a focus on clean water, efficient infra-structure, and sustainable energy solutions. Because of its decentralized approach Sweco doesn't have a separate sales organization. Rather, all consultants are client-driven and P&L (profit and loss) accountability is pushed out to the project level. "It means our people understand clients' drivers and needs better than anyone else," Åsa explains.

In Amsterdam, floating cities are a feasible option for areas that are repeat-edly flooded. One example is the floating neighborhood that is part of the IJburg Islands development, which Sweco helped to design. This collection of artificial islands on reclaimed land east of the city is transforming the city to meet future challenges: dealing with Amsterdam's housing shortage, while ensuring climate resilience. Projected to be a city of 18,000 residences and 45,000 citizens, it is already home to 10,000 people[4] (Fig. 7.1).

Define an Offering and Link It to the Core

Sweco's core business is to plan and design sustainable communities and cities of the future and its offering spans consulting engineering, environmental technology, and architecture. As the effects of climate change increasingly

Fig. 7.1 The IJburg Islands (© Sweco). The floating neighborhood that is part of the IJburg Islands development, which Sweco helped to design, is an example of how coastal regions of the world are preparing for a climate-constrained future

become a reality, Sweco is meeting growing demand by developing more solutions for climate adaptation such as effective storm water management and urban transport solutions. As such, addressing sustainability is an increasingly integral part of the urban planning that Sweco carries out for its clients, all of which can be applied at an overall national or regional perspective down to the individual building.

Åsa says:

> Everything we do is about delivering knowledge and solutions connected to our clients' needs, demands and questions. We've had sustainability on our agenda for a really long time, so whether or not a client is asking for sustainable solutions, we provide knowledge in line with that, and try to pull or push clients in the right direction. Fifteen years ago, clients didn't ask for that as much as they do now—today being in front and being relevant is all about delivering sustainable solutions, in all projects, and that is exactly where our knowledge and competence lie. We plan the sustainable communities and cities of the future and that means we need to have a long-term perspective.

From Core Business to Sales

Unless sustainability is anchored with customers, it will be difficult to achieve impact or scale with a sustainable solution or innovation, and to gain the financial returns so critical to success. While it's important to understand where customers are on their own sustainability journey, there is a great leadership opportunity in presenting a vision to customers about where that journey could lead and how to help them reach that destination.

In the Sweco case, sustainability is clearly embedded in the core offering, but this is often not the case for other companies, who often struggle to find such direct business linkages. Securing the link between sustainability and profitability, and sales can be a challenge, but as we discussed in Chap. 4, the links are growing stronger. Another hurdle has been a lack of tools and methods to directly connect a sustainability offering with sales results, or, to reflect sustainability in the sales process itself.

In order to successfully integrate sustainability with sales, we suggest a three-pronged approach. First, define a customer sustainability offering that is attractive, competitive and which customers find compelling, not least because it can help them achieve their own sustainability goals. Second, ensure the sales and marketing team is equipped and trained to use sustainability value arguments as a tool in driving sales and developing customer relationships.

Third, go out and sell it, and be sure to measure your success. It is not necessary to be a first mover—what matters is having a clear view of what is important within a company's own business ecosystem to get traction with customers. Once that is identified, the opportunity to leverage sustainability through innovative products or services is considerable and growing numbers of companies are succeeding in this space. We explore each of these areas in greater detail below.

Making the Sales-Sustainability Connection

Of 81 percent of FTSE (The Financial Times Stock Exchange) 100 companies with sustainability as a key objective, only 15 percent have processes in place to measure this. A smart sales team understands their customers' sustainability objectives so that they can support and measure the outcome for them.[5] Some companies like cloud-computing technology firm Salesforce, which specializes in customer relationship management (CRM), provide software solutions to manage and track nearly every aspect of the sales process, from pricing to personalized buying experiences to working smarter and faster. They have solutions for non-profits, startups, and large companies, yet their sustainability solution seems to be limited to tracking, analyzing, and reporting environmental data. This feature is a great tool for setting up the foundation of a sustainability journey, as described in Chap. 2, but it does not enable a company to understand how their own portfolio may be selling from a sustainability perspective, or to determine the relative significance of the sustainability features of their products or services relative to other features.

Despite the shortage of guidance and tools, some companies have devised their own methods for making the connection from a sales lead that might have been generated from a sustainability attribute to converting that lead to a deal. Elaine's team at Ericsson spent considerable time together with the sales team, and worked to create a method to track sales leads that were tied to sustainability features (in this case, energy or OPEX reductions, or to socioeconomic development benefits). Once this type of lead was captured and began to be tracked, the sales team soon found they had hundreds of leads from all over the world. The challenge was then to convert the leads to deals. Once they started to track leads, this brought important visibility to the sustainability aspects of the offering, and the team was able to establish supporting measurements and targets. This kind of indicator also generated a lot of interest from external stakeholders such as investors, who were keen to see the business-sustainability connection.

Scania has developed its own approach for integrating sustainability into their entire sales process, as we illustrate below in the discussion on the Scania sales funnel. Fundamental to Scania's approach is that sustainability transformation starts and ends with the customer. Some 95 percent of the company's carbon footprint occurs when its vehicles are in use. This means that no meaningful transformation of the company, or industry, is possible if customers are not prepared to buy and use its low-carbon products and solutions. In short, if customers don't reward Scania with their orders and their business, they won't be relevant for long in driving the shift.

Scania finds that its customers are focused on eliminating waste, saving resources, and reducing costs, for example, reduction of fuel consumption. The shift away from fossil fuels is a focal point for innovation and an opportunity to build demand for its most sustainable products. It is prompted not only by growing customer awareness of climate change and the desire to meet their own sustainability commitments, but by cities looking for sustainable public transport solutions. For example, four major global cities—Paris, Mexico City, Madrid, and Athens—have announced they will stop all use of diesel-powered vehicles by the middle of the next decade.[6] The Nordic countries are also in the lead, with Sweden, Norway, and Denmark all pledging to ban sales of diesel-powered cars within the next decade[7] (Fig. 7.2).

More broadly, consumers and customers are increasingly demanding more sustainable products. In the consumer packaged goods (CPG) industry, for example, recent data from the New York University Center for Sustainable Business (CSB) found that 50 percent of sales growth among CPG between 2013 and 2018 came from sustainability-marketed products, such as those advertised with criteria like non-GMO (genetically modified organisms), plant-based, or certified by a third party like the Rainforest Alliance or Fair Trade, despite the fact that such goods account for just under 17 percent of the market. While there might be a gap still between intentions and actual purchasing, "sustainability is where the growth is. There's been a massive shift in the past five years," Tensie Whelan, CSB Director, told *Fortune*.[8]

Among Swedes, the ability to choose more sustainable products has become the norm. A study by the European Commission found that 40 percent of Swedes have purchased eco-labeled food and consumer products in one month, higher than the European average.[9] The lesson to be drawn is that if companies consistently make the link to sustainability with their products and services, integrate the approach with the company's core KPIs such as gross margin, and these efforts are matched by real demand and interest in sustainability among customers and consumers, the investment quickly bears fruit.

Fig. 7.2 The Scania NXT is an example of innovation to meet the needs of fast-growing cities (© Scania). A battery electric self-driving urban concept vehicle, it is designed with the flexibility to shift from ferrying commuters to and from work in mornings and evenings, delivering goods during the day, and collecting refuse at night

Reaching the Customer

There are a number of ways to get customers to act on a sustainability offering. One fruitful approach is to convey the sustainability attributes clearly to customers. For leading global appliance company Electrolux, key factors influencing sustainable product sales are recycling and energy efficiency. Product energy use is responsible for over 80 percent of its climate impact over the life cycle, so product energy efficiency is where Electrolux can make the greatest contribution to tackling climate change. That drives the product development for appliances such as its Line 6000 tumble dryers that reduce energy by 60 percent.[10] Electrolux has used 20 times more recycled plastic in its products in 2019 compared with 2011, and has upped the amount of recycled steel from 7 percent in 2013 to 22 percent in 2019, which has reduced the annual CO_2 emissions by 17,700 metric tons.[11]

When it comes to sales, on-product energy and performance labeling and sustainability communication help raise consumer awareness of those products with the greatest resource and product efficiency. In turn this contributes to retailer sustainability goals and leads to more sustainable consumer choices.[12]

As Electrolux CEO Jonas Samuelsson explains, "In Europe, North America and an increasing number of countries, the sticker on the products—the energy rating—is one of the selling features. When we negotiate with our retailer partners about what the price should be, the energy rating becomes one of the parameters. If we have a product rated B or A+, those are different price points, or for Energy Star in the US, that becomes our part of our commercial association." Providing fact-based sustainability information, validated by an official program, has become an attractive purchasing factor for Electrolux consumers—an interesting takeaway for other companies.

Electrolux' most energy- and water-efficient products in 2019 accounted for 23 percent of total units sold and 32 percent of gross profit for consumer products.[13] While the performance of this group of products is a well-known sustainability success story, "We'd like to see that share of sales increase more, to be honest," Jonas confesses, "so we have more work to do."

The Brand Connection

The most energy- and water-efficient products in the Electrolux portfolio, as we explore in the next chapter, are excellent examples of how to use a specific product range to gain sales traction by creating a strong connection between the brand proposition and sustainability. When sustainability is infused within the brand, it can be extremely powerful.

Another example is the leading Swedish industrial group Axel Johnson, which comprises companies across several business and retail sectors including retail grocery company Axfood, beauty chain KICKS; Dustin, one of the leading resellers of IT products and additional services in the Nordics; and leading Swedish department store chain Åhléns. As CEO Mia Brunell Livfors explained, Axel Johnson's approach is to always offer a sustainable choice to customers.

Axel Johnson also tracks progress with sustainability KPIs. That includes measuring the share of sales coming from ecological products or a sustainable assortment (e.g., in foods, beauty), or growth in non-meat protein products. One of Axfood's sustainability targets is that by 2025, sustainability-certified products will account for at least 25 percent of sales.[14]

There is both a business case and a consumer demand for this kind of offering, according to Mia. "We've seen sustainability become more and more important for consumers, and it has accelerated over the past few years and even faster during the last year."

One of the brands sold in the Axel Johnson family of businesses, the fashion retailer Filippa K, has a strategy of encouraging consumers to choose "the hard

Fig. 7.3 Swedish fashion retailer Filippa K is working with a local farmer to produce products using Swedish wool that would otherwise be burned

right vs. the easy wrong," that is, to make it easier to make the right sustainable choice. That's an integral part of the brand, too, in which five elements are all interwoven with sustainability: always be relevant to customers, don't compromise between style, quality, fit and sustainability; focus on product longevity (Filippa K products are used on average 75 times versus seven times for the average fashion product, according to a quantitative consumers study in Sweden and the UK in 2019), resource efficiency, and to be transparent. In one example, Filippa K has partnered with a local farmer to produce products using Swedish wool that would otherwise be burned. Sweden's sheep provide over 1000 tonnes of wool every year, most of which go to waste. By partnering with the local farm, the fashion retailer gets a naturally organic raw material, turns waste into a resource, reduces carbon footprint, and supports good animal welfare (Fig. 7.3).

Selling a Solution

Scania's strategic positioning as a solutions provider rather than a heavy-duty vehicle manufacturer is the first layer of its sustainable sales approach. Scania has developed a granular understanding of both transport buyers and transport operators, not only in the purchasing moment but during operation, and then applies this knowledge to create a larger demand for sustainable solutions. By understanding what transport buyers and transport operators need, Scania can better support them in transitioning their own business to become fossil free; for example, to run the vehicles on biofuels or electric. Scania's insight also creates a level of comfort for the customer when it comes to purchasing a new vehicle type with requirements for new types of fuels. One approach is to partner with reputable alternative fuel providers. For example, by bundling products and services, Scania can offer a stable, predictable fuel price over the length of the contract which can help bridge resistance to a more sustainable solution.

When a company enjoys financial success while pursuing a strong sustainability agenda, the reward is more freedom to act and innovate. This has been important for Henrik, because positive market signals keep the team moving ahead and setting new ambitions. If sustainability trials and offers are not profitable, eventually they will be closed down, due to internal cost pressure or because the organization sees it as a failure. Sales of a sustainable offering must be visible to the rest of the organization, for example in R&D and production, to make the case for why the product was developed in the first place. Of course, R&D and product development must be closely tied to sales, in both performance and differentiated products, as we discussed in Chap. 4. Constant customer feedback close to product R&D is an essential ingredient for continuously improving the products, and in continually adapting to meet society's growing needs for more sustainable solutions.

Over the past few years Scania has seen an uptick in the number of customers and the customer's customers that are demanding sustainable transport. Scania is beginning to see evidence of this in its own income statements. For example, sales of Scania's low-carbon city bus solution (alternative fuel and/or hybrids) hit an all-time high in 2019 at some 40 percent of total sales.

Scania decided a few years ago to ensure that all vehicles being produced could run on renewable biofuels and to integrate sustainability as a standard part of the offering. Today Scania has the broadest range of vehicles ready for alternative fuels. While Scania's vision is ultimately to reduce use of fossil fuels in its vehicles to zero, in parallel it is helping customers to improve energy efficiency and reduce fuel consumption and CO_2 emissions for vehicles running on fossil fuels. A reduction of 10 percent of fuel consumption on vehicles running on fossil fuels would have a significant impact. To make progress and influence customers' purchasing behaviors, action is needed on both fronts: making the right products available and focusing on energy efficiency.

Raising Awareness

Simply asking the right questions can help to spark customer awareness of the potential benefits of more sustainable solutions. In 2010 Ericsson was looking at how to scale up renewable energy to power off-grid telecom sites in emerging markets. The sustainability team conducted a market assessment among key account managers to determine the existence of such sites in their markets. The results were surprising, showing some 2000 off-grid sites running on renewables. With Ericsson present in 180 countries, the study provided important insight into the market position and competitor situation in different regions of the world.

Swedish outdoor apparel company Houdini went a step further. According to Eva Karlsson, CEO of Houdini, sustainability is built into sales "in the most effective way by not offering anything but sustainable alternatives, encouraging a customer base that aligns with our philosophy and brand." Designed for longevity and multi-purpose use, Houdini's products are intended to upend the idea of "fast fashion." A Power Houdi, a type of hoodie, Eva explains, is used on average 1287 times during its lifetime, equivalent to more than ten years and several times a week for a great variety of activities. In comparison, in the Western world, the average number of times a garment is worn before it ceases to be used can be as little as seven to ten wears.[15] In addition, by offering services such as product care and repairs, Houdini ReUse as an alternative to new apparel purchases, and Houdini Rental as an alternative to buying, sustainability is built into the business model as well.

Houdini is onto something. There is growing interest in the circular economy, which could unlock $4.5 trillion in economic growth through circular business models, according to Accenture.[16] As one indication, the global online clothing rental market is expected to double, reaching $2.09 billion by 2025,[17] as consumer preferences shift away from fast fashion.

Linear vs Circular Economy

In a linear economy, we take resources from the ground to make products, which we use, and, when we no longer want them, throw them away. Take-make-waste. In a circular economy, we design out waste and pollution, keep products and materials in use, and regenerate natural systems.
—*Source: The Ellen MacArthur Foundation*[18]

Houdini's approach cleverly entwines sustainability stepchange with customer convenience and appeal, with the goal of creating a lifestyles solution: "Our latest project, the regenerative Lifestyles Initiative, is to evaluate our impact not only on nature, such as our carbon footprint or biodiversity impact, but also our impact on culture and lifestyle. How can we design lifestyle solutions that will lead people to live healthier, happier and more rewarding lives? The idea is to enable a much smaller and smarter wardrobe and garments that never limits us."

Create Impact, Together

One of the most effective ways of getting traction with customers on a sustainability solution, product, or service is to kindle an emotional connection around the potential to create positive impact together. Many Technology for Good initiatives were kickstarted this way at Ericsson, and Elaine discovered that what began as a feel-good exercise when approaching the sales team rapidly grew into new opportunities to engage with customers on an emotional level, to partner together for positive societal outcomes. Once the customer narrative was clear, demand began to flow from outside the company—from customers and governments—which further focused the attention and resources of the sales team. In 2007, Elaine was working with Ericsson in Uganda. Ericsson had just convinced mobile telecommunications operator MTN that together they should enable connectivity in a refugee settlement on the border to South Sudan, where many people were fleeing conflict in that country for the more stable Uganda. Ericsson worked jointly with MTN, the GSMA Development Fund (today called Mobile For Development), and the UN refugee agency, the UNHCR, to connect refugee settlements to affordable voice and data services via GSM through the extension of the existing network into previously unconnected areas, or upgrading the existing GSM network to provide 3G capabilities.

In the project, Ericsson committed to support the pilot by extending and upgrading the existing network to enable efficient voice and data capabilities. This included the required technical solution, including alternative power sources, and the development of mobile applications and the provision of phones. MTN Uganda committed to the expansion of the GSM network in order to provide coverage for "Shared Access to Voice" and "Shared Access to Data" services in the refugee settlement. UNHCR provide access to the refugee settlements and onsite support.

While it is hard to estimate the sales value, once the site was up and running, it became a very profitable site in the network, largely because the demand and the need for communication were so great. Ericsson and MTN continued to work on many such mobile-for-development cases. In this example the companies were able to do business while also addressing a serious societal need; that is, they were also doing good. The value of these types of public-private partnerships has evolved and is discussed further in Chap. 9 in the context of the SDGs.

Sustainability Across the Sales Funnel

Shortly after becoming CEO in 2016, Henrik set out a challenge to his sales organization to drive the shift in sustainable transport. His demand, supported by the Executive Board, was that every sales quotation would inherently include a sustainability component. This was intended to induce a change in mindset for the sales organization. Even if the customer said, "I think I want something else," Scania should offer something more sustainable for the customer and society—which was also a reflection of Scania's long-term vision and purpose. Of course, the sales team would still have to work with classic metrics, but this new component would drive change in the right direction.

To make that happen in practice, Scania used the sales funnel with its step approach to ensure sustainability considerations were built into each step of the sales process—mirroring the customers' buying process. Henrik's goal, to make sustainability the standard in every quotation, began happening in an increasing number of cases. And while the approach is still small scale, it is growing faster than anything else at the moment.

Tools and methods have been put in place—along with extensive training—to motivate, encourage, and equip the salesforce to meet this emerging area of customer demand for sustainability solutions. For example, changes to the sales system now enable salespeople to easily specify products suited to a customer's operations, including sustainability considerations.

The connection between the sales process and the product development process—to ensure a strong sustainable customer offering—is of course a precondition, and we examined the importance of a sustainability offering in Chap. 4. But then it comes down to sales. For Scania, like many companies, awareness, consideration, decision, and retention in the sales funnel are typical elements of a sales process. However, Scania has intentionally used the funnel to ensure that sustainability is integrated every step of the way.

Leadership within Scania's sales organization to pull more customers toward sustainable solutions to customers is exemplified by Jacob Thärnå, Director of Sustainable Transport for Commercial Operations at Scania Group, who has been instrumental in developing the approach. To encourage customer consideration of alternative fuels, the sales system enables the salesforce to map whether the sustainable alternative fuel and fuel infrastructure are available in a specific country, and to make a comparison between two or more alternatives based on total cost of ownership and CO_2 emissions. For example, in countries where some alternative fuels are less expensive, such as Spain, the salesforce can show the customer that a vehicle that runs on biogas, while costing more upfront, would pay itself off in a couple of years compared to purchasing a vehicle that runs on fossil fuel.

To push consideration further, Scania helps its customers find common ground with their customers, the transport buyers. This involves brokering discussion between the two interested parties—the direct customer and their customer—to agree on the most beneficial and sustainable transport solution. A transport buyer keen to lower its CO_2 emissions to meet climate targets might be interested in switching to vehicles that run on biofuels, but these vehicles have a higher upfront cost and longer payback period for the transporter. Instead of just asking the transport buyer to pay more, an alternative to is to build the relationship between buyer and supplier so they can agree to longer contracts for sustainable capital-heavy transport solutions than the typical two-year contract for traditional diesel vehicles. This is a win-win for buyer and provider alike, and a successful sustainable sale for Scania, which also creates security for customers, doesn't result in increased costs for transport buyers, and enables fuel providers to also invest in infrastructure.

One of the more successful risk-taking decisions for Scania was to standardize the fleet to connect all vehicles and for Scania to bear the cost of this investment, rather than trying to sell a solution which at that time was still quite intangible. In this approach, which also enhances customer retention, Scania uses real-time data from over 350,000 connected vehicles.[19] Data and analytics are a powerful way to visualize information, but also to track customer usage and preferences and thereby identify how to improve their fuel efficiency, profitability and carbon emissions. It also enables a close-up view of the activity of the entire fleet. Connectivity can put a spotlight on driver coaching for improved fuel efficiency, usually the biggest cost driver for the customer. The ability to show a wide range of real-time as well as historic data will, over time, help to convince customers (or customers' customers) to shift to new alternative solutions like biofuels.

Risk and cost-sharing arrangements are additional tools to create retention. In many cases Scania supplies not only the vehicle, but also the infrastructure and the fuel supply. For example, when it sells a bioethanol truck, Scania can sell it with new tank station, so the customer has fuel on the premises, as well as a ten-year supply of bioethanol at a fixed rate. The same is true for electrification. This removes the risk for the customer and gives them control over fuel costs as well as a guaranteed fuel supply.

Scania has found that once sustainable products, services, or approaches become integrated into the sales process, this creates significant momentum in driving uptake of sustainability throughout the company as a whole. It isn't always plain sailing, though, and at the outset, Henrik admits, CEOs need to be willing to take risks to try and shift behavior—not only among their own customers but their customers too. Scania wasn't sure at first what it would do with the data it collected, but was certain that it would present use cases and be of considerable value. Today the connectivity of Scania's vehicles is one of the main factors in its strategy to drive the shift in sustainable transport and customer profitability and retention and is also valuable in product development, specification, and follow-up.

Empowering the Sales Team

Having the sustainability commitment tied to core values with leadership from the top is an important driver for the entire organization, including the salesforce. This ensures that the commitment becomes real—not just to customers and the bottom line but for the brand promise and corporate DNA as well, all of which gives it lasting power. To succeed in the customer domain, though, proper training and education for the salesforce are a must. The salesforce needs to feel confident fielding questions about sustainability and putting forward the sustainability offering; otherwise, it can backfire.

Sweco, for instance, with the Sweco Model, uses the typical Swedish management approach of decentralized responsibility to empower consultants to solve customers' demands and develop customer relationships. Consultant teams are the basic building blocks of the organization: all consultants and managers are expected to be customer-facing and encouraged to do business. Team managers have full business responsibility, including managing customer relationships, projects, people, and financial performance. At the same time, Sweco acts as one company and operates under the same brand to capture the benefits of being a large, leading entity in Northern Europe.

There are many different approaches to bringing a sales team onboard. At Ericsson, a tactic was to create an annual sustainability award at the Top Sales conference. Winning awards at this event (which included several categories) was prestigious as it meant the winners were invited to attend the annual sales retreat. Monthly updates were also held with all sales and marketing people globally, and internal "points" could be earned for completing product and portfolio courses focused on sustainability offerings as well as taking part in specific sustainability training (sustainability was also integrated into a broader competence development program).

The upshot: don't be afraid to try different approaches to find what works best for the team and get the whole salesforce empowered and onboard.

A Tailored Approach

While Scania and the other company examples here can hopefully be an inspiration to others, it's not a case of one-size-fits-all. Each company will need to tailor their approach to the needs of their company, industry, and customer base. For Sweco, where this chapter began, the right approach is helping customers take the long view. Since sustainability is, by its very nature, long term, a potent customer hook is to help them think about the future when making decisions about products and services. Supporting customers to spot opportunities and potential challenges by examining their long-term needs is intrinsic to their approach, as Åsa Bergman explains:

> We see ourselves as advisors, providing our clients with solutions that are very much about the future. Whether we're designing a city district or a transport system or a hospital or a factory, we are helping customers to recognize not only what their need is today but what it will be in ten to fifteen years or longer. We have always had a long-term perspective, trying to look into the future, to understand what's coming next. How do we do that? Of course, no one can be absolutely sure about what the future holds but if you combine Sweco's collective competence, somewhere within the Group we have the solutions that will help our customers navigate the future.

Since every customer situation is unique, whether they're in Amsterdam, Paris, or Stockholm, Sweco's decentralized model of local, independent offices helps to ensure that sustainability is integrated into the sales approach as well as tailored to specific needs. "We understand the client and create local client relationships based around the challenges, issues and demands that our clients

Fig. 7.4 Barkarbystaden, Stockholm (© Sweco). Sweco has been involved in developing Barkarbystaden into a vibrant and sustainable district in northern Stockholm in Sweden. It will include housing for 30,000 people along with schools and playgrounds, libraries, stores, and public transport to and from Stockholm's inner city

have. That means we need to be local, to ensure we have the relevant competence close to our clients. If we can advise our clients in ways that contribute sustainable solutions through everything we do, we will make a huge difference," she explains (Fig. 7.4).

At the end of the day, a leader's actions must be directed at creating value for the customer, no matter the industry. Sales are crucial because they are tangible recognition that customers support the sustainable value proposition. In other words, they think a company's sustainable products and services have value and they're willing to pay for them. When a company has successfully merged sustainability and profitability, it's a testament that its business purpose is here to stay.

Key Takeaways

1. Sustainability can be an important aspect of the brand that increases loyalty and customer retention. Make sure your product offering meets your customers' needs, while also delivering on company goals and values.
2. Be willing to take and share risk with customers to help them overcome hurdles to closing the deal.

3. Train and empower the sales team, ensure sustainability criteria are embedded at every stage of the sales process, and incentivize results.
4. Make sure to measure sustainability sales leads and results. Remove obstacles and give the salesforce the tools to make it easy to sell the sustainable offering.
5. If sustainability isn't integral to sales and reflected in the numbers, it will be hard to bring the organization along on the sustainability journey.

Notes

1. Deborah Nicholls-Lee, "As sea levels rise, how long until the Netherlands is under water?" DutchNews.nl, Dec 23, 2019, https://www.dutchnews.nl/news/2019/12/as-sea-levels-rise-how-long-until-the-netherlands-is-under-water/.
2. Delta Programme, Government of the Netherlands, accessed Jan 18, 2020, https://www.government.nl/topics/delta-programme.
3. C40 Cities: Why Cities Are the Solution To Global Climate Change, accessed Jan 18, 2020, https://www.c40.org/ending-climate-change-begins-in-the-city.
4. "Sweco assigned to develop three major city districts in Amsterdam," May 9, 2017, http://mb.cision.com/Main/1356/2260282/670927.pdf.
5. "Sustainability in technology sales: what can we do?" ESP, Dec 17, 2019, https://esprecruit.com/news/sustainability-in-technology-sales-what-can-we-do/.
6. Matt McGrath, "Four major cities move to ban diesel vehicles by 2025," BBC News, Dec 2, 2016, https://www.bbc.com/news/science-environment-38170794.
7. Ethan Jupp, "Sweden to ban petrol and diesel cars, as Germany feels the pressure," Motoring Research, Jan 24, 2019, https://www.motoringresearch.com/car-news/sweden-ban-petrol-diesel-cars/.
8. Renae Reints, "Consumer Say They Want More Sustainable Products. Now they have the Receipts to Prove it," Fortune, Nov 5, 2019, https://fortune.com/2019/11/05/sustainability-marketing-consumer-spending/.
9. Ben Wilde, "How Sweden Became the World's Most Sustainable Country: Top 5 Reasons," ADEC Innovations, Jan 12, 2016, https://info.esg.adec-innovations.com/blog/how-sweden-became-the-worlds-most-sustainable-country-top-5-reasons.
10. Electrolux Line 6000 tumble dryers, accessed Jan 18, 2020, https://professional.electrolux.com/commercial-laundry-equipment/tumble-dryer-2/.
11. Electrolux Sustainability Report 2019, accessed April 13, 2020 https://www.electroluxgroup.com/sustainabilityreports/2019/.
12. Electrolux, Sustainability in Brief, 2018.

13. Electrolux Annual Report 2019, accessed April 5, 2020, https://www.electro-luxgroup.com/sustainabilityreports/2019/files/2019/PDF/Electrolux_Sustainability_Report_2019_final.pdf.

14. Axfood Annual and Sustainability Report 2018, accessed Jan 18, 2020., https://www.axfood.com/globalassets/startsida/investerare/rapporter-och-presentationer/axfood_ar18_eng.pdf.

15. A New Textiles Economy: Redesigning Fashion's Future, Ellen Macarthur Foundation, 2017, accessed Jan 18, 2020, https://www.ellenmacarthurfoun-dation.org/assets/downloads/publications/A-New-Textiles-Economy_Full-Report_Updated_1-12-17.pdf.

16. "The Circular Economy Could Unlock $4.5 trillion of economic growth, find new book by Accenture," Accenture.com, Sept 28, 2015, https://newsroom.accenture.com/news/the-circular-economy-could-unlock-4-5-trillion-of-eco-nomic-growth-finds-new-book-by-accenture.htm.

17. "Online Clothing Rental Market Worth $2.9 billion by 2025," April 2019, Grand View Research, accessed February 10, 2020, https://www.grand-viewresearch.com/press-release/global-online-clothing-rental-market.

18. What is the Circular Economy, Ellen MacArthur Foundation, https://ellen-macarthurfoundation.org.

19. Smart and safe transport, Scania.com, accessed March 12, 2020, https://www.scania.com/group/en/smart-and-safe-transport/.

8

Measuring Impact Beyond Profit

Up Close: Electrolux CEO Jonas Samuelsson on Combining Sustainability and Profitability

It's called the Great Pacific Garbage Patch, a rapidly growing hot spot for ocean plastic, carrying 1.8 trillion pieces of plastic in what is now the largest accumulation of ocean debris in the world.[1] That's one huge problem for marine life, wildlife, and human health. But for world-leading appliance manufacturer Electrolux, that gigantic floating pile of plastic debris was also an opportunity to get creative. So, in an effort to raise awareness about the global shortage of recycled plastics, Electrolux launched a campaign called Vac from the Sea.[2] Volunteers got to work, collecting plastic from oceans that were then turned into a number of special edition vacuum cleaners, each representing a specific ocean.

While this was a successful concept to shed light on an important issue, Electrolux has had a long-standing commitment to sustainable products. For many years, Electrolux has tracked the performance of its most energy and water-efficient products across markets, setting high standards for energy efficiency and energy labeling. More recently, Electrolux extended these bold metrics across its portfolio. And it's paid off. The company's most energy- and water-efficient products are by far the company's most profitable, consistently delivering higher margins. In 2019, these products accounted for 23 percent of total units sold and 32 percent of gross profit for consumer products in 2019.[3] Individual product efficiency targets are designed to contribute toward the company's bold 50 percent climate reduction targets.[4]

Impact matters to consumers, and that is obvious in the demand for more sustainable products. It also matters to other stakeholders when it comes to showing how a company can measure impact beyond profit—and that comes down to having the right numbers. Electrolux has a core set of targets and key

© The Author(s) 2020
H. Henriksson, E. Weidman Grunewald, *Sustainability Leadership*,
https://doi.org/10.1007/978-3-030-42291-2_8

performance indicators (KPIs) across its portfolio and operations that guide its everyday sustainability work. Take the plastics issue. In 2019, Electrolux used 6400 metric tons of recycled plastic, over 20 times more recycled plastic than when it started measuring in 2011[5]—when those concept vacuum cleaners made a big splash. However, as an indication that some targets are simply hard to reach, despite focused effort, Electrolux does not expect to meet its target to annually use 20,000 metric tons of recycled plastics by 2020—a lack of supply with sufficient quality outside Europe is part of the problem.[6] That said, it is stepping up its efforts to drive progress in coming years (Fig. 8.1).

But if there is one overriding target that keeps Electrolux CEO Jonas Samuelsson up at night, it is how to reduce the total carbon footprint of its products in manufacturing, distribution and use, and, most importantly, consumer use of its products.

"With an installed base of 400 million major appliances and 600 million in total, our products consume a lot of energy when used by families around the world and most of that energy is produced using fossil fuels. To the extent that we can impact that—and we can, very significantly—that is the biggest

Fig. 8.1 An Electrolux house (© Electrolux). Electrolux is a leading global appliance company that has shaped what it calls "living for the better" for more than 100 years. For many Swedes, that includes homes like this one which reflect a symbiosis with the natural world. Electrolux's emphasis on energy- and water-efficient appliances are part of that Swedish sensibility

contribution we can make and truly a strong focus for us everywhere across our business," according to Jonas.

Accounting for its sustainability impacts has long been an important aspect of sustainability performance for Electrolux, which for 12 consecutive years has been the Industry Leader of the Household Durables category in the Dow Jones Sustainability World Index (DJSI World).[7] In 2014, it created a target to halve the Group's climate impact, preventing the release of 25 million metric tons of carbon dioxide and its equivalents (CO_2e) over 15 years—between 2005 and 2020. When that target was launched, there was no standard approach for climate targets, as this was before the Paris Agreement and the Science-Based Targets (SBT) Initiative. As we describe later, the SBT is today the gold standard for corporate climate targets. Electrolux has since developed an SBT to build on their existing target and go beyond its 2020 timeframe.[8] In 2019, it reported a 75 percent reduction in absolute CO_2 emissions in its operations since 2005.[9]

In this chapter, we advocate for much greater business uptake of big, bold, stretch targets like the Electrolux carbon target. We make the case for why it's important to define sustainability metrics that match ambition, measure what matters, and expand key metrics for non-financial performance. Because there are literally hundreds of targets and KPIs a company can choose from, we focus on two leading areas where we want to see more action: one emphasizes impacts on the planet—science-based targets—and the other emphasizes impacts on society—human rights. Demonstrating serious and continuous improvement over time is one of the most critical aspects of measuring performance beyond profit. To make this process clearer, we also present criteria for distinguishing a good KPI from a weak one, which can be applied to other KPIs according to individual company priorities.

A caveat, though: reporting alone does not equal sustainability leadership or meaningful metrics. A sustainability report is of little use, especially to investors looking for concrete, verifiable, decision-useful numbers, if it doesn't involve meaningful action on sustainability issues. The bottom line is that investing time and resources into metrics should matter to a business leader, not for ranking or reporting awards, but because the data generated supports whether decisions are the right ones, evidences whether negative impacts are shrinking, and provides a solid basis for demonstrating the link between sustainability and profitability.

Listen to the Science, and Be Bold

Today, we are living in what American political scientist and economist Francis Fukuyama has described the emergence of a "post-fact" world, in which virtually all authoritative information sources are challenged by contrary facts of dubious quality and provenance.[10] Science has come under attack, particularly climate science in some parts of the world, like the US,[11] prompting in 2017 a worldwide global movement for science and justice called The March for Science.[12]

As we head into this new decade, the tipping points are all around us, painfully obvious, threatening natural systems and the people who depend on them (which is all of us). Many businesses are running a grand experiment with nature, some without even understanding their role or impact within those natural systems. We make the case for why we think business needs to think in terms of new societal ecosystems that include both a planetary and a societal lens in Chaps. 9 and 10. But in order to understand the outcome of these lenses, it is important to have metrics that can measure impacts and progress, that are robust and grounded in science. Given the scale of those tipping points that Johan Rockström and colleagues describe in their work on planetary boundaries,[13] business leaders must not be afraid to put forward big, bold, audacious goals. These are the kind of goals that will not only help a company move the needle on its own sustainability progress but also shift entire industries, which is the focus of 3.0 of The Sustainability Leadership Model, the next section of this book.

Aiming Higher

We are encouraged to see, at the start of this new decade, a number of companies really upping their game when it comes to setting targets. For example, tech giant Microsoft threw down the gauntlet when it announced in January 2020 that it aims to not only be carbon negative (removing more carbon from the atmosphere than it generates) by 2030, but that by 2050, it intends to remove all carbon the company has emitted either directly or by electrical consumption since it was founded in 1975. This is backed by a detailed plan that includes cutting its carbon emissions by more than half by 2030, both its direct emissions and for the entire supply chain and value chain. Further, it launched an initiative to use Microsoft technology to help suppliers and customers around the world reduce their own carbon footprints and a new $1 billion climate innovation fund to accelerate the global development of carbon reduction, capture, and removal technologies. Beginning in 2021, Microsoft will also make carbon reduction an explicit aspect of its procurement processes for its supply chain.[14] Its renewable energy target has been certified by the Science-Based Target Initiative as aligned to a 1.5-degree Celsius future.[15] In announcing the set of targets, Microsoft President Brad Smith said that reaching "net zero" emissions is "an ambitious—even audacious—goal, but science tells us that it's a goal of fundamental importance to every person alive today and for every generation to follow."[16] To create a momentum for change, more sectors need to adopt this kind of attitude and level of ambition, a theme that we return to in Chap. 9.

In another example from the food industry, a Swedish family company, MAX Burgers, has earned accolades from the UN for becoming the world's first restaurant chain to climate-label its menu and compensate for all CO_2 emissions to 100 percent, from farm to fork. In 2018, MAX Burgers began offsetting 110 percent of its CO_2 emissions with tree planting, making everything on the menu carbon positive. It decided to go beyond the global independent standard for carbon neutrality, ISO 14021, and consultancy EY performed an independent review of its methods.[17] In 2019, the UN gave the company a Global Climate Action Award, the only European company in the category "Go Climate Neutral Now."[18] These initiatives have not hurt business: with 120 restaurants worldwide and a turnover of over 220 million euro, it is the most profitable restaurant chain in Sweden, outperforming both McDonald's and Burger King.[19]

These companies demonstrate that to be trusted as credible contributors to a more sustainable and just world, in our view it must be rooted in science and backed by solid metrics. A sustainability-leading CEO who does not insist upon facts and scientific rigor to measure sustainability progress and performance will probably not be a leader for very long. Given the nature and complexity of the sustainability challenges we are facing, science-based leadership is crucial. Performance targets should follow the same rigor as any financial metric would, to make them tough enough to withstand the scrutiny of customers, investors, and other stakeholders, but, more importantly, robust enough to make a difference.

Targets should also aim to find that sweet spot (or dare we say "Swede spot"): to address both the risks (mitigate risks and negative impacts) and capture the opportunities (optimize performance and positive impacts).

Impact and Profit Must Go Hand in Hand

Non-financial metrics are growing in importance and should matter as much as financial metrics if the private sector is to show in a convincing way that it contributes to a world that is better off, not worse off, as a result of its products and solutions. Measuring impact beyond profits used to often be about showing voluntary corporate responsibility through philanthropy but that is now evolving into demonstrating how companies contribute through their core business to solving the biggest challenges of our time, for example, as articulated in the UN Sustainable Development Goals. With a growing number of companies designing targets and indicators to show progress toward achieving the SDGs, we explore this category of performance accounting further in Chap. 11.

In 1994, sustainability pioneer John Elkington coined the term Triple Bottom Line[20] which consists of the three Ps: people, profit, and planet. John argued early on that companies should look beyond the traditional measure of corporate profit—the "bottom line" of the profit and loss account—to consider three equally important bottom lines: economic (not just financial), social, and environmental performance. The idea was to put society and the environment on the same footing as shareholders in how a company measures its performance. The concept of the triple bottom line has influenced platforms like the Global Reporting Initiative (GRI), Dow Jones Sustainability Indexes (DJSI), and broader corporate accounting, stakeholder engagement, and strategy for over two decades.

As John explains: "When I introduced the Triple Bottom Line, it was meant to be a provocation. I didn't quite know how much of a provocation it was going to be. At the time the idea of a Triple Bottom Line wasn't obvious, even to many of those who worked with sustainability. It was based on two propositions: the system needs to change, and second, to do that you need to be aware of these three different dimensions."

However, as the financial bottom line continued to dominate the corporate mindset, John announced in a 2018 *Harvard Business Review* article[21] that he was "recalling" his own management concept, writing: "Fundamentally, we have a hard-wired cultural problem in business, finance and markets. Whereas CEOs, CFOs, and other corporate leaders move heaven and earth to ensure that they hit their profit targets, the same is very rarely true of their people and planet targets. Clearly, the Triple Bottom Line has failed to bury the single bottom line paradigm" (Fig. 8.2).

Fig. 8.2 Sustainability pioneer John Elkington (© Volans). John "recalled" his own concept of the Triple Bottom Line in 2018 because it had failed to bury the single bottom line paradigm. Today he talks about breakthrough Green Swan solutions, delivering exponential progress in the form of economic, social, and environmental wealth creation

While the practice of measuring and reporting sustainability performance has increased dramatically—most large companies now disclose some level of sustainability performance data—we think every company should set ambitious climate and other social and environmental KPIs and targets, given the overwhelming evidence of how critical this is to the long-term viability of their business.

And while many mainstream investors are still being driven by financial KPIs in the short term, savvy investors, concerned about climate and other sustainability risks in their portfolios, are increasingly pushing for more disclosure of ESG (Environmental, Social, and Governance) performance as a proxy for good management and innovation. In a strong signal from Larry Fink, CEO of BlackRock, the world's largest asset manager, his 2020 annual letter to CEOs called sustainability "its new standard for investing," stating that "where companies and boards are not producing effective sustainability disclosures or implementing frameworks for managing these issues, we will hold board members accountable." In Fink's view, the companies BlackRock invests in should disclose climate-related risks in line with the recommendations of the Task Force on Climate-Related Disclosures (TCFD),[22] and with industry-specific guidelines from the Sustainability Accounting Standards Board (SASB). "In the absence of robust disclosures, investors, including BlackRock, will increasingly conclude that companies are not adequately managing risk," Fink wrote.[23] Many stakeholders will be following how this plays out in practice, and we revisit the BlackRock journey later.

To meet the changing expectations of investors like Fink, corporate leaders need to know the facts and the science to understand the true implications of their firm's actions on people and planet, and minimize that impact. While the science tells us that climate change is clearly linked to sea level rise and an increasing number of severe weather events from storms to fires to droughts, it can be hard to draw direct causality between specific events and business activity. This can make global sustainability challenges appear distant or removed from the business, but our advice is to start by expanding the company's fact- and science-based knowledge of the scope of its sustainability impacts so it can put a plan in place to minimize them. Knowing the full impact of the company's sustainability performance, from both a risk and opportunity perspective, and reporting credibly and proactively on those impacts, is a powerful way to demonstrate true business integration and preparedness to key stakeholders.

In the future, we expect that non-financial, or sustainability, metrics will carry increasing weight as corporate and market understanding of both business opportunities and sustainability-related risks and opportunities grow. We also expect to see more requirements for disclosure of non-financial impacts. Companies need to be ready by investing the effort now. It is encouraging that those who tend to perform well on ESG metrics also tend to demonstrate strong financial performance for the long term. Numerous studies have shown that more sustainable companies outperform their peers economically. For instance, the STOXX Global Climate Change Leaders Index, which is based on the CDP A List, outperformed the STOXX Global 1800 by 5.4 percent per annum from December 2011 to July 2018.[24] An earlier study by Arabesque Partners and University of Oxford, which reviewed existing literature on sustainability and performance, found that 90 percent of 200 reviewed studies conclude that good ESG standards lower the cost of capital, 88 percent describe better operational performance, and 80 percent show a positive correlation between stock price and sustainability practices.[25] Any company that wants to be around in 50 years should pay close attention to this clear financial evidence that sustainability is a smart business move.

What Makes a Good Target?

The best and clearest targets are SMART—specific, measurable, ambitious yet achievable, relevant (or material), and time-bound. To ensure meaningful measurement, the choice of metrics or KPIs by which progress toward that target should be measured must be tailored to the activity and industry in question. For example, energy or water used per unit produced will be important for a manufacturing company like Electrolux, which includes these among its climate-related KPIs, or a beverage company like Coca-Cola or Pepsi. However, it is less relevant for a company like Ericsson, which typically uses water only for its facilities, that is, employee restaurants and toilets.

Finding the right metrics for the company or even industry is paramount. For a real estate company owning extensive property, measuring performance of an energy-saving cooling solution for buildings might be an effective KPI for capturing energy efficiency. By contrast, for a transport company, where real estate is a tiny fraction of the overall carbon footprint, that KPI will be insignificant compared to the per ton, or per kilometer, vehicle emissions. Of course, transport companies should also have targets to reduce emissions from their real estate. But when it comes to CO_2-based indicators of performance, a company should start with its most significant impact—in this case the emissions related to transport. The goal is to determine the most material topics and set KPIs that are truly representative of core business impacts.

Selected metrics or KPIs can be company-wide or specific to a department or to an individual. They can measure progress in implementing a policy, a process or the direct impact of a product or solution. An indicator on its own can be "good" or "bad," depending on other company indicators and how they are used. What matters is that the entire set of indicators provides a comprehensive overview of actual sustainability performance and impact, connected to the core business.

Sustainability targets should be woven into internal target setting processes rather than sidelined. Such targets should be prioritized, incentivized, and rolled out just like other business performance like other targets. Robust sustainability targets should ideally cover two dimensions: a company's positive impacts and the risks to mitigate. First, determine the positive impacts first and how to amplify them. Second, consider negative impacts or risks, and how to minimize them. Traditional business KPIs are typically measured by improved margins or growth targets (to amplify a positive target) or by reduced working capital (to minimize a negative impact). Just as there is no single magic number for financial performance, there is no holy grail by which to measure sustainability performance. The important thing is to strike a good balance between the positive and negative dimensions, while ensuring the targets are business-relevant. Keep in mind, too, that KPIs and targets are not meant to indicate perfection, but rather to measure continuous improvement over time.

Business targets are constantly evolving as the business expands or contracts, and simply meeting a target does not mean the job is done. The same can be said about sustainability targets. It is important to measure continuous improvements over time. Sustainability targets are not a PR exercise, either: often with sustainability, everyone wants to look good. However, if a business leader turns a sustainability goal into an actual, substantive target, connects it to the business, and measures it accordingly, then it becomes less of a beauty pageant but rather a target that really matters.

Determining the Most Important KPIs

How companies determine their most important KPIs comes down to what is most material to that company and its sector. The process for setting KPIs and targets can vary widely. Solving the challenge of measuring impact beyond profit is not an easy fix, so below we feature a variety of approaches which we hope will be instructive for any company looking to better understand how to measure their sustainability impacts.

A great starting place for companies looking to aspire to big, audacious goals and targets should have a look at Unilever's Sustainable Living Plan, launched in 2010, which sets out to decouple the company's growth from its environmental footprint, while increasing its positive social impact. It identifies three big goals to achieve, which are underpinned by nine commitments and targets spanning Unilever's social, environmental, and economic performance across the value chain. Unilever is on track to meet around 80 percent of its three big goals, which include improving health and wellbeing for one billion people, reducing environmental impact by half, and enhancing livelihoods for its millions of employees, suppliers, and retailers.[26] The results speak for themselves: Unilever's sustainable brands have grown 46 percent faster than the rest of the business and delivered 70 percent of Unilever's turnover growth.[27]

Companies with significant scale in their industries can have an outsized impact by setting ambitious targets, and inspiring others to follow. Verizon is one of the largest telecommunications providers in the US. Under CEO Hans Vestberg, Verizon launched a new operating model and strategy, Verizon 2.0, a transformation of the business intended to create the right platform to better serve customers and capture long-term growth opportunities.[28] Determining the right measurements to measure impact and progress was an integral part of the new strategy, and to understand how the company will reach its goals. As a major structural change in the company, the strategy had considerable implications for KPIs. While Verizon tracks a large number of metrics, Hans has brought rigor to responsibility measurement. Under his leadership, Verizon has set new sustainability goals to source half of its electricity usage from renewables, cut its water usage by 15 percent by 2025, and become carbon neutral for Scope 1 and Scope 2 emissions by 2035.[29] Network energy consumption is also part of those calculations. Given Verizon's prominence as one of the largest ICT companies in the world, the impact of its commitments is significant.

The aviation sector is facing increased pressure to account for its greenhouse gas (GHG) emissions and CO_2 footprint. Rickard Gustafson, CEO of the Scandinavian airline SAS, has wrestled with this area and points out that despite being a small carrier, SAS can still demonstrate leadership and position itself at the forefront of the airline industry's transition to low-carbon aviation—and that means setting challenging targets. As Rickard explains:

> We are setting clear and more aggressive targets for ourselves than what we see in the rest of the industry so far. For example, we said by 2030 we will reduce our emissions by 25 percent and that is not in relative terms, that is in real terms. By 2030 SAS has committed that it will operate all its domestic aircraft on bio-based jet fuel. That is close to 20 percent of our total fuel consumption which will require large scale production of sustainable aviation fuels, preferably in our part of the world, to get access to that amount of fuel. And we are talking about quite significant amounts, approximately 250,000 tons per year. And we are not the only carrier that wants to get access to these fuels.

Climate impact is important to Telia Company as well but according to former CEO Johan Dennelind, he would not single out one KPI out of the company's total SDG and sustainability metrics universe. "It's not just climate, it's many other parameters as well, so we try to be holistic in our measurements and reporting, but certainly we will have to report and measure and KPI ourselves on our 'Daring Goals,' and the ultimate goal of a zero-climate footprint."

Once the company's key parameters are clear, the next step is to make sure the supporting KPIs to track them are robust.

How to Avoid Poor KPIs

If good targets and KPIs are SMART, poor KPIs are those that are not tied to specific outcomes, have no baseline or clear units of measurement, are vague or of limited relevance to the core business, and have no clear endpoint. Worse, they do not lead to real performance improvement or impact in the real world.

In the area of carbon emissions, for example, poor KPIs might not break down information on operational GHG emissions (scope 1 and 2) versus indirect emissions (scope 3), or they may only be relative targets (absolute versus carbon intensity targets are discussed below).

Greenhouse gas emissions are categorized into three groups or "scopes" by the most widely used international accounting tool, the GHG Protocol.[30]

- Scope 1 covers direct emissions from owned or controlled sources.
- Scope 2 covers indirect emissions from the generation of purchased electricity, steam, heating, and cooling consumed by the reporting company.
- Scope 3 includes all other indirect emissions that occur in a company's value chain.

Operational GHG emissions (scope 1) might be used to measure progress toward a target of zero-net carbon growth in operational emissions by 2025. However, by focusing only on scope 1 emissions—and leaving out scope 2 and 3—the bulk of that company's carbon emissions may be missed, meaning that overall, its GHG footprint has not been significantly reduced.

When a big emitter does not set targets for scope 3 GHG emissions, in either relative or absolute terms, it's a problem, since scope 3 emissions are by far the largest proportion of most companies' overall emissions and climate impact. Likewise, companies should avoid hiding the actual numbers in favor of highlighting more positive but less meaningful metrics such as how much carbon was offset through offsetting projects, when scope 3 emissions may in fact be far larger than those offsets.

This list of common reasons for failed KPIs from the EY report "Metrics Matter" is instructive:

- *Miscalculation*—a KPI results in unintended consequences. For example, a KPI is designed to reduce payroll costs, but management achieves it through understaffing, which reduces employee and customer satisfaction, and eventually profit.[31]

- *Gaming*—Employees figure out how to meet the KPI without achieving the true goal. For example, a restaurant chain aiming to reduce the amount of chicken thrown away each day develops a KPI for efficiency. However, to meet it, workers cook less chicken and have to turn away customers.[32]
- *Sandbagging*—Employees delay reporting numbers once they have reached their goal for a period.[33]
- *Misalignment*—a KPI involves factors beyond the employees' control, leading to a decrease in employee satisfaction. For example, a factory may have KPIs relating to high throughput—producing as many products possible in the shortest possible time—but this makes it difficult to fulfil individual customized items. Through no fault of its own, the team responsible for customized orders is not likely to achieve its goals.[34]
- We would complement this list with some additional suggestions which address common pitfalls in setting KPIs:

  - *Lack of incentives or integration.* Sustainability targets should be integrated into existing target-setting processes, rather than bolted on or stand-alone. Consider incentivizing targets the same way financial and other metrics are incentivized. Give them the same priority as other targets.
  - *Lack of understanding.* Don't make KPIs too complex, or where this can't be avoided, make sure to build awareness and capacity when they are rolled out.
  - *Siloed.* Avoid setting sustainability targets in a silo—make sure they are broad and cross-functional—and that other KPIs aren't working against them to undermine progress.
  - *Too easy.* Targets should not be too easy to reach; stretch targets just might result in a real achievement.

At the end of the day, good measurement equals better decision-making, so it is well worth taking the time to get the metrics right.

Measuring Environmental Impact

There are hundreds of possible environmental KPIs to choose from, and the most important ones for a company will be dictated by its industry and business model. But given the universal state of urgency around climate change, we focus here on one of the most critical environmental metrics—GHGs or carbon dioxide emissions.

If a business is already setting ambitious targets on climate performance, it is ahead of the pack. A 2019 report from the Transition Pathway Initiative (TPI), a global initiative led by asset owners and aimed at investors, assesses the climate performance of 274 of the highest-emitting publicly listed companies. It found that only one in eight companies surveyed are aligned with a pathway that would keep global warming below 2 degrees Celsius. Almost 50 percent do not adequately consider climate risk in operational decision-making; and about 25 percent do not report their own emissions at all.[35] In fact, of the millions of corporations worldwide, only about 7000 companies disclose climate-related data via CDP, the global disclosure system. Of those that do report their numbers to CDP, only a third provide full disclosure, only a quarter set any type of emissions reduction target, and only an eighth actually reduce their emissions year-on-year.[36]

Also, according to the TPI, companies should have a long-term, quantified target to reduce their emissions. Long-term means more than five years in duration. Companies for whom scope 3 emissions from the use of sold products are significant—for example, the auto, coal, and oil and gas sectors—should disclose those emissions.[37] As a basic first step on metrics, companies should publish information on their operational GHG emissions (scope 1 and 2) and have some form of emissions reduction target.[38]

The Rise of Science-based Targets

The Science-Based Targets Initiative (SBTi), launched in 2018, is an initiative of CDP, UNGC, the World Resources Institute, and World Wide Fund for Nature (WWF) to encourage companies to set ambitious and meaningful corporate GHG emission reduction targets in line with climate science, referred to as Science-Based Targets (SBTs).[39] The targets are considered "science-based" if they are in line with the level of decarbonization required to keep global temperature increase below 2°C compared to preindustrial temperatures.

In 2019, the SBTi released new criteria to set a target in line with a 1.5°C pathway based on the latest IPCC report. At the UN climate negotiations in Madrid in December 2019, 177 companies pledged to set highly ambitious emissions targets in line with that pathway. The companies have a combined market capitalization of over US$2.8 trillion and represent annual direct emissions equivalent to the annual total CO_2 emissions of France.[40] They are among 754 companies that by end of December 2019 had committed to GHG emissions reductions that would limit global warming to well-below

2°C above pre-industrial levels and pursue efforts to limit warming to 1.5°C.[41] Science-based targets have been described as "the next generation of sustainability goals." A major benefit is to help businesses "get past incrementalism and make meaningful change."[42]

As noted at the start of this chapter, Electrolux has two approved science-based targets: reducing its greenhouse gas emissions from operations by 80 percent and its emissions from products by 25 percent by 2025 (base year 2015). The pathway to achieving its targets is by driving product efficiency, eliminating high-impact greenhouse gases from products, and improving efficiency throughout operations and supply chain. The focus on renewable energy sources for operations will also increase, with an aim to increase the share of those sources to 50 percent by 2020.[43]

In September 2019, at the Climate Action Summit in New York, Henrik signed the Business Ambition for 1.5 Pledge and committed Scania to science-based targets. The Scania SBTs are based on the current company targets, based on the Carbon Law,[44] to halve CO_2 emissions between 2015 and 2025 in scopes 1 and 2. The scope 3 targets are based on a 20 percent reduction of CO_2 emissions from the rolling global population of Scania vehicles between 2015 and 2025.

For Henrik it was never a difficult decision to commit to the Science-Based Targets Initiative. Scania is an engineering company at heart, which makes it natural to listen to science. Scania has committed to ensure that their climate targets are consistent with the pace recommended by climate scientists to limit the worst impacts of climate change.

Looking at the total climate impact of Scania's business, more than 95 percent of its carbon dioxide emissions are generated when products are in use, considered indirect, or scope 3, emissions. With the far-reaching leadership ambitions within the ecosystem of transport it was never an option for Scania to set climate targets only for this limited scope. For Scania, it is important to be transparent and to hold the company accountable to the highest standards, but to also ensure that climate targets help their customers to be winners in a sustainable transport system. With the SBTs, Scania is challenging business-as-usual in a hard-to-abate industry that has a significant impact on climate change.

Scania's SBTs are set to 2025, with 2015 as base year, and take all scopes into account. They are ambitious enough to influence strategic decisions— from investment decisions in production and logistics to product development and sales priorities. To be able to reach the targets Scania's customers will need to run their operations with less climate impact than their competitors and the industry at large. Hence, Scania will have to commit to actions taken by their customers to be able to fulfil the scope 3 targets. The aim is to support customers to choose vehicles that use biodiesel instead of fossil diesel, biogas instead of natural gas, and renewable electricity. The connectivity in Scania's vehicles provides a tangible and transparent approach to meeting scope 3 targets. Connected Scania vehicles send data as often as in one-minute intervals, making it possible to see how the current rolling fleet is performing and tracking progress toward the 2025 target. The progress on Scania's reduction can be monitored in real time—which creates internal motivation and also offers transparency to stakeholders.

Swedish companies have been among the earliest to sign up to the SBTi (with 31 companies in the SBTi as of early 2020, Sweden leads its Nordic neighbors).[45] Telia Company is among them. As former CEO Johan Dennelind explained, Telia Company's Daring Goals approach commits the company to be a zero-carbon and zero-waste company by 2030—and they expect that from their suppliers as well. "In the future, we will not work with companies who don't address the climate crisis in a meaningful way. It is essential that all organizations move from words to actions to deliver real impact."

The SBTs may not be suitable for everyone, especially smaller companies with fewer resources. The methodology for calculating SBTs is complex and it can be difficult for companies to obtain accurate data, especially for scope 3[46] as well as requiring considerable time and resources. In any case, we urge business leaders to know the science and numbers behind their products and processes, and to set quantified, evidence-based targets that will be taken seriously by customers, investors, and other stakeholders. Over time, we expect SBTs to become the norm. Many consider the SBTs to be the most ambitious targets currently available. They are designed to increase innovation; reduce regulatory uncertainty by staying ahead of future policies and regulations; strengthen stakeholder confidence and credibility, including with investors, customers, employees, policymakers, and environmental groups; and improve profitability and competitiveness by reducing energy consumption and volatility. When it comes to setting climate targets, we think they represent best practice and are definitely where climate reporting is heading.

The earlier science-based targets are adopted, the more a company will edge out competitors. In any event, whether a company uses the SBT framework, the planetary boundaries framework, or another framework for scientifically based targets, momentum is growing for an evidence-based approach to corporate performance measurement across all areas of environmental impact. Such approaches will be increasingly needed in the future.

Absolute Versus Carbon Intensity Targets

In determining a science-based target, companies typically look at two leading types of KPIs for carbon emissions: absolute GHG emissions and emission intensity. The absolute number shows the company's total (actual) direct and indirect emissions. To be robust it should include scopes 1, 2, and 3 and also ideally be a science-based target approved by the SBTi. Intensity targets are only eligible under the SBTi when they lead to absolute emission reduction targets in line with climate scenarios for keeping warming to within the temperature goals of 2°C, well below 2°C or 1.5°C, as set out within the SBTi criteria or when they are modeled using an approved sector pathway or method by the SBTi (e.g., the Sectoral Decarbonization Approach).[47]

The metric of carbon intensity can be appealing because it is relative and normalizes emission measurements for company size and growth, enabling carbon emissions to be compared or benchmarked by using metrics like CO_2 per employee, or unit of sales, or per kilometer. However, absolute emission reductions are needed to achieve the targets set out in the Paris Agreement— so while a good set of KPIs might include both relative and absolute reductions targets, we think absolute emissions should be non-negotiable.

Finding the right balance in KPIs can be challenging. Rapidly growing industries like ICT face inherent difficulty in setting such targets, because if the industry is growing, emissions are going to grow as well, and in the case of ICT, growth may be beneficial in order to offset emissions in other sectors. Reducing emissions year-on-year when a company is growing is complicated, leading to Ericsson's decision to establish carbon intensity targets: If absolute emissions are growing exponentially, a company faces a challenge in not being able to show a target that focuses on absolute reductions. Starting with intensity targets can be a good way to get everyone onboard, because these targets are normalized to the company's business. Ericsson continuously evolved its approach to setting carbon dioxide emission reduction targets, eventually setting an SBT in February 2018. The Global Enabling Sustainability Initiative (GeSI), an ICT industry group, has also published a sector-specific decarbonization pathway that allows ICT companies to set targets in line with SBTIs.[48]

On Being Net Positive

Net positive is a way of doing business which puts back more CO_2 into society, the environment, and the global economy than it takes out.[49] The concept of net positive for CO_2 emissions, or climate positive, has existed for several years, especially in the ICT sector where technology makes it possible to offset more emissions than are emitted. For example, Ericsson estimated that while the ICT sector accounted for about 2 percent of total GHG emissions, ICT-enabled technologies could enable reductions in the other 98 percent of global GHG emissions.[50] GeSI, in its SMARTer 2030 report, found that by 2030, ICT has the potential to hold global CO_2e emissions at 2015 levels and to reduce consumption of scarce resources.[51] Put another way, smart use of broadband-enabled services could reduce CO_2 emissions by a factor of 10–100; that is, the use of a telecom service that emits 1 kg of CO_2 may enable a reduction of 10–100 kg of CO_2.[52]

While we provided a deep dive on CO_2 emissions reduction targets, it is important not to forget about other environmental indicators. The GRI, for example, provides a complete list of indicators that could be relevant to report.

Measuring Social Impact

The third of the triple bottom lines, social impact, captures one of the main tenets of our leadership model, what we call the societal lens (see Chap. 7). Social impact can be defined as how an organization affects people and encompasses a wide range of topics from Workplace or Occupational Health and Safety (WHS/OHS) and labor conditions such as working hours, as well as issues around inclusion, equal opportunity, liveability, and broader community wellbeing. In many of these areas, there are already well-established metrics and KPIs for reporting on corporate impacts—such as Total Recordable Incidents (TRI) for OHS in the forestry sector, for example. But other social impacts can be harder to capture.

Ericsson provides an interesting example of how to tackle an area of social impact that can be challenging to measure: human rights performance. As part of its serious and comprehensive look at improving measurement and accounting of human rights performance, Ericsson was an early adopter of the UN Guiding Principles on Business and Human Rights established by the UN in 2011. When the UN Guiding Principles Reporting Framework was launched in 2015, Ericsson was the first ICT company and among the first entities globally to report to the framework.[53] It is comprised of 31 questions that enable companies to report meaningfully on their human rights performance.[54] Nonetheless, developing appropriate human rights metrics proved a challenge. It is an area of sustainability in which experts agree it can be difficult to define "statistically reliable metrics on such a qualitative, contextual topic,"[55] despite the guidance offered by the UN Guiding Principles Reporting Framework, GRI, and others on setting KPIs for human rights. However, for sustainability leaders, to not report because it is difficult is simply not an option.

Finding the Right Human Rights Metrics

As a way to address that challenge, and to improve its management of and reporting on human rights, Ericsson worked closely with Shift, a leading center of expertise on the UN Guiding Principles on Business and Human Rights.

According to Shift, the most common errors companies make in reporting on human rights include:[56]

- Not clarifying which human rights are most relevant to their operations and value chains: this means they are not managing their most severe potential risks to people.
- Lack of oversight: not clearly identifying who is responsible and accountable for managing human rights risks.
- Lack of clarity about internal controls: 90 percent of companies do not explain how risk/impact assessments inform mitigation actions taken, decisions are made, or if senior management is involved.
- Silence on governance: providing no information about governance of human rights.

With guidance from Shift, Ericsson set about addressing these questions and, crucially, took a full value chain perspective on human rights. Human rights reporting can be a tricky area to navigate, one that many business leaders don't know much about, and if they do, it's typically in the supply chain domain, that is, labor conditions. But just as there are potential downstream supply chain risks, Ericsson also took that view upstream to the sales process. As an equipment provider, Ericsson could not ensure that the products sold to customers would not be misused in ways that could negatively impact human rights. Ericsson also tied the organization's human rights targets to the sales process, an area often overlooked by companies in the context of human rights and created the Sales Compliance Process as a means to mitigate risks, including specific targets.

Three main criteria were established to address what Ericsson sells, where, and to whom. This meant having a system for understanding which markets posed the highest risk, which aspects of the portfolio might be subject to overuse or misuse, and it also meant knowing the customer and the context in which they operated (e.g., government owned or privately owned).

Through this approach, Ericsson was able to determine the main metric to be "adherence to the sales compliance process." This meant that in some cases the company turned down business deals where the risk was perceived to be too great, tracking as a KPI the total number of approved cases, cases approved with conditions, or rejected cases. The goal was to support the sales process with informed decision-making designed to reduce risks and help ensure that there weren't inadvertent instances of impacting negatively on human rights.

Measuring human rights impacts is still in a relatively early stage, and many companies are on a learning curve. Even Unilever—which created a human rights report in 2015 that was the first to use the UN Guiding Principles Reporting Framework comprehensively—admits they "constantly" came across gaps around the need for better metrics for progress and impacts reporting, confirming that "social impact measurement is inherently more complex than environmental."[57]

Today the concept of net positive, most typically applied to climate targets, is being applied to social impacts. A growing number of investors, as we discussed earlier, are wrestling with how to determine which targets best assess a company's societal impact. One of them is Niklas Adalberth, founder of Norrsken Foundation, the leading tech impact investor in the Nordic region. Norrsken receives about a thousand requests for funding a year, from which it has selected 19, meaning that when they measure impact, they are looking for nine out of ten or ten out of ten in terms of impact. According to Niklas: "To evaluate whether an investment has an impact on society, we are quite selective. We have that luxury since the deal pipeline is so broad. It has to be clear it's net positive, otherwise we don't do it."

Niklas sees it as a return spectrum.

On the one hand you have charity where there are no returns from a financial perspective, then you have private investment groups and everything in between. We have different products and funding depending on who the beneficiaries are. So, the foundation can actually make donations—and we have done that in a few cases—where we don't expect anything in return. Then in our next fund we are trying to have competitive returns of up to three times the money in ten years while also doing impact, and that we can really qualify as impact investing. We try to cover the whole spectrum, because we think it's needed. But where we will have the most impact is when you can promise financial returns that are competitive. That is how you move the trillions and not only having it as a niche.

Niklas explains that their criteria for net positive have different lenses.

First of all, we look at what seems to be the gold standard, which is the theory of change. You look at each business from three perspectives: output, outcome and impact. A classic example from the transport industry is if you look at Tesla, the *output* is over 720,000 cars sold (end Q2 2019),[58] the *outcome* is over 3.5 million tons of CO_2 saved by Tesla vehicles globally,[59] but the real *impact* of Tesla is that they transform Volkswagen (and other automakers) to move into the electric vehicle business as well. You can't only look at the direct impact, you need to look at indirect impacts as well, and that could be negative or positive for each entity that we look at. Our main qualification is the probability of success times impact. Success is mainly looked at in terms of how good the entrepreneurs are behind the venture.

No Magic Bullet

Non-financial measures of performance will only grow in importance; the best practices being demonstrated by many businesses today offer valuable guidance. There is no magic bullet for determining credible KPIs and robust metrics, but the intention of this chapter is to underscore why effectively measuring impact beyond profit is essential for companies aspiring to transformative sustainability—and how to go about it. After a company has determined metrics that are credible, meaningful, and targeted toward the sustainability performance it wants to achieve, it's time to turn to the third phase of the Sustainability Leadership Model, the Leap, for exponential impact.

Key Takeaways

1. Impact and profit go hand in hand, and non-financial metrics are growing in importance. Consider how to best elevate your sustainability targets to put them on par with the financial ones.
2. There is no one single golden metric. Develop a comprehensive set of sustainability targets that address the company's most important impacts across the value chain. Choose targets that will stretch and challenge the organization (it's not just about looking good; it's about making a difference).
3. Targets should be relevant to the business, quantifiable, and fact-based. Listen to the science and be bold. For climate action, aim for science-based targets, and don't shy from social metrics like human rights. These will be key to understanding your impact on society.

4. Anchor KPIs firmly in the organization by connecting them to the core business and normal performance reporting of the company. Make it clear who is accountable for ensuring they are met.
5. Be aware of—and avoid—the common pitfalls that lead to weak targets; you will only land as high as you aim.

Notes

1. Amina Khan, "The Great Pacific Garbage Patch counts .18 trillion pieces of trash, mostly plastic," *Los Angeles Times*, March 22, 2018, https://www.latimes.com/science/sciencenow/la-sci-sn-garbage-patch-plastic-20180322-story.html.
2. Electrolux unveils five Vacs from the Sea, Nov 1, 2010, Electrolux.com, https://www.electroluxgroup.com/en/electrolux-unveils-five-vacs-from-the-sea-8687/.
3. Electrolux Annual Report 2019, accessed April 5, 2020, https://www.electroluxgroup.com/en/electrolux-sustainability-report-2019-30989/.
4. Improve product performance and efficiency, Electrolux.com, accessed March 13, 2020, https://www.electroluxgroup.com/en/improve-product-performance-and-efficiency-22055/.
5. Electrolux Annual Report 2019, accessed April 5, 2020, https://www.electroluxgroup.com/en/electrolux-sustainability-report-2019-30989/.
6. Electrolux Annual Report 2019.
7. Electrolux retains position as industry leader in Dow Jones Sustainability Indices, Electrolux.com, Sept 3, 2018, https://www.electroluxgroup.com/en/electrolux-retains-position-as-industry-leader-in-dow-jones-sustainability-indices-26095/.
8. "Our climate targets," Electrolux, accessed August 5, 2019, https://www.electroluxgroup.com/sustainabilityreports/2018/key-priorities-and-progress-2018/our-climate-targets/.
9. Electrolux Annual Report 2019, accessed April 5, 2020, https://www.electroluxgroup.com/en/electrolux-sustainability-report-2019-30989/.
10. Francis Fukuyama, "The Emergence of a Post-Fact World," Project Syndicate, Jan 2, 2017, https://www.project-syndicate.org/onpoint/the-emergence-of-a-post-fact-world-by-francis-fukuyama-2017-01.
11. Coral Davenport and Mark Landler, "Trump Administration Hardens Its Attack on Climate Science," *New York Times*, May 27, 2019, https://www.project-syndicate.org/onpoint/the-emergence-of-a-post-fact-world-by-francis-fukuyama-2017-01.
12. Unite Behind the Science, March for Science, https://marchforscience.org.

13. Planetary boundaries research, Stockholm Resilience Centre, accessed April 5, 2020, https://stockholmresilience.org/research/planetary-boundaries.html.

14. Brad Smith, "Microsoft will be carbon negative by 2030," Microsoft, accessed March 2, 2020, https://blogs.microsoft.com/blog/2020/01/16/microsoft-will-be-carbon-negative-by-2030/.

15. Lucas Joppa, "Ambition is good: action is better: Making progress on our climate commitments," Sept 22, 2019, Microsoft.com, https://blogs.microsoft.com/on-the-issues/2019/09/22/ambition-is-good-action-is-better-making-progress-on-our-climate-commitments/.

16. Brad Smith, "Microsoft will be carbon negative by 2030."

17. Climate-positive burgers, MAX Burgers, accessed Dec 11, 2019, https://www.maxburgers.com/climate-positive/climate-positive/.

18. The UN praises MAX and climate positive, MAX Burgers, Sept 27, 2019, https://www.maxburgers.com/about-max/news/news-and-press-releases/the-un-praises-max-and-climate-positive/.

19. MAX Burgers, accessed Dec 11, 2019, https://www.maxburgers.com/about-max/about-max/.

20. Triple Bottom Line, *The Economist*, Nov 17, 2009, https://www.economist.com/news/2009/11/17/triple-bottom-line.

21. John Elkington, "25 Years Ago I Coined the Phrase "Triple Bottom Line." Here's Why It's Time to Rethink It." *Harvard Business Review*, 2018, https://hbr.org/2018/06/25-years-ago-i-coined-the-phrase-triple-bottom-line-heres-why-im-giving-up-on-it.

22. Task Force on Climate-related Financial Disclosures, accessed Dec 11, 2019, https://www.fsb-tcfd.org/.

23. Larry Fink, "A fundamental reshaping of finance," BlackRock, Jan 14, 2020, https://www.blackrock.com/corporate/investor-relations/larry-fink-ceo-letter.

24. "World's top green businesses revealed in the CDP A List," January 22, 2019, https://www.cdp.net/en/articles/companies/worlds-top-green-businesses-revealed-in-the-cdp-a-list.

25. Gordon L. Clark, Andreas Feiner, and Michael Viehs, "From the Stockholder to the Stakeholder: How Sustainability Can Drive Financial Performance," updated version, March 2015, https://arabesque.com/research/From_the_stockholder_to_the_stakeholder_web.pdf.

26. "Unilever's Sustainable Living Plan continues to fuel growth," Unilever.com, Oct 5, 2018, https://www.unilever.com/news/Press-releases/2018/unilevers-sustainable-living-plan-continues-to-fuel-growth.html.

27. "Unilever's Sustainable Living Plan continues to fuel growth."

28. Verizon releases recast segment results in alignment with its new operating model, Verizon.com, June 18, 2019, https://www.verizon.com/about/news/verizon-releases-recast-segment-results-alignment-its-new-operating-model.

29. "Verizon goes carbon neutral by 2035," Verizon.com, April 22, 2019, https://www.verizon.com/about/news/verizon-goes-carbon-neutral-2035.

30. "What are Scope 3 emissions, how can they be measured and what benefit is there to organizations measuring them?" Carbon Trust, accessed Oct 24, 2019, https://www.carbontrust.com/resources/faqs/services/scope-3-indirect-carbon-emissions/.

31. "Metrics matter," EY, 2015, accessed August 15, 2019, https://www.ey.com/Publication/vwLUAssets/Metrics-Matter/$FILE/EY-Metrics-Matter.pdf.

32. "Metrics matter," EY, 2015.

33. "Metrics matter," EY, 2015.

34. "Metrics matter," EY, 2015.

35. Simon Dietz, Rhoda Byrne, Dan Gardiner, Valentin Jahn, Michal Nachmany, Jolien Noels, and Rory Sullivan,. "TPI State of Transition Report 2019", Transition Pathway Initiative, 2019, accessed Dec 11, 2019, http://www.lse.ac.uk/GranthamInstitute/tpi/wp-content/uploads/2019/07/TPI_State_of_Transition_Report_2019.pdf.

36. The Net-Zero Challenge: Fast Forward to Decisive Climate Action, World Economic Forum in collaboration with Boston Consulting Group, January 2020, http://www3.weforum.org/docs/WEF_The_Net_Zero_Challenge.pdf.

37. Dietz et al., "TPI State of Transition Report 2019", 12.

38. Dietz et al., "TPI State of Transition Report 2019", 12.

39. Science Based Targets, accessed Feb 5, 2020, https://sciencebasedtargets.org/.

40. "At COP 25, corporate climate movement grows exponentially as new companies announce plans to align with a 1.5C future," Science Based Targets, December 1, 2019, https://sciencebasedtargets.org/2019/12/11/at-cop-25-corporate-climate-movement-grows-exponentially-as-new-companies-announce-plans-to-align-with-a-1-5c-future/.

41. Science Based Targets, accessed Dec 11, 2019, https://sciencebasedtargets.org/.

42. Tim Greiner, "Goals with Impact: How to Set the Next Generation of Sustainability Goals", Sustainable Brands, 2019, https://sustainablebrands.com/read/new-metrics/goals-with-impact-how-to-set-the-next-generation-of-sustainability-goals.

43. Achieve more with less, ElectroluxGroup.com.

44. The Carbon Law: A roadmap for rapid decarbonization, Stockholm Resilience Centre, accessed Dec 11, 2019, https://www.stockholmresilience.org/research/research-news/2017-03-23-curbing-emissions-with-a-new-carbon-law.html.

45. Companies Taking Action, Science Based Targets, accessed Dec 11, 2019, https://sciencebasedtargets.org/companies-taking-action/.

46. Uwe G. Schulte, "Science Based Targets—What Is It All About?", The Conference Board, 2018, accessed Dec 11, 2019, https://www.conference-board.org/blog/postdetail.cfm?post=6783.

47. Science Based Target Initiative criteria, Science Based Targets.org, accessed Dec 11, 2019, https://sciencebasedtargets.org/faq/.

48. Guidance for ICT Companies Setting Science-Based Targets, GeSI, accessed April 5, 2020, https://gesi.org/research/guidance-for-ict-companies-setting-science-based-targets.

49. Net Positive, Forum for the Future, accessed March 26, 2020, https://www.forumforthefuture.org/net-positive.

50. Ericsson Energy and Carbon Report, Ericsson, November 2014, https://www.ericsson.com/assets/local/about-ericsson/sustainability-and-corporate-responsibility/documents/ericsson-energy-and-carbon-report.pdf.

51. SMARTer 2030, Global e-Sustainability Initiative, accessed Dec 11, 2019, http://smarter2030.gesi.org/the-opportunity/.

52. Ericsson and WWF Sweden partner to promote climate-positive solutions to reduce global CO2 emissions, Ericsson, May 4, 2009, https://www.ericsson.com/en/press-releases/2009/5/ericsson-and-wwf-sweden-partner-to-promote-climate-positive-solutions-to-reduce-global-co2-emissions.

53. "Guiding Principles on Business and Human Rights," United Nations Human Rights Office of the High Commissioner, 2011, https://www.ohchr.org/Documents/Publications/GuidingPrinciplesBusinessHR_EN.pdf.

54. UN Guiding Principles Reporting Framework, Shift and Mazars LLP, accessed August 7, 2019, https://www.ungpreporting.org/framework-guidance/.

55. Agathe Derain, "Human rights and business: Could performance measurement be premature?" The London School of Economics and Political Science, 2016, https://blogs.lse.ac.uk/businesshumanrights/2016/02/01/agathe-derain-human-rights-business-performance-measurement/.

56. Michelle Langlois, "Human Rights Reporting: Are Companies Telling Investors What They Need to Know?" Shift, 2017, https://www.shiftproject.org/resources/publications/corporate-human-rights-reporting-maturity.

57. "Unilever Human Rights Report 2015," Unilever, 2016, https://www.unilever.com/Images/unilever-human-rights-report-2015_tcm244-437226_en.pdf.

58. Nikola Djurkovic, "26 Most Fascinating Tesla Statistics—2020 Edition," Carsurance.net, Dec 30, 2019, https://carsurance.net/blog/tesla-statistics/.

59. Tesla.com, accessed Dec 11, 2019, https://www.tesla.com/carbonimpact.

Part III

Sustainability Leadership Model 3.0: The Leap

After working through the first two phases of the Sustainability Leadership Model, you're ready to make the Leap to 3.0. This implies a move from incremental to exponential solutions and impact—or, as we've dubbed it with a Swedish flair, Expönentiality. The path to Expönentiality depends on a few essential concepts: applying a societal and planetary lens, having society as your stakeholder, and using tools and accelerators like digitalization to amplify your ambition, or your X-factor. A simple but powerful Expönentiality Formula helps business leaders identify their own path for creating change at the scale necessary to shift direction or increase the ambition not just on your company, but on your industry and even the world. In this section, we urge leaders to think big and bold, gather the right partners (even if these are unconventional), and find the personal influencing platform that will allow them to bring their purpose to bear on an even larger stage. The level of ambition depends, as always, on the willingness and appetite to demonstrate true leadership.

The companies and organizations featured in this section are Houdini, Scania, Ericsson, Trine, Kinnevik, Verizon, Telia Company, Electrolux, Axel Johnson, EQT, Investor and the Wallenberg Foundation, Norrsken Foundation, NetClean, the GSMA, and the AI Sustainability Center.

9

The Path to Expönentiality

Up Close: Eva Karlsson, CEO of Outdoor Wear Company Houdini on Operationalizing the Planetary Boundaries Framework for Business

A peek at a clothing catalogue for Swedish outdoor wear company Houdini immediately lets the prospective customer know that a commitment to sustainability is no mere marketing claim. At the back of the catalogue, three dense pages of tables list all 130 clothing items by country of manufacture, type of fabric, composition (percentage recycled), and whether it is certified by Bluesign, an independent verifier of sustainable manufacturing of textile consumer products.[1] There is also information on recycled fibers, recyclable fibers, biodegradable and renewable fibers, and circular product lifecycle for each product.

That's a pretty comprehensive account of what exactly goes into its Power Air Houdi, for example, a type of hoodie made of Polartec Power Air, a new type of fleece that sheds up to 80 percent less microfibers.[2] But it's also a reflection of just how serious Houdini is about sustainability. In 2018, Houdini published a pilot study of company performance based on the planetary boundaries framework—to their knowledge the first-ever corporate planetary boundaries analysis.[3] The planetary boundaries framework was conceived by a group of Earth system and environmental scientists led by Johan Rockström, formerly of the Stockholm Resilience Centre, and Will Steffen from the Australian National University. The framework presents nine planetary boundaries within which humanity can continue to develop and thrive for generations to come.[4] Houdini's aim was to operationalize the planetary boundaries framework in a business context in order to understand its entire impact on the earth system and how to reduce its negative impacts and reinforce the positive ones.

H. Henriksson, E. Weidman Grunewald, *Sustainability Leadership*,
https://doi.org/10.1007/978-3-030-42291-2_9

That kind of big-picture view is necessary if Houdini is to meet its targets: By 2020, 100 percent of what it has identified as transitional fibers will be transitioned into recycled alternatives. By 2022, 100 percent of its products will be circular by design—made from recycled or biodegradable fibers and recyclable or biodegradable for next life. And by 2030, its entire ecosystem will be circular—which means not taking any of its resources from the earth's crust and eliminating the concept of waste in its value chain.

"We need to embrace complexity and acquire holistic, robust and in-depth understanding of the complex systems we are part of in order to understand how to engage in, contribute to or change them," Houdini CEO Eva Karlsson explains. "The planetary boundaries pilot study is one example. In order to minimize and eliminate our negative impact on the planet we need a holistic and science-based understanding of it—that we not only have a carbon impact but also an impact on biodiversity, novel entities, land systems and fresh water. These different parts of the system affect each other and the system as a whole. And so we need to adjust and transform our way of doing business in order to eventually contribute to the planet rather than take from it."

As Eva sees it, a massive design flaw in today's business logic is accepting degenerative practices. She believes that centuries of degenerative business practices have taken the world to the sixth mass extinction, destabilized ecosystems, and accelerated a climate breakdown. "It is coming to a point where the business community needs to prove its long-term relevance," she says bluntly. "By transforming to regenerative, corporations would become the planetary and societal caretakers—innovate technologies that work in partnership with nature rather than at the expense of it, design value chains that have local communities and ecosystems flourishing rather than degrading, and no longer accepting profits at the expense of others. Imagine the surge of creativity, entrepreneurial spirit, solutions orientation and positive power if regenerative became mainstream in the business community." The pioneering work at Houdini under Eva's leadership is a shining example of when a CEO takes responsibility for understanding the planetary impacts, catapulting the company well on its way toward achieving Expönentiality—not just for the company but for the industry as well.

The concepts presented in this chapter involve a shift in corporate mindset toward exponential, rather than incremental, change—and Houdini embodies that journey. Achieving exponential change starts with incremental growth; the latter is a subset of the former. Business leaders who want to create systemic change need to think in entirely new ways about how to view and manage their impacts. "Most leaders are trained to optimize the current model. They are not trained to transform the model," says Osvald Bjelland, founder of Xynteo, an Oslo-based advisory that helps large business transform themselves and the systems in which they operate.

Osvald's observation cuts straight to the purpose of this chapter. Simply optimizing current models—making incremental improvements—is never going to be enough for transformative change. We're not downplaying the importance of incremental change. To move past incrementalism doesn't mean there isn't a place for continuous improvement. In fact, optimizing is what generates meaningful, continuous growth in a way that can be called "exponential." For example, 10 percent from effort A this year, another 10 percent from project B next year, and so on, and pretty soon you have something which grows by an increment that is a factor, not a fixed increment, every year. Rather it's a call for business leaders to push their sights beyond the conventional boundaries of their factory gate, sector, business model, and immediate value chain. Our model defines those accelerators that can help you achieve your vision, and presents a way to grasp the broader social, economic, and environmental systems in which business operates. In doing so, it becomes possible to identify new or better ways of working, and the significant new business opportunities that accompany these changes, and ultimately drive positive change.

Each business leader needs to decide for himself or herself how far to take their journey of exponential impact—and to what degree it makes business sense. Each journey will be unique and will depend on the level of ambition of the leader. But rather than waiting for this to be asked of a leader, we would argue there is a compelling case for business to seize the initiative. As Harry S. Truman once said, "In periods where there is no leadership, society stands still. Progress occurs when courageous skillful leaders seize the opportunity to change things for the better."[5] Like Truman, we believe that society cannot stand still, and that leadership is key to driving change. Yet it can be difficult to find the right nexus or intersection between a company's profitability and societal prosperity.

To help, we have created a simple formula that brings to the fore the building blocks of strong sustainability leadership, along with guidance on how to combine and turbocharge those building blocks to achieve impact at scale. Again, as noted in the Introduction, this is not a mathematical exercise, but a conceptual leadership approach, a thought process.

The Expönentiality Formula

Expönentiality is a company journey to achieve significant positive sustainability impact. It is founded on purpose-driven leadership, integration with the core business, and finding what we call the "X-Factor."

Applying or achieving exponentiality is different for every company. It depends on the resources on hand, their networks, and their respective markets. While the need for sustainability transformation is recognized by many business leaders, there is very little guidance available on how to go about this, and how to make such a transformation relevant in a corporate context. To guide leaders on their journey to exponential impact, we have developed a formula that sets out a conceptual framework they can use as they progress through all phases of our Sustainability Leadership Model (Fig. 9.1).

The *Footprint* is captured in 1.0 of our model, the first part of this book: how a company can minimize its negative sustainability impacts, and maximize positive ones, and set its direction (purpose) in every aspect of the business.

The *Value proposition* refers to section 2.0 of our model, where we describe some effective approaches to credibly integrate sustainability into the core business, address customer needs, and bring customers onboard to create an even stronger value proposition.

Many companies stop here, content with doing no harm, and making incremental and often important improvements. In our view that is simply

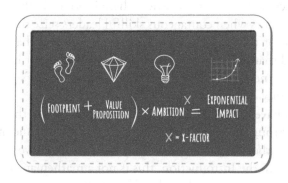

$$\left(\text{FOOTPRINT} + \text{VALUE PROPOSITION} \right) \times \text{AMBITION} \overset{X}{=} \text{EXPONENTIAL IMPACT}$$

$$X = \text{X-FACTOR}$$

Fig. 9.1 The Expönentiality Formula. This simple but powerful formula shows how leaders can reach sustainable exponential impact, or Expönentiality. The *footprint* focuses on minimizing negative and maximizing positive sustainability impacts. The *Value proposition* is how sustainability is integrated into the core business. By upping their *ambition*, leaders can discover their *X-Factor* through a set of unique tools and accelerators. The *exponential impact* you create delivers long-term value for business and for society

not enough. We believe it is possible for business leaders to take a further Leap by upping their *ambition* and discovering their *X-Factor*. The X-Factor is a set of leverage points—unique tools and accelerators that enable you to drastically ratchet up your ambition and achieve world-changing levels of impact. The X-Factor is what helps you avoid meeting an exponential problem with an incremental response and falling short. It is a multiplier that enables you to amplify your ambition, and, when combined with footprint and value proposition, makes it possible to reach exponential impact. The *exponential impact* you create delivers long-term value for business and for society, while meeting your customers' real needs.

In our model there are many accelerators that either a company or a leader can draw on to find their "X." Each business leader must decide how "exponential" his or her ambition will be, and how they want to use their personal platforms to amplify their influence. Here are a few examples we highlight as part of our model that are covered in this last section of the book:

- *Societal and planetary lenses*, which help generate a radically enlarged but yet accurate representation of your company's ecosystem and impact on society.
- *Unconventional partnerships*, which can create new value and unprecedented reach for your business.
- *Digitalization*, which leverages efforts and investments to achieve greater impact faster, as new solutions and business models emerge from an array of new technologies.
- *Personal influencing platform*, in which leaders use their personal platforms to amplify their voice and impact on issues.

With this toolbox, the influencing arena expands, bringing new possibilities for exponential change that extend far beyond one's industry vertical. Finding the X-Factor will result in a different exponentiality journey for each leader and for each company because it is fundamentally tied to personal leadership and ambition, organizational aspiration and the resources and capabilities at your disposal. The nature of the industry, and the degree to which a leader is willing to look outside in, instead of inside out, play a critical role, too. We think the formula can be applied to any company or sector, from startups to well-established, harder-to-abate sectors. In Chap. 10, we take you on the journey of how Henrik and Scania found their X-Factor, a journey that brings the formula to life.

At the heart of our thinking is that companies need to shift their mindset, to re-focus on achieving exponential impact. What does this mean in practical terms? Climate scientist Johan Rockström uses a simple analogy to illustrate this idea of the power of exponential change to get to scale quickly. As he explains, "If you take 30 linear steps you might reach across a classroom or meeting room. If you instead take exponential steps, your speed doubles with every new step you take. If you start in Sweden, you will have reached New York in 13 steps. After 16 steps you would have walked around the world and with step 28, you will be close to landing on the moon."[6]

Building on this analogy, the following is an instructive company example which was one conceptual input for arriving at the Expönentiality Formula. Several years ago, Elaine was working with former Ericsson Chief Technical Officer Håkan Eriksson to try to visualize the relative significance of CO_2 emissions reduction activities at Ericsson. Each of the following options underlines the possibility for exponentiality, at different levels of ambition.

- If Ericsson reduced CO_2 emissions in its offices, facilities, travel, and IT, it would have an impact of 1. While such measures are important to demonstrate commitment and "walking the talk," these emissions represented some 2 percent of the company's total life cycle carbon footprint (*the footprint*).
- If Ericsson addressed CO_2 emissions associated with energy consumption in the use phase of its equipment over an average of 10- to 15-year product life cycle, that would have an impact of 10 (*life-cycle thinking, and total cost of ownership, that is, the value proposition tied to the core business*).
- If Ericsson, through its technology, enabled smarter ICT-based solutions to offset CO_2 emissions in society, in areas like smarter transport or smart grids, that would have an impact of 100 (*digitalization as an accelerator, which led to new partnerships with new industries, and a transformational impact on society*).

It was this thinking that ultimately helped to shape Ericsson's climate strategy, set relevant targets, and conduct related research and other work at Ericsson. It also led to new business opportunities in other industry verticals, such as transport and energy. If Ericsson had only focused on its direct carbon footprint, it would have totally missed the big picture—and biggest potential—in terms of its most impactful contribution as a company. While today this type of thinking forms the basis of science-based targets, at the time it was groundbreaking.

In contrast to the Ericsson example, a fully digitalized startup might have different preconditions to reach exponential impact. For example, Trine, an investment platform connecting investors with solar companies in emerging markets, has in a few short years been able to provide access to electricity to more than two million people.

We look more closely at Trine, Scania, and other companies in Chap. 10 when we delve further into understanding how to assess and quantify impacts on society and how these companies have attempted to accelerate their ambition. But first, we introduce a few concepts that can be seen as tools to help accelerate the X-Factor as described in the formula. These tools include a new set of goggles (or lenses) through which a company can view its true impacts on the planet and society from a broader societal ecosystem perspective. We also look at some powerful enablers, such as digitalization.

A Shifting Definition of Ecosystems

Natural ecosystems are well known—the large community of living organisms (plants, animals, and microbes), for example, the flows and interactions within a food chain. With increased globalization over the past few decades, the ecosystem concept has been extended and applied to *business ecosystems*, comprising a company's direct value chain, the major players within it, and the physical flows associated with that system (including products and services). James F. Moore, who coined the term "business ecosystem" in 2012, explains that the members of the business ecosystem include those we've always considered to be part of a corporation: those inside the organization's walls plus distribution channels and direct suppliers. They also include the extended enterprise including direct customers, standards bodies, and suppliers of complementary products. Finally, they include those who can have a significant effect on the core business but who are often considered afterthoughts or pesky outsiders: trade associations, regulatory bodies, unions, and investors, among others.[7]

This is the definition of a traditional business ecosystem. But *a societal ecosystem*, as we present in part of 3.0 of our Sustainability Leadership Model, is a business ecosystem that applies *a planetary lens* and a *societal lens* to understand the science and impacts of business activities on people and planet while engaging with other actors in the system, and finding new value chains and solutions. In other words, if you declare society as a stakeholder, a societal ecosystem allows you to put that commitment into action, to find new solutions and partners in order to do things differently. In Chap. 10, we explain these concepts in greater detail and, in our analysis, how some companies apply them on the ground.

Companies do not exist in a vacuum. In our view, business leaders will increasingly need to view their role—indeed, their future survival—through planetary and societal lenses. This has become obvious after nearly six decades of corporate development predicated in large part on natural resource exploitation, where, as planetary boundaries teach us, we are nearing many tipping points.

The societal ecosystem takes a broad perspective, addressing positive impacts, such as innovative, energy-saving products for customers or jobs created for new business partners, which directly or indirectly benefit from business activities. It also includes any negative impacts on people, communities, society, or nature arising from these same activities. It's a concept that has its roots in environmental economics, where the idea of positive and negative "externalities" has long been established. In his milestone book, *Blueprint 2: Greening the World Economy*, David Pearce argues that all of the negative impacts from business arise out of economic failures to internalize those costs (which are then borne by society or the planet).[8] Managing your societal ecosystem is about understanding the full scale of those impacts from both the social and planetary lenses, and ensuring adequate engagement and mitigation are in place to address those impacts. But the societal ecosystem concept goes beyond negative externalities to include positive impacts, new solutions, and value creation. With these lenses in place, the path to exponentiality and finding your X-Factor comes into view.

We unpack these concepts beginning with the planetary lens—aptly illustrated in the case of Houdini's work with the planetary boundaries.

The Planetary Lens

The planetary lens is a way to view and understand a company's impact on the environment and the planet. It is about understanding the impacts caused by business on natural resources without which the world, including business, could not survive. These resources include sufficient water, energy, and land, mineral and other resources, clean air and oceans, and a stable climate.

How companies view their impact on the planet is changing—and with good reason. Most companies that are at 2.0 of the Sustainability Leadership Model think about environmental impacts in terms of manufacturing, or the energy impact of their facilities. That might include end-of-pipe solutions to address pollution after it is has occurred, or, in more advanced thinking, considering how to shift away from a linear way of producing products to a more circular economy. Both are necessary, but not necessarily exponential in their effects.

Unfortunately, the planet is under such pressure today that these kinds of solutions are simply not enough. Under the planetary boundaries framework, there are nine global planetary boundaries beyond which we face catastrophic threshold effects in the environment and climate.[9] These are: (1) climate change, (2) pollution by novel entities (an expansion of the chemical pollution boundary),[10] (3) stratospheric ozone depletion, (4) alteration of atmospheric aerosols, (5) ocean acidification, (6) perturbation of biogeochemical flows (nitrogen and phosphorus inputs to the biosphere), (7) unsustainable freshwater use, (8) land-system change, and (9) changes in biosphere integrity (or destruction of ecosystems and biodiversity).

The "tipping point" in these processes poses a risk that the planet and its ecosystems enter new states, some of which are likely to be less hospitable to our current societies, and possibly irreversible. According to Johan Rockström and his colleagues, four of the nine have now been crossed: climate change, loss of biosphere integrity, land-system change, and altered biogeochemical cycles (phosphorous and nitrogen),[11] which has direct business implications. Surpassing the climate change boundary, for example, affects all sectors of society, with sea levels rising and the many other effects that require us to adapt or mitigate. The planetary boundaries dictate that if we are to remain in the "safe operating space" for the planet and humanity, carbon dioxide levels should not rise above 350 parts per million (ppm) in the atmosphere. This boundary is consistent with a stabilization of global temperatures at 1.5 degrees Celsius above pre-industrial levels. At this level, research suggests that humanity faces climate adaptations, but that the risk of catastrophic shifts is not imminent. However, carbon dioxide levels have already risen into the riskier "zone of uncertainty."

From a systems perspective, the interdependencies quickly become apparent. On a planetary scale, there are many interactions among the different planetary boundaries. The Earth is a single, complex, integrated system where the boundaries interact in ways that can create stabilizing or destabilizing feedbacks. Multiple interacting environmental processes must be addressed simultaneously (e.g., stabilizing the climate system requires sustainable forest management and stable ocean ecosystems).[12]

But what does this mean for business? For Scania, as we address in the next chapter, the planetary lens applied at a business level clearly showed it wasn't enough for Scania to shift from diesel to biofuel in addressing climate change. Scania needed to understand how the biofuel was being generated and sourced, in order to avoid inadvertently causing massive effects in other planetary boundaries. A well-to-wheel perspective was paramount, especially linked to land and water use. The well-to-wheel analysis is commonly used to assess total energy consumption, or the energy conversion efficiency and emissions impact of marine vessels, aircraft, and motor vehicles, including their carbon footprint, and the fuels used in each of these transport modes.

For Houdini, the planetary boundaries provided a useful framework to assess and understand where and how a company might be impacting on the planet, and to what degree. And to do that, Houdini recognized it needed unconventional partnerships to achieve its aim. "We look at Houdini as an interconnected system, where it is about forming partnerships and collaborations in every direction to enable a continuous flow of materials, products, knowledge, ideas and experiences where all can prosper and evolve. We form partnerships for innovation, production and sourcing and collaborate with our peers, academia and of course with our customers and end-users. It is clearly a co-creative process," CEO Eva Karlsson explains (Fig. 9.2).

The planetary boundary assessment highlighted opportunities for Houdini to take this systematic thinking into its supply chain, armed with a better understanding of the impacts of different fiber suppliers and different

Fig. 9.2 Tents under the Northern Lights (© Houdini). Swedish outdoor wear company Houdini has a vision of regenerative corporations, social and planetary caretakers that work in partnership with nature rather than at its expense

production methods; for instance, the thinner the fiber the higher the impact. It also led to further development, in dialogue with suppliers, of the company's supplier questionnaire, eventually working toward a full planetary boundaries analysis based on the actual fiber, fabric, and garment production of Houdini's value chain. Not only was this a co-learning process for Houdini and its suppliers, it has the potential to change the industry with regard to transparency and data accessibility.

The assessment also confirmed that Houdini should continue developing its circular/collaborative business model as circularity tends to reduce the overall impact on all planetary boundaries—and to continue to analyze the effect of business strategies on the planetary boundaries. This deep dive into planetary impact led to benefits for Houdini, gleaning more information on processes for developing new materials. As a result, steps under consideration include developing fibers that are biodiversity positive or finding ways to remove excess nutrients or plastic particles from the oceans. Sustainable business strategies that don't take this kind of holistic approach run the risk of creating unintended trade-offs as well as missed opportunities to innovate.

The Societal Lens

The societal lens is a way to view and understand a company's impact on people, communities, and society. It goes beyond traditional stakeholder engagement: by acknowledging society as a stakeholder in its own right, a company significantly deepens its understanding of how to maximize the positive impacts or minimize the negative impacts of its core business on society.

Just as the planetary lens is changing, so is the societal lens. The classic definition of a company's most important stakeholders typically encompasses employees, customers, and shareholders, as well as NGOs, governments, and so on, and many companies have solid systems and metrics in place to track the views of these particular stakeholder groups.

Embracing society as a stakeholder represents a shift in company mindset that is much more than how stakeholders perceive your activities, or doing no harm. Rather our approach opens the company up to a broader context to consider how business operations affect the wider society, including both direct and indirect impacts on the local and/or global community. With this mindset, companies take into account not only their direct impacts, but how they balance the needs and expectations of "society" with those of employees, customers, and shareholders. Balancing potential trade-offs between different stakeholders and impacts is a complex exercise that cuts to the heart of 3.0 of our leadership model—where the aim is to minimize, mitigate, or offset negative impacts by ensuring much bigger positive impacts, or even aspiring toward net-positive impact.

The societal lens is clearly illustrated in the context of human rights impact assessments in accordance with the UN Guiding Principles for Business and Human Rights. Among other things, the Principles require companies to describe the social, operational, and human rights context for doing business, to identify "rights holders" potentially impacted by operations as well as actions to mitigate or adapt to any risks and to avoid complicity in human rights violations and in any unintended use of products, services, or solutions.

It is critical for business leaders to look beyond their own operations when identifying the risks associated with the impact of their product or services on society and the environment. In short, we advise leaders to look not only at their organization, but to pay attention to those risks they might inadvertently inflict on others. In addition, companies should have a system in place for forecasting, assessing, and mitigating those risks before they occur. For example, a company might look at privacy in a classic sense, that is, privacy risks related to how they handle employee or customer data. But what might be more relevant for a technology company, however, are the implications around privacy in the use of their products and how users are affected. Focusing on the people or communities affected, that is, a societal stakeholder perspective, is quite different for companies that are typically accustomed to looking at how risks affect *them*.

Leaders who care about what they and their company can contribute to the world's greatest social and environmental challenges see society as a primary stakeholder. They see their company as a global citizen, a responsible member of a shared planet. That does not mean downplaying the importance of financial performance as a driver, but rather connecting value creation to societal needs. This is the essence of purpose.

Hans Vestberg, CEO of Verizon told us, after he took over the helm and introduced the Verizon 2.0 organizational strategy,

One of the big changes we made immediately (at Verizon) was to make serving society and being a responsible business part of our strategy. I wanted to ground our four major stakeholders: society, shareholders, customers and employees. I put out a north star for all of them. Sometimes, when I talk with shareholders it can be hard to articulate why it is important to focus on society. But if you are not focusing on society, you are failing. Nowadays I usually argue that I have four stakeholders and I do not compromise between any of them. Because the moment I compromise for example on society and there is a negative outcome, that affects our customers, people will not buy from us anymore, and it will affect our financial position in the long run. And it's the same for employees, if you don't treat them well, then pretty fast you will have no shareholder value at all. It all hangs together, and you need to manage it.

Hans' efforts to eliminate trade-offs at Verizon by putting all stakeholders on even footing are a powerful illustration of 3.0 of our model in practice. While companies may talk about stakeholders in a wider sense, most are still fundamentally focused on their shareholder returns, and the impact their decisions will have on finances or reputation, not the broader, interlinking impacts of their business on the economy, on society, and on the environment. Yet it is not only financial performance that determines business success.

Returning to the unique tools that can enable you to advance your ambition and achieve world-changing levels of impact, in the next section we take a closer look at one of the most potent and pervasive accelerators of all—digitalization.

Digitalization as an Accelerator

When contextualizing societal ecosystems, an important dimension to consider is that we're in an increasingly digital world: digitalization is a driver and accelerator across every industry, and the pace of change has never been faster. That is the case today more than ever before. Consider that it took one hundred years for the telephone to connect one billion people, beginning before 1900.[13] By 2020, almost 75 percent of the world population will be connected by mobile devices, according to data from GSMA.[14] In December 2018, the internet reached its "50–50 moment," where, for the first time ever, more than half of the global population had access to the Internet.[15] With 5G, the powerful, high-speed, next-generation of mobile technology, and the Internet of Things (IoT), it's not just people, but entire industrial networks that are being connected, building the foundation for AI and advanced uses of data. Harnessing this force of digitalization can also be an important driver for sustainability.

Digitalization affects companies in different ways, and there are two main reasons that a company embarks on a more digital, or automated track. First, to optimize and improve their own core processes and operations to achieve efficiency gains. This could be as simple as installing a Customer Relationship

Management (CRM) system, or as advanced as a fully automated production line. The second track is to explore new revenue opportunities. That could include the use of data and analytics to provide new insights to customers, as Scania has in connecting all of its vehicles. Or, in another example, it could involve shifting from selling physical products such as a computer, to virtual products such as the cloud and software-as-a-service. Technology company IBM's transition from a business machine manufacturer to an information technology (and increasingly a cloud) company is a case in point.[16] Going digital can also create new revenue opportunities by introducing new business models, as we see quite broadly in the sharing economy, and new partnerships, with the potential to transform entire industries.

In both of these tracks, fundamental questions emerge that affect an entire organization, such as how to handle data, new types of security required, implementation of new systems to be put in place, and extensive training and competence development, often demanding an entirely new set of competencies.

In the sustainability context, digitalization can without doubt deliver a multiplier effect that can be harnessed for Expönentiality. Digital technologies can drive decarbonization and cost savings across industries, enabling great gains in material, energy, process, and logistical efficiency. That includes zero-carbon design, reverse logistics, and real-time tracing of material, new breakthroughs in components and products to increase the efficient use of consumer goods, vehicles, and physical infrastructure. This paves the way for a sharing economy and circular economy models, which will in turn cut huge amounts of material waste. Digitalization also provides opportunities to drive novel use of data which can be used to draw insights that make us smarter, better informed about customers' needs, or lead to scientific breakthroughs. But digitalization also carries risks, as we explore further in Chap. 12.

The role of digitalization as an accelerator was evident in The Exponential Roadmap,[17] a collaboration between academia, business, and civil society groups led by Johan Rockström. It outlined 36 solutions to cut greenhouse gas emission by 50 percent by 2030 worldwide including partners Scania, Ericsson, Telia Company, Fossil Free Sweden, and the Swedish Energy Agency. Looking at six sectors—energy, industry, transport, buildings, food consumption, and nature-based solutions—digitalization accelerated innovation in every area. Further, the Roadmap delivered some good news: that with existing technologies, halving GHG emissions could be done within the framework of today's economy while generating new jobs and good economic growth.

Cities are often at the forefront of the digitalization trend. The services cities provide to their citizens are increasingly built on ICT, not only to increase efficiency and explore innovation but to support positive societal development, from healthcare to transport to utilities. Stockholm has been a city with high ICT maturity[18] for many years, and has used its digital infrastructure to realize benefits to economic, social, and environmental development. Stockholm enjoys extremely well-developed open data and e-services with some 98 percent of the population having high-quality access to both fixed and mobile broadband,[19] thanks to extensive infrastructure rollouts. The city of Stockholm's vision is to become the world's smartest city by 2040, defined as a city that utilizes digitalization and new technology to improve the lives of its residents, visitors, and businesses.[20]

For local and national government and business alike, internet and broadband technological deployment is now so widespread that it can be an effective infrastructure platform for societal development objectives, such as achieving the SDGs. According to Anna Felländer, Co-Founder of the AI Sustainability Center in Stockholm and a digital economist:

We can think of technological paradigm shifts as basically having three waves. In the first wave, the technology is immature and this is usually when we focus on the positive impacts it brings. In the second phase, there is a widespread use of the technology and that is where its risks or downsides start to become more apparent. In the third wave, there is a cross fertilization between sectors and change becomes systemic. In the case of digitalization, this will be essentially technology-driven, with AI as the underlying and most powerful force. We need to ensure that this acceleration is both society- and planet-centric.

Having a societal ecosystem perspective is one way to ensure this. At the same time, as a company becomes increasingly digital, business leaders need to exercise caution and to avoid new types of digital "pollution," as we argue in Chap. 12.

Each Expönentiality Journey Is Unique

Expönentiality starts with knowing your Footprint and developing the Value Proposition; that will get you part of the way along the journey. Once that is accomplished, the X-Factor comes into view with some options to turbocharge your Ambition. The societal and planetary lenses illuminate a broader world-view, and the ability to interact with society in new ways. For this interaction to achieve the desired system change, it has to create societal value as well as business value—as we explore in Chap. 10.

Your impact on the planet or society depends on the nature of your business. If you are in transport or telecom, or an industry that is driven by energy consumption, climate change may be the critical impact area revealed from a planetary lens. If you're a beverage company you might look at water use, or sugar consumption, and if you are in healthcare or pharma, you might look at health outcomes. This is ultimately about determining what is material to each company and its core business. No matter the sector, the planetary lens and the societal lens together provide a holistic framework for understanding a company's transformative potential and leadership role.

But just how do you deliver on an exponential ambition which holds society, the planet, and profit in balance? At the start of this chapter, Houdini's and Eva Karlsson's journey focused on the need for regenerative models. Every company will need to find their own pathways, and our formula is intended to serve as a roadmap or guide to help companies mainstream exponential impact. In the next chapter, we learn how Scania and other companies are applying the formula to find that pathway and putting the societal ecosystem into action.

Key Takeaways

1. You cannot solve an exponential problem with an incremental response—it's time to think differently.
2. Each Expönentiality journey will be unique—it is about identifying where your most significant positive sustainability contribution lies.
3. Using the societal and planetary lenses helps business understand its most relevant issues and impacts; the societal ecosystem helps you find the sweet spot of where profitability and societal wellbeing lie.
4. Finding your X-Factor is like discovering your own special recipe—it is that unique cocktail of accelerators that enables you to achieve positive change at scale. Each business leader must decide how exponential his or her ambition will be, and how to use their personal platforms to amplify their influence.
5. Technologies like digitalization can be extraordinary accelerators to create impact that extends far beyond traditional industry verticals into new ecosystems.

Notes

1. The Blue Way, Bluesign, accessed March 8, 2020, https://www.bluesign.com/en.
2. M's Power Air Houdi, accessed March 8, 2020 https://houdinisportswear.com/en-us/men/fleece-and-mid-layer/ms-power-air-houdi-229094.

3. Planetary Boundaries Assessment 2018, Houdini, accessed March 8, 2020 https://api.houdinisportswear.com/storage/2A69199BFCBA925CC9260D6 1F41301EA566C760FB9A727B5DABB2C330C13D1BC/08df8496f36 f49f0bb821fdeafdd775e/pdf/media/e5eec5e201b242e9a2aa14aba9c3b696/ Houdini_Planetary_Boundaries_Assessment_2018.pdf.

4. The nine planetary boundaries, Stockholm Resilience Centre, accessed March 14, 2020, https://www.stockholmresilience.org/research/planetary-boundaries/planetary-boundaries/about-the-research/the-nine-planetary-boundaries.html.

5. AZ Quotes, accessed March 8, 2020, https://www.azquotes.com/quote/297319.

6. Summer & Winter in P1, Swedish Radio, Johan Rockstrom, Dec 27, 2019, https://podcasts.apple.com/us/podcast/sommar-vinter-i-p1/id284610981.

7. Maya Townsend, What are Business Ecosystems? Aug 9, 2012, Business2community, accessed January 8, 2020 https://www.business2community.com/strategy/what-are-business-ecosystems-0245275.

8. David Pearce, *Blueprint 2: Greening the World Economy*, Routledge, 1991, https://doi.org/10.4324/9781315070247.

9. Rockström, J., et al, 2009. Planetary boundaries: exploring the safe operating space for humanity. Ecology and Society 14(2): 32.

10. Planetary Boundaries, Novel Entities. These include emissions of toxic compounds such as synthetic organic pollutants, and radioactive materials, as well as genetically modified organisms, nanomaterials, and micro-plastics. Accessed from http://www.anthropocene.info/pb2.php.

11. Steffen et al. 2015. Planetary Boundaries: Guiding human development on a changing planet. Science Vol. 347 no. 6223.

12. Steffen, W., K. Richardson, J. Rockström, S.E. Cornell, I. Fetzer, E.M. Bennett, R. Biggs, S.R. Carpenter, W. de Vries, C.A. de Wit, C. Folke, D. Gerten, J. Heinke, G.M. Mace, L.M. Persson, V. Ramanathan, B. Reyers, S. Sörlin. 2015. Planetary boundaries: Guiding human development on a changing planet. Science, 15 January 2015. DOI: 10.1126/science.1259855.

13. Source: Telephone, Encyclopedia.com, accessed April 9, 2020, https://www.encyclopedia.com/science-and-technology/computers-and-electrical-engineering/electrical-engineering/telephones.

14. Half of the world's population connected to the mobile internet by 2020, according to new GSMA figures, GSMA, Nov 6, 2014, https://www.gsma.com/newsroom/press-release/half-worlds-population-connected-mobile-internet-2020-according-gsma/.

15. New ITU statistics show more than half the world is using the Internet, ITU, Dec 6, 2018, https://news.itu.int/itu-statistics-leaving-no-one-offline/.

16. Will Healy, Where Will IBM Be in 5 Years?, The Motley Fool, Feb 5, 2020, https://www.fool.com/investing/2020/02/15/where-will-ibm-be-in-5-years.aspx.

17. J. Falk, O. Gaffney, A. K. Bhowmik, P. Bergmark, V. Galaz, N. Gaskell, S. Henningsson, M. Höjer, L. Jacobson, K. Jónás, T. Kåberger, D. Klingenfeld, J. Lenhart, B. Loken, D. Lundén, J. Malmodin, T. Malmqvist, V. Olausson, I. Otto, A. Pearce, E. Pihl, T. Shalit, Exponential Roadmap 1.5. Future Earth. Sweden. (September 2019).

18. Networked Society Index 2016, Ericsson, June 20, 2016, https://www.ericsson.com/en/press-releases/2016/6/stockholm-tops-ericsson-networked-society-city-index-2016.

19. Internet user penetration Sweden 2009-2019, Statista, accessed April 15, 2020, https://www.statista.com/statistics/543324/sweden-access-to-the-internet/.

20. Smart and connected city, City of Stockholm, accessed April 15, 2020, https://international.stockholm.se/governance/smart-and-connected-city/.

10

Society as a Stakeholder

Up Close: Jacob Wallenberg of Sweden's Leading Business Family on A Century of Having Society in Focus

In 1856 André Oscar Wallenberg founded Stockholms Enskilda Bank (SEB) bank. Today his great-great grandson Jacob Wallenberg is among the fifth generation of the Wallenbergs, the preeminent Swedish business family that is behind many large Swedish industrial companies. Jacob is the chair of Investor AB, the industrial holding company arm of the family, which is also Sweden's largest investment company. For him, a basic principle underlies Investor's investment philosophy, one that dates back 160 years. "We are long-term, engaged owners and that means we develop companies with a focus on long-term competitiveness and their relationship with society at large," he explains. "That includes of course employees, shareholders, and customers. The better you deal with all the different stakeholders the better a company will perform. This is not rocket science. Historically, the emphasis has been about maximizing shareholder value, but if you ask me, most successful companies have always been the ones who could balance all the different stakeholders, because they are all important and over time this leads to long-term shareholder value."

Jacob's view, despite its historical roots, is about as modern as you can get. The concept of shareholder primacy as the main driver for business has in recent years been challenged by progressive business movements such as B Corporations and Benefit Corporation legislation,[1] and even by the business mainstream, like the *Financial Times*.[2] The vocabulary may have changed, but what we today call sustainability has for Jacob always been about putting society at the center of everything a company does, from its culture and values to its operations, products, services, R&D, and innovation because "we are convinced this is a prerequisite for creating long-term value."

© The Author(s) 2020
H. Henriksson, E. Weidman Grunewald, *Sustainability Leadership*,
https://doi.org/10.1007/978-3-030-42291-2_10

The approach seems to have worked. The Wallenbergs today hold a leading stake in many of Sweden's most successful international blue-chip firms such as ABB, Ericsson, Atlas Copco, and SAS, among others. For Jacob, what these successful Swedish multinational companies have in common is that they are world leaders in their respective fields. Not, he says, because their focus has been exclusively on shareholder returns, but because value creation for these companies is synonymous with what's important to society and they align their research and innovation with that world view, which brings sustainable shareholder returns over time. "Business is—and has always been—highly impacted and affected by the rest of the society and its stakeholders," he says.

Each company in the Wallenberg holdings must have value creation plans that include sustainability issues. Company progress is tracked against parameters in three areas: business ethics and governance, climate and resource efficiency, and diversity and inclusion. Progress reports in 2018 included these highlights: 100 percent of portfolio companies had anti-corruption policy and training in place, 75 percent of listed companies report carbon emissions to CDP, and 42 percent of listed companies have science-based targets. A quarter of management groups and board members were women. "In order to be successful longer term, the company has to satisfy and take into consideration the demands and expectations from all relevant stakeholders," Jacob says. This thinking dates back to the late 1800s when the Wallenberg family, as founders of SEB, the country's first commercial bank, were the first organization to employ women and also the first organization to offer a pension scheme to all its employees.

As Jacob points out, a business leader that does not pay attention to every stakeholder—not just shareholders but all those in society impacted by the business—risks missing out on a huge opportunity to bring creativity, energy, innovation, and purpose to product development, R&D, and new business models. Whether we look back to the dawn of the industrial era over a hundred years ago or forward to the emerging outlines of tomorrow's Industry 4.0, it's imperative that a company remains in tune with societal expectations.

The more inclusive concept of stakeholder primacy, as the Wallenberg business approach illustrates, has long held sway in Sweden where an inclusive society and economy is not just a matter of principle but a way to be more resilient and successful in the long term.

Today the idea of moving beyond just allegiance to shareholders is gaining acceptance even with those who have been resistant. In 2019, a powerful business group known for its allegiance to shareholder primacy shifted course. In a new statement of purpose, the Business Roundtable (BRT), comprising some 200 CEOs from major US corporations, said they were committed to lead their companies for the benefit of all stakeholders—customers, employees, suppliers, communities, and shareholders.[3] It remains an aspirational statement rather than a plan of action. But it was significant in signaling change even among those previously committed to the doctrine that corporations should maximize shareholder value (meaning profits and share prices) as their primary duty.

That the shareholder-centric view should have taken so long to be knocked off its pedestal is surprising to Jacob: "Implicitly thinking about sustainability and different stakeholders always had to be important to any reasonable business person. That is something we have been saying and acting on for a long time."

As noted in Chap. 9, our Sustainability Leadership Model moves beyond the classic definition of stakeholder to embrace the broader perspective of society as a stakeholder. The scope includes everyone affected by business operations as well as the natural environment.

In this chapter, we make the link between the Expönentiality Formula presented in Chap. 9 and how those concepts can be applied in practice to gain a much deeper understanding of a company's impact on society. The societal ecosystem may go by other names; the intention here is to be inspirational rather than prescriptive. In addition to the societal and planetary lenses, in this chapter we go deeper in exploring the value of unconventional partnerships, and how some companies are using digitalization to accelerate their impacts. There are many ways to gain insight into a company's impacts. The chosen path doesn't matter, as long as the end result delivers a more exponential impact. Scania is a prime example. In its journey to drive the shift toward sustainable transport, Scania dove into the latest science and brought together a diverse set of partners to take on a big challenge: decarbonizing heavy transport. By understanding and deepening its role within the broader perspective of the world of mobility, and applying both planetary and societal lenses, Scania's view expanded to embrace new business opportunities and new players—what we call unconventional partnerships.

In another case, Trine, an investment platform connecting investors with solar companies in markets such as Africa, Asia, and Latin America, leverages three powerful and converging trends to create exponential impact to help bring electricity to millions of households. Three other firms owned by Swedish investment company Kinnevik—Bima, offering mobile micro-insurance for emerging markets; digital healthcare startup Babylon Health, and online fashion platform Zalando—each showcase how digitalization can accelerate the positive impact on society.

We offer these examples as a jumping off point for business leaders to envision their own societal ecosystem by taking a similarly expansive view. Depending on the type of company, the suppliers, customers, and key stakeholders may be quite different.

How Scania Found Its X-Factor

Frustration can be a productive emotion when paired with a mission. For Henrik that frustration was rooted in the slow pace of global action to halt climate change—and the deepening sense that in his role as CEO of Scania he needed do much more to drive the necessary shift in his own industry. The question was, what could he do that was big enough to move to the needle, and how?

The recognition that Scania is part of the problem but also an essential part of the solution had long been Henrik's burning platform. It is what sustains his commitment to the kind of radical change he believes is possible within the heavy transport industry to help bring its impact on global warming in line with the Paris targets. But he faced a huge challenge. The transport sector is the second largest source of global CO_2 emissions and currently contributes nearly a quarter of global emissions.[4] To meet the Paris targets, this figure needs to be radically reduced. Although trucks stand for around 5 percent of vehicle stocks globally, they represent 20 percent of road transport fuels, a third of global diesel demand.[5]

In harder-to-abate industries like transport it is a much tougher proposition to demonstrate sustainability leadership than, for example, a clean tech company. Companies face new obstacles and need to do things radically differently in order to counter public perception and sentiment that may see them as polluters. But the path to a zero-carbon future won't be achieved without paying significant attention to these sectors. Large-scale transformation of the transport system can't be achieved by any single entity, company, or organization: it is an ambition that by its very nature demands exponentiality. Shifting an entire system requires overcoming huge logistical and technical challenges, and new partnerships are essential. Addressing these challenges meant that Scania had to think beyond its own industry vertical.

Under Henrik's leadership one of the fundamental mindset changes that Scania made in the past few years was moving toward the idea of an ecosystem, although it had not defined it as a societal ecosystem at that time. The idea was for Scania to move away from the mindset of belonging to an industry vertical—in this case "heavy commercial vehicles"—and instead to think outside this silo. That meant putting on 360-degree goggles to see Scania's role as much larger, part of an ecosystem of mobility rather than a vehicle manufacturer. That thinking enlarged Scania's view of stakeholders in both number and context. The business scope, ability to make an impact, and opportunity to take responsibility grew tenfold when Scania saw itself as part of something much bigger. Suddenly, not only its traditional competitors, suppliers, and customers were in focus. The threat of new entrants to disrupt its narrow industry vertical became obvious. At the same time, new opportunities were revealed: new ways to create exponential change in the company's value proposition by working with other stakeholders such as its customers' customer along with policymakers and academia. These unexpected alliances, along with the 360-degree view with its societal and planetary lenses, meant that Scania's ambition was no longer limited by conventional boundaries. It was clear the company had the opportunity—but also the obligation—to do something that could change its industry and society and deliver on its higher purpose. "To Drive the Shift."

In the following pages we apply the Expönentiality Formula (see Fig. 10.1) retrospectively to the Scania journey over the past several years.

Footprint and Value Proposition

The journey begins with Scania's purpose to drive the shift in sustainable transport, anchored in the company's core values. The first sections of this book describe in detail how Scania tracked and managed its footprint (1.0 of the Sustainability Leadership Model) and created a better value proposition through more sustainable solutions (2.0). In Scania's vocabulary, this is simplified as "doing things right" and "doing the right things." Doing things right (the footprint) is all about responsible business and making sure you walk the talk. It's about diversity and inclusion, engagement and ethics while at the same time knowing your carbon footprint and safeguarding resource- and energy-efficient operations. "Doing the right things" (the value proposition) acknowledges that to achieve more sustainable transport solutions, there are no simple, stand-alone solutions that can solve all the challenges. Therefore, Scania's work over the past several years to drive the shift is expressed in its three pillars:

Energy efficiency: Optimizing the vehicle itself. Making more efficient use of energy involves improving vehicle powertrain (the engine, gearbox, axles, and software in the vehicle), but also longer and heavier vehicles to ensure more efficiency. Other elements include features that reduce fuel consumption,

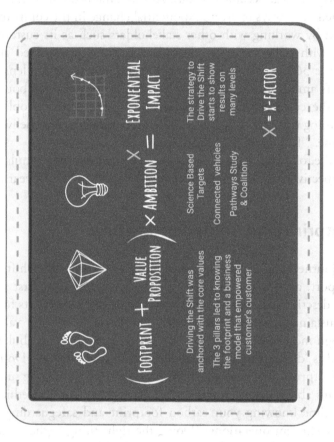

Fig. 10.1 Scania's Expönentiality Formula. An Expönentiality retrospective on Scania's journey over the past several years to drive the shift in sustainable transport. Doing things right (the footprint), and doing the right things (value proposition), presented a solid platform to raise the ambition level and deliver on an industry-changing and potentially world-changing impact

driver training for more fuel-efficient vehicle operation, and regular follow-up of drivers.

Renewable fuels and electrification: Optimizing the energy from a wheel-to-wheel perspective by phasing out fossil fuels and replacing them with types of energy that have a lower net impact on the climate.

Smart and safe transport: Optimizing transport and mobility flows in order to minimize waste. Connectivity is a key enabler for both creating more efficient logistical flows and greater filling rates as well as enhancing vehicle and driver safety.

Individually or together, the pillars helped Scania to better understand its footprint and optimize sustainability in its value proposition and create a solutions-based offering (as described in Chaps. 6 and 7). Scania's business model evolved to engage not only customers, but customers' customers in developing more sustainable solutions.

By looking at the industry flows and understanding not only the business of their own customers but the challenges facing the transport buyers, Scania could offer ways for both its customers and their customers to improve energy efficiency and remove waste and inefficiencies. This typically leads to greater profitability and a lower carbon footprint, usually through greater fuel efficiency. Scania has applied this approach to a number of industry applications, including pulp and paper, mining, construction, agriculture, energy, and consumer goods. The business success of the approach was combined emissions reductions with cost savings.

Ambition

Henrik's and Scania's ambition to get to the next level of a truly transformative impact on mobility and transport required deeper planetary knowledge and new partnerships. That's where the societal ecosystem perspective came into play, yielding new insights and advancing the overall journey.

Delivering on Scania's purpose to drive the shift in sustainable transport meant understanding and influencing the many alternative systems and actors that play a key role in mobility: from renewable fuel production to electric vehicle charging to electrification infrastructure. It also meant establishing an in-depth understanding of the societal and planetary impacts of those different alternatives (or pathways).

For Henrik, elevating Scania's ambition translated into four crucial elements:

1. The Pathways Study, led by a distinguished group of experts, provided the science.
2. The Pathways Coalition, a constellation of unconventional partners, carved out a realistic roadmap to make it happen.
3. Connectivity, as part of digitalization's powerful role in business and society (see Chap. 12), made it possible to accelerate the impact.
4. A commitment to set science-based targets in line with a 1.5°C pathway based on the latest climate science showed the company took climate change seriously.

Scania's science-based targets are described in Chap. 8. We take a closer look at the first three elements below.

The Pathways Study: Scania's Planetary Lens

Applying the three pillars to the entire ecosystem of transport demanded more in-depth knowledge and insights, so in 2018 Scania commissioned the Pathways Study.[6] The study was a way for Scania to apply a planetary lens to evaluate whether achieving fossil-free commercial transport by 2050, within the Paris Agreement timeframe, would be both scientifically possible as well as financially attractive from a business and societal perspective.

For any company, a science-based study diving into perspectives that are relevant for a specific industry or sector is a compelling way to gain new knowledge, guidance, and credibility and to identify the enabling factors that can translate into a formula for Expönentiality (Fig. 10.2).

The Pathways Study was developed with an academic review panel led by experts including Johan Rockström, author of this book's Foreword, and director of the Potsdam Institute for Climate Impact Research in Germany. The study took a backcasting approach, looking at the viability of concurrent pathways to phase out carbon emissions in commercial transport by 2050. The study examined systems costs and CO_2 emissions abatement for the three commercial transport segments responsible for 90 percent of commercial vehicle carbon dioxide emissions in four diverse markets, Sweden, the US, Germany, and China. Four different scenarios for achieving the required emissions savings were studied, including full electrification; maximizing the use of biofuels; growth in the use of hydrogen fuel cells, and a mix of all these different technologies.

What became crystal clear in the Pathways Study is that decarbonizing the commercial transport sector is not only possible, it has societal benefits and

Fig. 10.2   Why fly a Scania truck with 2000 drones? (© Scania). The idea behind this concept was to trigger ideas. If you want to be part of developing the future and sustainable transport, you need to come up with some bold ideas. Not all of them are going to fly. But some will, and, when they do, they will change the world

can potentially be profitable for business. Further, it emphasized that this was an exponential journey, dependent both on technology and innovation and on striking strategic and often unconventional partnerships. But this shift to fossil-free commercial transport wouldn't necessarily happen on its own.

The Pathways Study found that more than 20 percent in emissions abatement can be achieved by optimizing systems currently available today, along with non-powertrain vehicle improvements and improving routing and load management. Energy efficiency is often the low-hanging fruit, and is typically one of the first opportunities identified. But exponentiality requires going beyond these more incremental savings.

In summary, it found that while a quick introduction of electrification is the least expensive scenario for society overall, biofuels provide the fastest way to achieve the reduction because the technology is available here and now. We take a look at the key findings for each of the four pathways to understand how they apply the planetary and societal lenses of the societal ecosystem—and how Scania is working with each pathway in its strategy to drive the shift toward sustainable transport:

Electrification offers the most cost-effective route and delivers almost 20 percent total system cost savings by 2050 compared to business-as-usual but will require four or five times more infrastructure investment relative to the present situation.

Here, batteries are a crucial piece of the puzzle. For the electrification pathway to take off, particularly for electrified heavy vehicles, battery cell production, which is typically energy intensive and dependent on mined raw materials, must be more sustainable, more robust, and offered at a more competitive cost than today. Scania is working to address this barrier through a technological partnership with lithium-ion battery manufacturer Northvolt (see Chap. 6), working to develop the world's greenest battery by deploying a circular economy model to recycle and extract materials from its batteries to lower costs and reduce environmental and social impact. Electrical highways could also be an alternative to carrying large quantities of batteries on the vehicles.

Maximizing use of sustainable biofuels is by far the fastest path to decarbonizing commercial transport, the Pathways Study found. If maximizing carbon abatement over the coming decades is the chief objective, biofuels will be critical, since they can play a near-term role in reducing emissions by making it possible for internal combustion engine vehicles (the dominant engines on the road) to easily shift to these fuels. Biofuels have the potential to reduce CO_2 emissions by up to 90 percent compared with fossil fuels.[7]

Biofuels also present a number of controversial dilemmas, primarily focused on whether biofuel feedstock decreases food production and influences food prices and if biofuel production competes for agricultural land and increases deforestation. However, second- and third-generation biofuels, which use feedstock not suitable for human or animal consumption, pose a smaller threat to the food chain, produce less waste, and are more efficient.[8] Viewed from a societal and planetary lens in a science-based and factual way, biofuels provide a number of benefits. Chief among these is the ability to significantly reduce the carbon impact of heavy transport. Further, the volumes produced can be shifted to aviation and shipping, which are harder to electrify, once the heavy transport sector has moved further into electrification. Large-scale investments in production of sustainable biofuels are therefore urgent. Timely and positive interventions from policymakers can help, in the form of tax incentives and other measures. One such action would be to remove subsidies for fossil fuels and divert these funds toward biofuels.

Fuel cell vehicles, powered by pure hydrogen, emit no tailpipe GHGs, only heat and water,[9] which is a huge positive from a planetary perspective. But while relatively clean, depending on the production method (fossil fuels vs renewable energy), the fuel can be expensive and difficult to store and distribute.[10] In addition, the fuel cell vehicle technology is currently expensive. Over the next decade, they may become attractive alternatives to battery electric powertrains in markets where regulatory support for hydrogen technology is high, and supply of hydrogen is plentiful and available at low cost. In 2019 Scania delivered the first fuel cell vehicle to the Norwegian food wholesaler

ASKO, which has established its own production facility for sustainable hydrogen gas.[11]

Mix of all technologies: Multiple powertrain technologies and infrastructures will coexist, with a mix of battery electric, fuel cell, and biofuel-powered engine vehicles.

The success of each carbon abatement pathway requires not only an unprecedented rate of technological change but also adjacent industries to innovate, for example a high mix of renewables in electricity generation and continued falling battery prices. Dramatic changes will be called for across all sectors in the form of new technologies, new infrastructure, and completely new business models. To achieve full sales penetration of fossil free powertrain technologies by 2040 requires an adoption growth rate of at least 5–10 percent annually across regions.[12] As noted, the right taxation policies could help make sure this happens.

The Pathways Study does not have all the answers; it is meant to start a discussion with external stakeholders and experts to better understand the choices Scania can make and how it can influence the development of the transport system. Åsa Pettersson, Head of Public Affairs & Sustainability at Scania and one of the initiators of the Pathways Study, was key to coming up with this approach and implementing it. Certainly, the study helped Scania to understand the complexity of its industry-changing ambition, delivering a planetary and societal lens and a business roadmap for Scania. That led to a better foundation for decision-making and raised a much-needed debate on how to scale. It also underscored the importance of new partnerships as an accelerator. Crucially, it showed that Scania was on the right track in terms of its approach to driving the shift but could elevate that even more by harnessing all three core elements of its strategy: the technology push, the customer pull, and ecosystem partnership.

The Pathways Study was the first input in Scania's efforts to increase its ambition, or find its X-Factor, by applying a societal ecosystem approach. The next was to challenge its conventional view of partnerships.

The Pathways Coalition: Unconventional Partnerships

Scania has long worked in partnership to unlock technological or commercial challenges. Through its holistic way of working across boundaries, the so-called diamond takes the whole transport system into consideration, including Scania, transport companies, buyers of transport services, and infrastructure partners, as a way to leverage the strengths of key players in the ecosystem (Fig. 10.3).

But to take it to the next level, Scania needed to influence and work not only with customers and suppliers, but also with the broader industry, governments, cities, research organizations, and NGOs, and even biofuel producers and energy suppliers. As the Pathways Study made clear, no single entity can address a massive challenge like fossil-free transport on its own. System and equipment providers will need to adopt new powertrain technology; transport providers must adopt emerging technology; retailers and transport buyers need to drive CO2 reductions in their supply chains; energy providers must continue to drive renewables penetration and ensure grid stability. And policymakers must work with industry to remove the barriers and to accelerate bringing decarbonizing technology to market. That's a tall order, but with the right constellation of partners, the impact could be exponential.

In short, Scania needed partners who could span the entire societal ecosystem for sustainable mobility. Enter the Pathways Coalition. Created in 2018, it brings together Scania, H&M, Siemens, and E.ON with the mutual goal to achieve fossil-free commercial transport by 2050. The choice of partners was

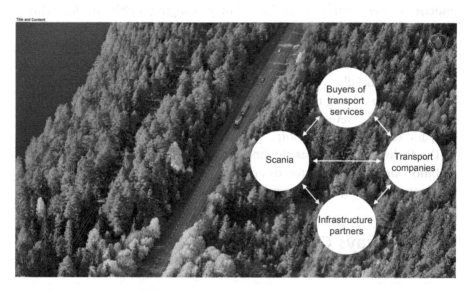

Fig. 10.3 Scania's partnership approach (© Scania). Scania has long worked in partnership to unlock technological or commercial challenges. Through its holistic way of working across boundaries, illustrated here, Scania leverages the strengths of key players in the ecosystem including transport companies, buyers of transport services, and infrastructure partners

strategic, with representatives from infrastructure provision, energy solutions and supply, vehicle manufacturing, and a major retail transport buyer. Each partner brings key assets and gains significant business benefits, but each partner is also key to achieve the sustainability benefits: a new kind of value exchange. As a large retailer and transport buyer with strong sustainability ambitions, H&M, the world's second largest fashion retailer, wants to decarbonize their logistics, which in turn creates demand for sustainable transport. As the transport provider, Scania supplies the transport solutions (vehicles and services) and satisfies customer demand for sustainable transport services. Electrification systems provider Siemens builds the electric highways and charging infrastructure. And electricity producer E.ON ensures that the grid is filled with sustainable electricity to meet the demand for renewable energy and that there is enough grid capacity available.

The Pathways Coalition makes the case that solutions are available today to decarbonize transport. It has made recommendations for how transport buyers and decision-makers can speed things along, including enabling policy to remove obstacles such as taxation on biofuels. The coalition is calling on other players along the value chain to join them in advocating for a mutually beneficial roadmap that would lead to real system change.

The Coalition has spurred initiatives in other markets such as in France, including a partnership with recycling giant SUEZ and with the French transport operator Citram Aquitaine, which is running a Scania Interlink bus on bioethanol that comes from locally produced wine residue. Scania also is expanding its partnerships with large transport buyers who have global reach and influence to specify alternative fuels and boost infrastructure initiatives, such as Unilever—demonstrating that Scania's approach to unconventional partnerships is creating ripples across the global transport market. For Scania, the goal is to support these companies in making the shift to sustainable transport using alternative fuels here and now, as well as long-term considerations for future technologies such as electrification.

Where the Exponential Rubber Hits the Road

The key lessons from Scania's societal ecosystem journey can be applied to any major change process, or exponential journey—not least, that a leader has a responsibility to understand the facts. It begins by having leadership with a higher ambition that has society in focus. A conventional approach would argue that that the indirect emissions from Scania's products are the customer's problem. But Scania now has a means to take into account the societal and planetary ecosystem perspective, consider the carbon law boundary, scope 1, 2 and 3 emissions and the cumulative lifetime emissions from Scania's products in use. In short, Scania was able to take on the issue as a systems and design challenge.

Viewed from the perspective of the Expönentiality Formula presented in Chap. 9, Scania's value proposition has evolved. That has taken the form of new products and solutions linked to biofuels and electrification, and new ways of selling and charging for the added value by including energy and infrastructure in solutions. This, in turn, lowers barriers for customers to adopt the new solutions.

The following simple yet illustrative example shows the CO_2 emissions savings presented in the Pathways Study versus different scenarios in which Scania would attempt to achieve carbon emissions reduction on its own (i.e., without the societal ecosystem). This highlights the relative significance in terms of CO_2 emissions represented by the study and the Coalition.

In a first scenario, a tailor-made and more energy-efficient truck could improve fuel consumption and reduce CO_2 emissions by some 10 percent compared to an older truck or competition. Better engine technology and aerodynamics could be the main factors. This is an improvement that Scania could arrange with most of its customers currently and serves as baseline. This option enables important but still incremental emissions reductions.

In a second scenario, if Scania could ensure availability of renewable biodiesel produced sustainably, CO_2 emissions could be reduced up to 90 percent compared to fossil diesel. If the taxation of the fuel takes a "well-to-wheel" perspective along with a price on carbon, then the tax would be lower on the renewable fuel alternative than the fossil fuel. The result would be that the customer would have no cost disadvantage and society would gain a transport solution that would reduce CO_2 emissions dramatically. But—and this is critical—Scania cannot provide this second option without a societal ecosystem approach, because it needs the partners and policy decisions to enable the societal ecosystem approach.

In a third scenario, the average truck in Europe (although the region has the world's most efficient transport system) is typically loaded to some 60 percent of its capacity, based on Scania internal data. That means there is 40 percent waste in the whole transport system that can be addressed by smart solutions available now. (It should be noted, however, that the 10 percent improvement in the first scenario is at the vehicle level, whereas the 40 percent reduction in this scenario is at the system level.) Through connectivity and real-time tracking Scania can together with its customers and their customers improve the fill rate and reduce empty runs, a perfect example of digitalization as an accelerator. This scenario envisions fewer trucks on the road, reducing the impact of transport itself. This reduction of CO_2 emissions would not be possible for Scania to do on its own, because, again, the enabling partner ecosystem is absolutely necessary.

In summary, frustration at the lack of progress on climate action was one trigger that accelerated the ambition to do something bigger and better, for Henrik personally and for Scania. The societal ecosystem approach (the Pathways Study) provided a new way of seeing the world. And with digitalization as an accelerator and coalitions of unconventional partners (the Pathways Coalition), Scania could further accelerate impact. This is a journey, and Scania does not claim to have reached full exponential impact yet. But the company is on its way, and we hope that in tracing the journey, we've illuminated the path for others.

The following company examples aren't as complete as Scania's in terms of applying the Formula, but each illustrates how the individual parts of the Formula can be applied in practice.

Trine: Turning the Lights On

Transformation was certainly on the radar for Sam Manaberi, CEO of Trine, a Sweden-based investment platform for connecting investors with solar companies in markets such as Africa, Asia and Latin America, founded in 2015. With his previous experience as a Director at Bosch Solar Energy North America, he saw a huge problem demanding a creative solution. Some 860 million people globally lack electricity, the majority (600 million) living in sub-Saharan Africa.[13] Millions rely on kerosene for cooking and heating, which contributes to climate change as well as adverse human health impacts. But how to make solar bankable in sub-Saharan Africa? (Fig. 10.4)

Sam describes how they tackled that challenge:

> At Trine we fund solar energy companies where it does the most good. That means that we bring funding in to scale the solar entrepreneurs, the majority of which are in sub-Saharan Africa. They use that money to scale their business, which consists of a multitude of systems that are quite small, tens of thousands of systems in the field which replace kerosene lamps and provide electricity where there is none. The companies we've funded typically have a couple of hundred or a couple of thousand employees, and we fund them with a couple of millions of euros. But their customers represent a massive amount of people. They are not the ones taking the loans; they are not our direct customers but

Fig. 10.4 One of Trine's solar roof installations (© Trine). In a typical village solar installation, households in emerging markets that formerly relied on kerosene for cooking and heating benefit from Trine's innovative approach to connecting solar entrepreneurs in need of capital with investors in Europe

rather our customers' customers. The end user is the person who lives in the countryside, for example, in Kenya, and uses their cell phone to pay for their electricity with very small micropayments, maybe a couple of dollars a week.

In essence, Trine is creating the foundation for micro-financing for its customers' customers. As we see it, from an ecosystem perspective, Trine is applying both the societal and planetary lenses, and bringing unconventional partners like retail investors and solar entrepreneurs to the table. Compared to the kind of hard-to-abate sector that presented specific challenges for Scania, the clean energy sector faces other hurdles, including cost of capital infrastructure and lack of supportive public policy in some instances. This prompted a different, but not necessarily easier, pathway for Trine.

With a societal lens, Trine recognized that the mostly small- and medium-sized solar energy companies in sub-Saharan Africa faced barriers in gaining commercial finance. At the same time, crowdfunding for retail investing had taken off, and public support for sustainability was rising. Trine seized on these different elements for its ecosystem approach. For unconventional partners, it brought together sustainability-minded retail investors in Europe and solar entrepreneurs in Africa in need of capital. The retail investment platform could give solar partners the injection of capital they needed to bring solar energy to the millions who needed it. And investors would earn a profit (once loans to solar partners were repaid) while making a social and environmental impact. Trine invests in solar entrepreneurs that build small home systems as well as commercial and industrial solar installations and mini- or micro-grids.

Another crucial element for Trine's ecosystem approach was to leverage existing mobile technology on their digital platform, which helped them to accelerate their ambition. While much of sub-Saharan Africa may lack access to electricity, mobile penetration is high, making it easy for customers to pay for their energy via mobile payments. According to Sam, a number of trends aligned to allow Trine to exist. One was the rapidly declining costs of solar and wind energy, now the cheapest form of energy in two-thirds of the world, expected to produce half of the world's energy in 30 years.[14] The rate of increase is exponential, from a few percent a few years ago to double digits in just a few years.

Digitalization is another powerful accelerator, paving the way for mobile payments that enabled the off-grid electricity industry to really take off. Thirdly, sub-Saharan Africa is the fastest-growing market for mobile communications, with some 43 percent of the population having a mobile subscription.[15]

All of this has led to a successful business model for Trine. According to Sam: "We are able to determine that we've provided electricity to roughly 2 million people because we get the data from each of the solar power units. It's very tangible."

Identifying business opportunities at the bottom of the pyramid, and the transformative impact of mobile communications in developing countries, certainly is not new. But Trine illustrates how a purpose-driven Swedish startup can gain significant traction and success when certain essential elements come together at the right time to solve a critical problem.

At the time of publication, Trine had provided over 2.7 million people with electricity and avoided 63,302 tons of CO_2 through the replacement of kerosene lamps. Over 10,000 investors have joined its platform where it operates in Europe, investing more than EUR 31 million as of January 2020. The minimum investment is EUR 25, so the entry barrier is low, and investors are repaid with interest when solar partners repay the loans.[16] "Electricity really does change everything—societies prosper and are built on electrons. And by financing off-grid solar solutions, we're replacing expensive fossil fuels in Africa," Sam explains.

It was no coincidence that Trine chose to start its venture in Sweden, where risk willingness was higher than in other countries, according to Sam. Several elements were working in Trine's favor: a high degree of interest in sustainability as well as an excitement around the use of solar energy and an enabling legislative environment in Sweden that allowed Trine to build a minimum viable product without building a massive financial institution first—thanks to the new business models of crowdfunding and retail investment that had taken off. Globally, this phenomenon had existed for more than a decade and was well tested and scaled. Trine could then consider that "a given," and focus its efforts and limited resources on innovating elsewhere in the value chain. And not least, Sweden's social security net, providing free high-quality education and healthcare, meant that for Sam, his family, and the Trine team, the risk they were taking would not cost them everything if it should fail.

Trine's purpose, "to make the world a bit better, as fast as we can," is a motivating force in shaping its ambition and Sam acknowledges that being purpose-driven from the start, as a young company, might make it easier to move more quickly but the challenges to scale as a startup can be harder than for a larger company. "To use a solar energy analogy, it is sometimes better to retrofit and sometimes to build new. When we create something new, we can have the benefits of shortcuts speed, and flexibility and not hindered by legacy issues. But I can't see a reason why a more established company can't have the same societal purpose. The most important thing is that both types of companies get it done no matter how hard it is. We just have to figure this out."

We would say that for Trine, having a societal ecosystem approach was the only way to achieve its purpose—in fact, it's woven into its name. Trine means triple, threefold, or trinity in Middle English. "It reflects our triple bottom line thinking, where our impact is threefold: people, planet and profit," according to Sam.

A prevailing attitude is that there is a polar axis in which you do good on one side and make money on the other. And somewhere in the middle is venture philanthropy. The implication is that doing good means you need to compromise, with more risk and less return and it sounds really bad. So why would anyone do it? And this thinking makes sustainable investing seem like a fringe phenomenon. But actually, in reality, that's just an illusion. The point is that you can have a sustainable business full stop. No compromises. As I look at it, we are painting on a new canvas. We want to reinvent investment—to eliminate the distinction between sustainable or impact investing and investing. When we're done, it is going to be either investments in people, planet, profit, or evil investments.

We think that Trine is also illustrative of the Expönentiality Formula in that they have challenged traditional business models and created something entirely new and impactful between the crossroads of the traditional sectors of energy suppliers and banks. Their value proposition provides financial and societal benefits to all the relevant stakeholders within the societal ecosystem, while at the same time bringing value to the company itself. And it has created this value by using all the advantages of digitalization. Leveraging his personal experience from the solar energy industry, with a healthy dose of impatience, Sam has used the societal lenses to identify a missing link and a gap in the market waiting to be filled with an innovative approach. Trine's roots are entrepreneurial, and it is early days, but it has planted the seeds for exponential leadership.

There is a Swahili word, *hatujafika*, which means "we have not arrived yet." This is the phrase Sam Manaberi and his colleagues at Trine think about when they assess their progress, despite being enormously proud of what they've accomplished so far. As Sam explains:

> To keep building something that is massively valuable over time, which has the opportunity of making a large improvement on the planet and on the people living on the planet. That's what keeps me going on the dark days when tackling this problem feels really complicated and hard because we're a small team and there are constant challenges. But we hang onto this idea of building something of value. Our job is to bring this product at scale to the world.

When Digital Meets Societal Challenges

Our third example is Kinnevik, an industry-focused investment company which focuses its investments on three sectors, healthcare, financial services, and e-commerce, all in the process of significant technological disruption. It primarily invests in Europe, with a focus on the Nordics, the US and other selected markets. For Kinnevik, using digitalization to accelerate a positive impact on society is part of their long-term approach as owners.

For Kinnevik CEO Georgi Ganev, transformation and change are critical to everything that they do. From a business perspective, he says it is vital to "drive change and take big bets" and that "we are not sentimental." In our analysis, three of Kinnevik's portfolio investments illustrate (a) how considering society as a stakeholder is critical to their business success—in fact, the business success depends on the use of technology to make the services available and accessible to more people and (b) the power of digital as an accelerator of sustainability. All three cases also illustrate how digitalization is changing value chains, customer bases, and conventional business partnerships.

The first case is Babylon Health, a digital healthcare service company based in the UK, whose aim is to make healthcare services available to a broader part of the population. Combining mobile technology and artificial intelligence, its mission is to make healthcare more accessible and affordable for people everywhere. Babylon Health is also engaged in unconventional partnerships, as noted below, to explore how the same technology can apply not just to the richest markets, but emerging markets as well.

As Georgi explains, "Babylon Health provides a telemedicine solution with very powerful AI in order to diagnose people remotely and to give medical advice; it's more about healthcare delivery. And they have proven that they can serve the richest people and also use the technology to serve the poorest."

In Rwanda, Babylon Health has partnered with the Rwandan Ministry of Health and the Bill & Melinda Gates Foundation to provide a mobile phone app that gives any citizen instant, free access to expert health advice. Rwandans can download the app, called "babyl," and register to be connected to a chatbot that uses AI and machine learning to triage medical problems. The app offers treatment recommendations for simple conditions or, when appropriate, sets up an appointment to talk to a physician by phone or video. Consultations typically cost about 65 cents each. Patients without access to a mobile phone can visit babyl booths equipped with tablets and phones at various pharmacies.[17]

As Georgi describes,

> This underlines the importance of unconventional partnerships. Some would say why is a company like Babylon Health which has shareholders looking for profit, have a cooperation with the government of Rwanda. If you're building long-term businesses, you want to attract the best talent in the business. And if you are a good AI engineer and you're switching from Google Deep Mind to Babylon Health, of course you care about what the technology is used for, and you want to work for a company that has a clear vision that it wants to help not only the richest people but also the poorest people. I think that also helps to create the right culture.

Digital health solutions also have implications for the risks associated with AI, which we explore in Chap. 12.

In another Kinnevik example, Zalando, Europe's leading online fashion platform, is looking at its business not only from financial returns, but through the lens of planetary impacts. It recently bucked the trend of most e-commerce platforms, which are predicated on volumes and deliveries. Many e-commerce retailers face similar pressure, as exemplified in the case of New York City, where the delivery of 1.5 million packages per day from Amazon and other online retailers is clogging streets and contributing to GHG emissions.[18] With its Do.More strategy, Zalando's vision is to have a net-zero carbon impact for people and the planet which means looking at those volumes and deliveries and to address the negative environmental impacts of "fast fashion." Its commitments include that from October 2019 onward, its own operations and all deliveries and returns will be carbon neutral. Zalando is setting science-based targets in 2020 to reduce its environmental impact. It is also exploring new business models to change behavior, including reducing the number of returns, and encouraging customers to use what they buy and not return it.

According to Georgi Ganev, the new strategy is triggering new kinds of innovation with products, services, and even business models. "We will see significant progress in how to work with sizing to minimize the number of returns. Zalando is also experimenting with pre-owned goods, both pre-owned goods for purchase and the ability to return those goods for re-use" (Fig. 10.5).

This approach goes counter to most people's expectations, including investors, according to Georgi:

Fig. 10.5 Leading online fashion platform Zalando is experimenting with new business models as part of its sustainability strategy (© Zalando). This includes selling pre-owned goods and offering consumers the ability to return those goods for re-use

Some would assume a company like Zalando needs to fuel the fast fashion sector, meaning that we should buy more and buy more often in order to increase the frequency and average order value. Whereas I would say that a lot of the future profitability from Zalando can come from reducing the number of returns, which is really a cost for them. And they would do that by finding ways to get people to actually use the goods they buy instead of buying and returning them. And secondly, working with alternatives such as renting or pre-owned. If you're long term in your thinking, you would see more opportunities than challenges by focusing on sustainability. You can actually pull your customers towards another choice that is more sustainable and still make more money, especially if you have some kind of recurring revenue, for example, the ability to rent clothes or return clothes.

While Georgi says it is still too early to see any volumes growing in the pre-owned space, he adds "I think just the fact that Zalando is experimenting with these new models shows that they are keen and see profitability in the long run for this approach. Experimenting, even at the risk of failure, is far better than doing nothing at all, he reasons. "I think the biggest risk is that people don't do anything differently. They say, 'Well, we tried to change,' but then they don't actually do anything differently tomorrow than they did yesterday."

The third Kinnevik example is Bima, which offers affordable health insurance products via mobile phone in 13 countries across Africa, Asia, Latin America, and the Caribbean. Its aim is to bring insurance and health services to people who never had it before. To date it has reached 31 million customers, adding 575,000 new customers each month. About 75 percent of their customers are accessing insurance for the first time and 93 percent live on less than $10 per day.[19] The business model relies on a range of partnerships—between mobile operators, microfinance and banks, and corporations and consumers. Bima pioneered the mobile-delivered insurance model in which customers can pay for insurance via deduction of prepaid airtime credit.

According to Georgi,

What is unique about Bima is that the business model as such is based on strong unit economics, meaning that it is a company where you need a lot of users because the average customer spend is low. But with a digital setup you can achieve scale over time. That is a result of a number of innovations in product design and distribution, compared to the traditional insurance industry. And while Bima's products are built around having a real positive social impact for society, from Kinnevik's perspective they have the same targets for financial returns as for any other business.

All three examples from Kinnevik show how digitalization is accelerating a sustainability transformation. For Zalando, applying the planetary lens puts a different spin on the value proposition. While it is still early days, the company is finding new recurring revenues in business models that go against the tide of traditional e-commerce strategy. By understanding societal needs, Bima and Babylon Health are able to create solutions that are adapted for inclusion and accessibility—and they do so with the help of unconventional partnerships.

Customize Your Own Journey

The cases presented in this chapter illustrated different ways that companies can embrace society as a stakeholder. When we apply our model, it is clear to see how each company can adopt different elements of the journey and combine different accelerators and enablers for Expönentiality (Fig. 10.6).

The Formula provides a roadmap to identify each part of the journey. Each phase is unique, and, when taken in its entirety, it can guide you to see gaps, or areas for improvement. With that big-picture view, business leaders can better formulate action plans that lead to a successful, impactful sustainability journey. If someone had provided us with this kind of roadmap years ago, it would have saved time and effort and allowed us to achieve a more sustainable exponential impact that much sooner. This doesn't mean the work won't be hard—but with a plan to follow it's a far more manageable undertaking.

The companies profiled in this chapter show how the formula can work in practice. Yet every Expönentiality journey will be unique. For Scania, applying (retrospectively) the entire formula was the key to achieving exponential gains in sustainability leadership. In the Trine case, applying the societal lens was the gateway to greater impact. The Kinnevik examples focused on how digitalization, new business models, and unconventional partnerships could address societal challenges—with planetary impacts particularly relevant for Zalando.

In our analysis, these companies each adopted key elements of a societal ecosystem approach. They applied societal and planetary lenses to different degrees to better understand the science and impacts of business activities on people and the planet, while still conducting a profitable business. This is the very core of having society as your stakeholder, where the aim is to maximize positive impacts and minimize negative ones—and ideally to do so at scale.

It comes down to a mindset that embraces the entire ecosystem rather than the more narrow view of an industry vertical, and which brings new and

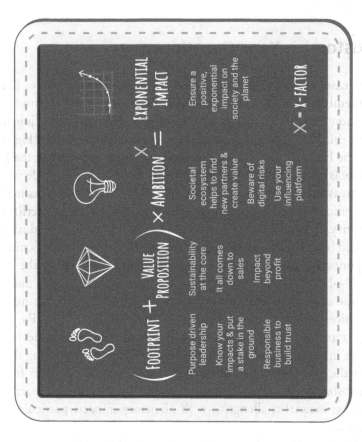

Fig. 10.6 The Expönentiality Formula: breaking it down. This illustration breaks down the Expönentiality Formula, tracing the Sustainability Leadership journey from mapping your footprint and creating a successful sustainable value proposition to ratcheting up your ambition to find your X-Factor

unconventional partners to the table to forge potentially industry-changing or world-changing solutions. As noted by Jacob Wallenberg at the start of this chapter, for reasons deeply rooted in the culture and values, Swedish companies seem particularly accustomed to thinking in terms of their impact on society and stakeholders. Of course, we're not all Swedish, so how do others adopt the same mindset? We think the answer is to adjust your lens to bring society and planet into focus. With that new perspective, you are able to challenge your business model, rethink your value proposition, and marshal the necessary partners to realize your vision.

If you see a bigger role for your company than belonging only to an industry vertical, this is the path to changing your industry and maybe the world. It is not necessary to be a first mover. But a leader needs to be intentional in adopting this approach, ready to leap, if necessary, to trial new business models. While we applaud the pioneers, companies that start later on this path than others can still make an impact—as long as they are clear on what's most important to them in their own ecosystem. But if a leader is struggling to find the societal and planetary lenses in which to view their path to Expönentiality, the next chapter explains why the UN Sustainable Development Goals might be helpful to illuminate the way forward.

Key Takeaways

1. To make society your stakeholder, don't look at only what your stakeholders think of you, but rather what impact you have on them. Assume responsibility for maximizing the positive impacts and minimizing the negative impacts of your business on people, communities, and society more broadly.
2. Build a deeper scientific knowledge base about your business ecosystem.
3. Seek unexpected partnerships and alliances where together you can overcome obstacles to get things done.
4. Consider how your value creation can be synonymous with what's important to society.
5. Create your own societal ecosystem to explore unconventional partnerships where every member can be an essential part of solving systemic challenges.
6. Think outside-in, not inside-out, to ensure your leadership approach is resonating with stakeholders, and is gaining traction capable of exponential impacts.

Notes

1. Benefit Corporations, accessed February 12, 2020, https://benefitcorp. net/?_ga=2.20458488.1586091844.1576703970-1160153567.1576703970.
2. Andrew Hill, "The limits of the pursuit of profit," FT Series The Company of the Future: Profit and Purpose, *Financial Times*, accessed September 24 2019, https://www.ft.com/content/c998cc32-d93e-11e9-8f9b-77216ebe1f17.
3. Business Roundtable, "Business Roundtable Redefines the Purpose of a Corporation to Promote 'An Economy That Serves All Americans'," Aug 19, 2019. https://www.businessroundtable.org/business-roundtable-redefines-the-purpose-of-a-corporation-to-promote-an-economy-that-serves-all-americans.
4. Sims R. et al, 2014: Transport. In: Climate Change 2014: Mitigation of Climate Change. Contribution of Working Group III to the Fifth Assessment Report of the Intergovernmental Panel on Climate Change, Cambridge University Press, Cambridge, United Kingdom and New York, NY, USA, https://www.ipcc.ch/site/assets/uploads/2018/02/ipcc_wg3_ar5_chapter8.pdf.
5. Fossil-free alternatives for commercial road transportation in Sweden, The Pathways Coalition, April 2019, accessed November 10, 2019, https://www. thepathwayscoalition.com/wp-content/uploads/2019/06/Fossil-free-alternatives-for-commercial-road-transportation-in-Sweden_ny-logga.pdf.
6. The Pathways Study: Achieving fossil-free commercial transport by 2050, May 2018, Scania.com, https://www.scania.com/group/en/wp-content/uploads/sites/2/2018/05/white-paper-the-pathways-study-achieving-fossil-free-commercial-transport-by-2050.pdf.
7. Alternative fuels and electrification, Scania.com, accessed March 8, 2020 https://www.scania.com/global/en/home/products-and-services/articles/alternative-fuels.html.
8. Oseweuba Valentine Okoro, Zhifa Sun and John Birch, "Catalyst-Free Biodiesel Production Methods: A Comparative Technical and Environmental Evaluation," *Sustainability* 10, no. 1 (2018): 127–149, https://doi. org/10.3390/su10010127.
9. US Department of Energy, Office of Energy Efficiency & Renewable Energy, www.fueleconomy.gov, accessed March 29, 2020, https://fueleconomy.gov/feg/fcv_benefits.shtml.
10. Hydrogen storage challenges, Office of Energy Efficiency and Renewable Energy, Energy.gov, accessed April 7, 2020, https://www.energy.gov/eere/fuelcells/hydrogen-storage-challenges.
11. Norwegian wholesaler ASKO puts hydrogen powered fuel cell electric Scania trucks on the road, Scania.com, January 2020, retrieved from https://www. scania.com/group/en/norwegian-wholesaler-asko-puts-hydrogen-powered-fuel-cell-electric-scania-trucks-on-the-road/.

12. The Pathways Coalition, accessed March 8, 2020, https://www.thepathway-scoalition.com/about-the-coalition/.

13. SDG 7: Data and Projections, IEA, Flagship report November 2019, https://www.iea.org/reports/sdg7-data-and-projections.

14. B. Ewers et al., Divestment may burst the carbon bubble if investors' beliefs tip to anticipating strong future climate policy. (preprint arxiv available at: http://arxiv.org/abs/1902.07481) (2019).

15. The Mobile Economy: Sub-Saharan Africa 2017, GSMA, accessed March 8, 2020   https://www.gsmaintelligence.com/research/?file=7bf3592e6d75014 4e58d9dcfac6adfab&download.

16. The progress of making change, Trine.com, accessed March 8, 2020, https://trine.com/our-progress.

17. Lia Novotny, "3-minute case study: The doctor will chatbot you know," Athena Health, June 20, 2018, https://www.athenahealth.com/knowledge-hub/healthcare-technology/3-minute-case-study-doctor-will-chatbot-you-now.

18. Matthew Haag and Winne Hu, "1.5 Million Packages a Day: The Internet Brings Chaos to N.Y. Streets," The New York Times, Oct 28, 2019, https://www.nytimes.com/2019/10/27/nyregion/nyc-amazon-delivery.html.

19. Bima.com, accessed March 19, 2020, http://www.bimamobile.com/about-bima/about-us-new/.

11

Making Business Sense of the SDGs

Up Close: Niklas Adalberth, Founder of Klarna and Norrsken Foundation, on Scaling Social Impact

In 2005, when Niklas Adalberth was 23, he co-founded the hugely successful e-payments firm Klarna. Today Klarna Bank is one of Europe's largest banks and provides payment solutions for 80 million consumers across 190,000 merchants in 17 countries.[1] Before Klarna, his only job experience had been flipping burgers at a Burger King, yet he managed to turn Klarna into that holy grail for entrepreneurs: a fintech unicorn, a privately held startup company valued at over $2 billion. Then, three years ago, Niklas decided to leave Klarna and invest his own resources to start Norrsken Foundation, an incubator for some 300 social impact entrepreneurs based in Stockholm, with a new tech hub opening soon in Kigali, Rwanda.

Where other tech billionaires might have continued to ride the gravy train of a skyrocketing startup, Niklas had a nagging sense that he had another purpose in life. He was worried about the future and wanted technology to be optimized for people and the planet, not simply to enrich owners and investors or to push forward with the latest financial goal, blinders on. At the bright and airy Norrsken House in downtown Stockholm, a converted former tramway workshop, Niklas sat down one gray November afternoon, his five-month-old son on his lap, to explain what changed for him:

> I used to think that once I was financially independent, I would reach nirvana and be the luckiest guy alive. The problem with that goal was that once you reach it, what then? The timing of Klarna was super lucky just when e-commerce took off. But if I can't feel any marginal return from extra wealth, why should I continue to chase that? Especially given how lucky I have been? And if I can't give back in one way or another, who should?, I asked myself. Given the

© The Author(s) 2020
H. Henriksson, E. Weidman Grunewald, *Sustainability Leadership*,
https://doi.org/10.1007/978-3-030-42291-2_11

challenges we face, am I part of the problem or part of the solution? As an entrepreneur, I am used to taking risks. So why not take a risk with tech startups that can solve real global issues.

For Niklas, who has personally invested $82 million in Norrsken Foundation,[2] entrepreneurs and startups are going to have to play an even greater role in the UN Sustainable Development Goals (SDGs). That's the motivation behind Norrsken Foundation's new EUR 100 million early-stage impact investment fund announced in 2019, Europe's largest, which will focus on early-stage tech startups in Europe. The founders of Swedish firms Minecraft, Candy Crush Saga, and Klarna and the family behind H&M are also backing the fund.[3] The idea is to show that companies seeking to solve the world's greatest challenges, including poverty, food waste, and climate change, can also generate market returns. To assess whether a company is impact-driven, the fund will use an impact framework inspired by the SDGs[4] (Fig. 11.1).

"We need to involve governments, other public agencies, large companies, entrepreneurs and academia to tackle the SDGs to create actual impact and bring it to the next level," Niklas says.

Fig. 11.1 Norrsken House in downtown Stockholm (© Norrsken). A converted former tramway workshop, the building now serves as an incubator for some 300 social impact entrepreneurs. Founder Niklas Adalberth has launched Europe's largest impact invest fund to support startups solving global sustainability challenges

The SDGs: A Complete Framework for Identifying Societal and Planetary Lenses

The work that Niklas and the social impact entrepreneurs are doing at Norrsken is a great example of the way businesses of all types—no matter the size or the sector—can use the SDGs as a societal and planetary lens to guide how they can make an impact on the world's greatest sustainable development challenges. As noted in Chaps. 9 and 10, there can be many types of societal and planetary lenses. If a company has not been able to identify its own lens through which to view its sustainability priorities, the SDGs can provide a useful framework for doing so.

The 17 SDGs, adopted by the global community in 2015, span economic development, environmental sustainability, and societal inclusion (see Table 11.1).[5] These Global Goals, to be achieved by 2030, marked the first time

Table 11.1 The UN Sustainable Development Goals

Goal 1: End poverty in all its forms everywhere
Goal 2: End hunger, achieve food security and improved nutrition, and promote sustainable agriculture
Goal 3: Ensure healthy lives and promote wellbeing for all at all ages
Goal 4: Ensure inclusive and equitable quality education and promote lifelong learning opportunities for all
Goal 5: Achieve gender equality and empower all women and girls
Goal 6: Ensure availability and sustainable management of water and sanitation for all
Goal 7: Ensure access to affordable, reliable, sustainable, and modern energy for all
Goal 8: Promote sustained, inclusive, and sustainable economic growth, full and productive employment, and decent work for all
Goal 9: Build resilient infrastructure, promote inclusive and sustainable industrialization, and foster innovation
Goal 10: Reduce inequality within and among countries
Goal 11: Make cities and human settlements inclusive, safe, resilient, and sustainable
Goal 12: Ensure sustainable consumption and production patterns
Goal 13: Take urgent action to combat climate change and its impacts
Goal 14: Conserve and sustainably use the oceans, seas, and marine resources for sustainable development
Goal 15: Protect, restore, and promote sustainable use of terrestrial ecosystems, sustainably manage forests, combat desertification, and halt and reverse land degradation and halt biodiversity loss
Goal 16: Promote peaceful and inclusive societies for sustainable development, provide access to justice for all, and build effective, accountable, and inclusive institutions at all levels
Goal 17: Strengthen the means of implementation and revitalize the global partnership for sustainable development

Source: United Nations Sustainable Development Goals, https://sustainabledevelopment. un.org/sdgs

the world had articulated a common vision and shared language for sustainable development. They capture the scope and complexity of global sustainable development problems and the bold actions and commitments necessary to solve them. At Norrsken, Niklas understands the challenges laid out by the Global Goals and is directing his impact funding to tackle them head-on—there is a clear linkage. For other companies, they might be misunderstood or even hyped. But one thing is for sure: the SDGs demand transformative solutions that can be delivered at scale only with the engagement of the private sector.

For business leaders committed to sustainability, not placing a company's agenda into the context of the SDGs is a missed opportunity. The Global Goals offer a readily adaptable platform for moving into the societal ecosystem, because solving them requires collaboration. They can help companies identify key sustainability issues where business can contribute, from the big, scalable actions to the low-hanging fruit. The SDGs are a perfect backdrop for deciding whether you want to transform your company, your industry, or the world. A single company acting alone may be able to impact a Goal, but perhaps not solve the achievement of the broader Goals. However, if an entire industry moves, as illustrated by the mobile industry later in this chapter, the impact can be far more significant. This was also the case with the combined efforts within and between sectors to tackle broader social and environmental challenges, as illustrated in the Pathways example in Chap. 10, where the aim is to make an exponential difference.

This chapter looks at how the SDGs provide that broader sustainable development context, although how to relate the Goals to business is not always obvious. To effectively use the SDGs as your societal and planetary lens, it's important to understand what the SDGs are—and aren't, and how to make them relevant for business. We look at how to link a company's bold goals to the SDGs, and how to ensure in doing so that you can distinguish a credible business contribution from "SDG-washing." We also take a deep dive into how the ICT industry leveraged its role as a game-changer in accelerating progress toward the SDGs.

The Basics: The SDGS and the Role of Business

First and foremost, the SDGs provide a context for the challenges within which any business will operate, now and in the future. The 17 SDGs, also known as the 2030 Agenda for Sustainable Development, underpinned by 169 targets and 232 indicators, call for several ambitious breakthroughs by 2030, including an end to extreme poverty and hunger while improving access to healthcare and education, protecting the environment, and building peaceful, inclusive societies.[6] No single sector of society can solve these challenges alone.

In fact, the UN's preamble to the 2030 Agenda for Sustainable Development recognizes that "private business activity, investment and innovation are major drivers of productivity, inclusive economic growth and job creation."[7] But five years on, with inadequate progress, a much deeper, faster, and transformational response is needed to get the world on track to achieve the Global Goals. Increasingly, the role of business is recognized as fundamental to success. Calling on all sectors to work together, UN Secretary António Guterres has called for a Decade of Action starting in 2020: "We know the great task before us. We need all hands on deck. We need to move together, leaving no one behind."[8]

The 2030 Agenda is ambitious and transformative. It is not about business-as-usual. Achieving the SDGs means being bold and sometimes making tough decisions. This is the kind of leadership mindset that's called for in 3.0.

The SDGs were ratified by—and are the ultimate responsibility of—governments around the world. Yet there is growing recognition that the private sector needs to engage, and many companies have adopted the Goals as a responsible business roadmap. Organizations like the UN Global Compact, the World Business Council for Sustainable Development (WBCSD), and the Global Reporting Initiative (GRI) offer a variety of tools to help navigate the business contribution.

The Goals provide a means to frame and anticipate current and future market and societal needs. Aligning strategy with the SDGs can enhance supply chain resilience, attract investors, and help ensure a license to operate by better managing risks and meeting regulatory compliance. Not least, it makes companies more attractive employers for the growing number of people who want to work for companies that contribute to a better world. In short, the SDGs are an invitation for business to be part of solving global challenges, rather than perpetuating them.

It's a huge business opportunity as well. According to the WBSCD, there is significant business value to be captured across at least four economic systems by 2030.[9] These include food and agriculture, at US$2.3 trillion; cities and urban mobility at US$3.7 trillion; energy and materials at US$4.3 trillion, and health and wellbeing at US$1.8 trillion. Yet despite the overwhelming case for business action, a 2019 CEO Study from Accenture and the UN Global Compact found that just 21 percent of CEOs believe business is playing a critical role in contributing to the Global Goals, and they recognize their own businesses could do more. So, what will it take for more companies to step up?

It can be difficult to translate these business opportunities to specific actions a company can take on such wide-ranging topics as eliminating poverty and hunger and promoting peaceful, just, and strong societies. The SDGs, and their underlying targets and indicators, were conceived for governments. Since business had limited input in their design, it can be challenging for corporations or industries to measure and track their progress against the Goals. To further complicate matters, a sizeable number of SDG indicators are classified as "Tier 3," which means that internationally established methodologies or standards do not yet exist for the indicator and are yet to be developed or tested.[10] Many companies are starting to make the links and report on their priority Goals. But there are still substantial gaps in measuring direct and potential impacts of the private sector. To date, it has largely been up to each company or industry sector to figure out how to operationalize the SDGs and where to direct the biggest effort and resources for maximum impact.

Making the Goals Fit for Business Purpose

While the SDGs invite leadership on a global scale, the SDG indicators are not always relevant for business. Yet given the enormity of the challenges the world faces, the Global Goals cannot be achieved without the resources, skills, innovation, and economies of scale of the private sector. There is as yet no clear blueprint on moving from a mere SDG branding exercise to substantive, ideally scalable solutions that are business-relevant and impactful. Ultimately, companies must define how they can best contribute to the Goals and measure progress. What distinguishes a real contribution from "SDG-washing," where slick slogans and alluring, colorful SDG logos become just another public relations exercise?

It starts with making sure every commitment to an SDG is fact- and evidence-based. A company claiming to be making a meaningful contribution to Goal 13, Climate Action, for instance, without setting a science-based target is unconvincing. The contribution must also be ambitious, transformative, and material: a renewable energy business aligning its strategy with Goal 7: Affordable and Clean Energy, makes complete sense—but a retailer that draws the line at installing LED lighting cannot claim to be making an adequate or significant contribution to Goal 7.

As a way to understand how a company can be consistent and effective, and consider the big picture in approaching the SDGs, a look at Goal 3 (Good Health and Wellbeing) is instructive. For example, to make a meaningful contribution to Goal 3, a pharmaceutical company needs to go beyond a general statement of commitment and first articulate and then measure what it is actually doing to support the underlying targets for that goal. Is it providing access to life-saving drugs in emerging markets? Does it educate community health workers to deliver health services? Commitments are most effective when detailed and supported by real programs and initiatives that have the potential to be scaled. Additionally, at first glance, from a business perspective, Goal 3 seems targeted for the healthcare sector. Yet in fact, it makes sense for every employer to advocate for Goal 3 and create supportive structures and policies for employee wellbeing. For example, greater awareness and prevention through health education, even at a corporate level, can have a significant impact on health outcomes.

Substantive corporate actions are at their best when they succeed in delivering co-benefits or positive impact across multiple goals. A notable example is Adidas, which has pledged to replace virgin polyester in its products with 100 percent recycled polyester primarily from recycled ocean plastic.[11] That initiative contributes to SDG 12—Responsible Consumption and Production and SDG 14—Life Under Water by leveraging a market-based solution to ocean plastic. There are hundreds of examples of companies that are making contributions to the SDGs, both large and small, so this chapter does not attempt to capture them all. But what successful commitments have in common is that they are fact-based, actionable, and, to the greatest extent possible, relevant to the company's core business.

A caveat, however: supporting the Goals can also simply be the right thing to do; for instance, reducing waste, transitioning to clean energy, or contributing to greater access to health or education. With children and young people among the most avid tech users today, digital education has helped to vastly improve access to learning for all (Goal 4). But this same group is vulnerable to risks as well—offering another opportunity for companies to do the right thing. One example is Swedish companies' leadership in supporting technology that can detect child sexual abuse material in corporate IT environments.

Everyone's Responsibility to Safeguard Children

Online child sexual abuse is escalating at a startling rate. A record 45 million illegal images of children being sexually abused (both photos and videos) were flagged last year alone—exposing a system at a breaking point and unable to keep up with the perpetrators, according to a *New York Times* investigation.[12] More than a decade ago, when the reported number was less than a million, the proliferation of the explicit imagery had already reached a crisis point.[13] The National Center for Missing and Exploited Children (NCMEC) Cyber Tipline, the national repository for child abuse materials detected by US-based tech companies, reported a 541 percent increase in the amount of video depicting child abuse between 2017 and 2018.[14]

(continued)

(continued)

The business environment is far from immune; one in 500 work computers is used to handle child sexual abuse material.[15] It is estimated that 50 percent of those who consume child sexual abuse material abuse children physically, and that 80 percent of the offenders abuse children that they have a close relationship with.[16]

Companies are in a powerful position to do something about this horrifying crime, yet it is an often-overlooked aspect of responsible business, perhaps because it is a difficult topic to discuss. In 2003, four tech-savvy Swedes, alarmed at the rise in child sexual abuse material on the internet, devised a technology that could detect child sexual abuse material on corporate computer networks. Called NetClean,[17] based in Gothenburg, Sweden, it had support from the start from Her Majesty Queen Silvia of Sweden's World Childhood Foundation, dedicated to safeguarding children against sexual abuse and exploitation. Today over 200 Swedish companies have NetClean installed in their organizations globally, with around one million end-points in 110 countries.

The technology, similar to an anti-virus software, reacts when it detects the digital fingerprint of an image or video that law enforcement has classified as child sexual abuse material. The company alerts law enforcement who initiate an investigation.

"By following the trail of the detected image in a business environment, material can be found, offenders can be prosecuted, and children can be rescued," according to NetClean CEO Anna Borgström. "This is a really amazing positive impact to society. Companies are in a unique position to stop crimes from being committed with the use of company devices, while acting as an ethical corporate citizen and safeguarding children. We have found that policies alone are not enough; you need the right technology to root out the problem."

As an idea incubated in Sweden that has proven effective in dealing with a serious societal problem, NetClean is currently expanding to other markets to spread the approach globally. Such efforts have a direct impact on sub-goal 16.2 of the SDGs: to end abuse, exploitation, trafficking and all forms of violence and torture against children.[18] Companies can and must do more in this area of responsible business. Protecting an organization's IT environment by using software to detect child sexual abuse crime is a concrete action that sustainable, ethical businesses can take to protect children's rights.

It also makes sense to find out how specific national governments are working toward the Goals, and if there are any private sector outreach activities to support those efforts. Sweden is a long-time supporter of the UN system and an early advocate for the SDGs. Sweden ranked second in the world in how close it has come to achieving the Goals, in the 2019 Sustainable Development Report from the non-profit Bertelsmann Stiftung and the UN Sustainable Solutions Development Network. It was just slightly behind Denmark and followed by Finland, showing once again Nordic leadership on the SDGs.[19] No country however can claim to be completely on track, and Sweden and

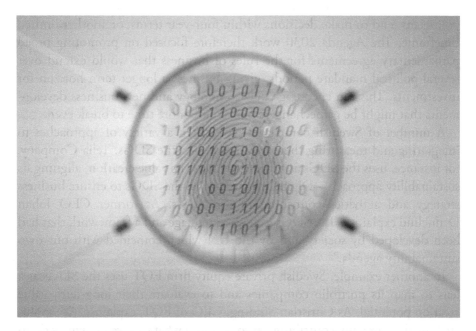

Fig. 11.2 Swedish firm NetClean has devised a solution (illustrated by this digital fingerprint, © NetClean) that detects child sexual abuse material on corporate computer networks. Adopted widely by Swedish companies, it demonstrates how business can directly impact the SDG sub-goal 16.2: to end abuse, exploitation, trafficking, and all forms of violence and torture against children

the other Nordic countries will need to focus particularly on transitioning their energy systems from high-carbon to low-carbon sources (Fig. 11.2).

Sweden has also been a leader in bringing the private sector to the table. One example is the Swedish Leadership for Sustainable Development,[20] which Elaine actively supported and helped to form. This network, coordinated by the Swedish International Development Cooperation Agency (SIDA), comprises over 20 leading company CEOs and expert organizations to share knowledge and collaborate on joint projects to advance progress on the SDGs.

Henrik participated as the industrial business voice in the Swedish government's work to advance Agenda 2030.[21] This was an in-depth look at how the government could implement Agenda 2030 broadly across all sectors of society. Another aim was to analyze how the government could be better organized and create the right processes to ensure that the Agenda was present in all aspects of governance. By working together, the public and private sectors were able to overcome hurdles to accelerate Agenda 2030. The business community encouraged the government to consider long-term decisions to ensure policy stability and coherence. In Sweden, as in many other countries, politicians tend to make decisions within four-year terms, or another limited timeframe. The Agenda 2030 work therefore focused on promoting broad parliamentary agreements for the rules of business that would extend over several political mandate periods, giving business a longer-term horizon for investments. This can encourage new technology and new business developments that might be gamechangers but require more time to break even.

A number of Swedish companies have taken a variety of approaches to integrating and measuring their contribution to the SDGs. Telia Company, for instance, uses the SDGs as a lens to measure its value creation, aligning its sustainability approach—Digital Impact—with the SDGs to ensure business strategy and activities contribute to the SDGs. As former CEO Johan Dennelind explains: "The SDGs gave us a language and a framework that had been developed by society and by the UN which coincided with our own sustainability agenda."

In another example, Swedish private equity firm EQT uses the SDGs as a lens to map its portfolio companies and to evaluate their long-term value creation potential. As Christian Sinding, CEO of EQT, explains, "We evaluate how the company contributes to society and what can we as owners do to accelerate that positive impact." EQT is among a group of investors who have joined SDG Impact, an initiative from the UN Development Programme, with the goal of advancing a unified, global effort to authenticate SDG-enabling investment—a good fit with EQT's core business. The initiative aims to set SDG Impact Standards as principles and tools for investors and enterprises. According to Christian: "We feel it is important to contribute to the definition and common measurement of progress toward the SDGs and a measurement of sustainability. We've joined to see if we can actually have an impact in a positive way, because we find it quite complex now to measure progress. Our goal is two-fold, to help simplify it but also to get some inspiration on how our own measurement can be improved." While the language of the SDGs is starting to become known in some parts of the investor community, among many private equity and venture capital firms there are still considerable gaps in understanding their value in assessing companies.

Global appliance manufacturer Electrolux has adapted a holistic view of the Global Goals. According to CEO Jonas Samuelsson: "The SDGs are an important part of our materiality analysis for sustainability issues, and our sustainability framework—For the Better—supports several of the goals. Crucially, I believe the correlation between our sustainability framework and the SDGs highlights that our agenda reflects societal objectives."

As well as embedding the goals in their own organizations, companies wanting to increase their reach and impact to tackle complex problems can look to alliances and partnerships to achieve scale. Scania has embraced an approach to ensure attention is given to all the SDGs, to ensure that there is no suboptimization. There are always a few Goals where a global company can have a major impact, depending on the nature of its business. Every company needs to have a process to evaluate which goals are most relevant for their business and what they can really deliver on, keeping in mind that all the Goals are interlinked. For Scania these are Goals 9 (Industry Innovation and Infrastructure), 11 (Sustainable Cities and Communities), 13 (Climate Action), and 17 (Partnerships for the Goals). Often work is aimed at addressing one of the goals, but partnership can bring about greater scale.

One example that hits all of the above goals for Scania at once is its solution for more sustainable urban public transport—so called Bus Rapid Transit (BRT) systems (like an above-ground subway system using buses). One such system can be found in Ghana's capital city Accra. The project included not only delivery of some 250 sustainable buses but also construction of bus terminals, bus stops and bus depots, an electronic, cash-free ticketing system, and a workshop for servicing and maintaining vehicles and training for 600 bus drivers. To encourage the recruitment and training of more female bus drivers, a related Scania initiative, together with partners, called "Women Moving The City" is providing a six-month training to women. Initially, 60 women have been selected for the program. Without a strong partnership between local and national governments and the private sector, there would be little, if any, progress in achieving any of these Goals.

To understand how a company—or industry—can truly impact the Global Goals, we look at how the ICT industry took an early role in shaping the role of mobile communications to accelerate the SDGs.

Pushing for ICT's Pivotal Role in SDGs

Elaine in her former role at Ericsson felt strongly that ICT could be a gamechanger for countries in achieving the SDGs. This grew out of hands-on experience working with the Millennium Development Goals (MDGs) in Africa between 2006 and 2010. The eight MDGs set out in 2000 to halve extreme poverty rates by 2015, among other goals, and preceded the SDGs.[22] Although they can be credited with the most successful anti-poverty movement in history for developing countries, the MDGs lacked the universal, interconnected global development framework that defines the SDGs. In 2007, Elaine met with Joanna Rubinstein, President and CEO of World Childhood Foundation USA. At that time, Joanna was Chief of Staff to

Professor Jeffrey Sachs of Columbia University, who was then Special Advisor to UN Secretary-General Kofi Annan on the Millennium Development Goals. As they discussed the dramatic impact of telecom in responding to natural disasters, the conversation turned to the still-untapped role of telecom for global development. A plan was hatched for Jeffrey to meet then Ericsson CEO Carl-Henric Svanberg. It was a fruitful connection, bringing together Jeffrey, who had the ear of the UN, and Carl-Henric, who had access to global technology in 180 countries. Together they could try to prove the premise that ICT could have an impact on development. Elaine and Joanna put the plan in motion, and the result was Ericsson's multi-year $10 million commitment to the Millennium Villages Project (MVP), an integrated approach to fighting poverty at the village level through community-led development in sub-Saharan Africa.[23] Although there are mixed research findings on whether the MVP actually achieved its vision after ten years—or not—it is clear that it did foster global awareness in a way never seen before in the global development community, stimulated technological innovations, and forged new groundbreaking types of public-private partnerships between the private sector, NGOs, and local governments.

Over the next few years, in the context of the MDGs, it became clear that mobile communication and later broadband proved themselves as powerful enablers of social and economic development and for environmental sustainability. It started with a basic premise: even in the poorest corners of the planet, if you had a phone, you had a business. Broadband was quickly becoming a twenty-first-century infrastructure that could unleash sustainable development in fields as diverse as education to energy and banking. Yet governments were still thinking about infrastructure in the more limited terms of physical infrastructure.

Through her role at Ericsson, Elaine was part of launching many firsts: supporting the One Million Community Healthworkers Campaign with mobile phones,[24] using mobile communications to revolutionize Africa weather information,[25] and extending mobile coverage to improve safety and security for fishermen on Lake Victoria,[26] to name a few. With the help of a diverse array of partners, these projects provided on-the-ground evidence of the power of technology. They also served to teach Ericsson first-hand about the possibilities—and challenges—in global development, from establishing projects in remote areas without sufficient infrastructure to finding the right set of public-private partners to back an initiative.

Gradually ICT's potential to have an outsized impact on global sustainable development became clear. With its presence in 180 countries, Ericsson had tremendous reach to scale technology. Ericsson began to advocate for governments worldwide to establish broadband and digital strategies to achieve the Global Goals, and it also moved ahead with specific targets, initiatives, and engagement with governments to align its commitment to action. Advocating the role of broadband as a way for governments to achieve the Goals was a core business issue for Ericsson (since sustainability and the core business were synonymous), and it evolved into an industry-wide movement. In 2014, Elaine led an initiative within the Broadband Commission that resulted in an Industry Manifesto, signed by 55 members of the Broadband Commission for Sustainable Development, calling for broadband to be "acknowledged at the core of any post-2015 sustainable development framework, to ensure that all countries are empowered to participate in the global digital economy."[27]

The role of ICT became increasingly clear. For example, delivering quality education for all by 2030 depended on a well-functioning broadband infrastructure that would allow national governments to harness digital education. And similarly, tackling Goal 3 would not be possible without e-health or telemedicine. Making progress on the SDGs hinges on making technology accessible and affordable to everyone. The ICT industry therefore has enormous potential to champion, drive, and scale the SDGs. The industry still is working actively to help governments understand how to leverage technology to achieve their SDG commitments.

Hans Vestberg, CEO of Ericsson at the time the SDGs were being formulated, explains,

> At first we were fighting for the Goal 18, which would be a digital vision of how to scale up solutions in every country and city. We lost that game and instead settled on acknowledging that ICT could be embedded in individual goals, and that we needed to focus on Goal 17: Partnership to Achieve the Goals, to make it happen. But our vision is still that digitalization is the enabler for all 17 Goals. I remain very excited about technology and the good it can do in the world.

Ericsson continued to lead its industry in advocating a role for ICT in delivering and accelerating achievement of the SDGs. The company also worked to embed the Goals into the business strategy and connect them with the product portfolio. For instance, using ICT to advance mobile money in underserved markets—"banking the unbanked"—addressed financial inclusion and social and economic empowerment, contributing to Goal 1 (No Poverty) and Goal 8 (Decent Work and Economic Growth). Switching to renewable energy in off-grid telecom sites was a way to link to Goal 7 (Affordable and Clean Energy), and champion sustainable energy for all. In addition to broadband's role as a key infrastructure for development, Internet of Things (IoT) products and services could enable digital urban environments in support of Goal 11 (Sustainable Cities and Communities). An understanding of how products and services can impact the Goals is the foundation for using the SDGs effectively as a societal and planetary lens.

GSMA—A Whole Industry Response

Given the complex and far-reaching nature of the SDG agenda, it sometimes takes an entire industry to move the needle. While the ICT sector, including Internet Service Providers (ISPs), telecom providers, software companies, and more, rose to this challenge, as noted in the Broadband Commission example above, the mobile industry was the first industry sector to broadly commit to the SDGs, in 2016. Under the leadership of Mats Granryd, Director General of the GSMA (the mobile communications industry group), the industry grasped that the Global Goals provided a sustainability framework for many of the activities that its member companies were already doing. He is now spearheading initiatives to amplify and accelerate the mobile industry's impact on all 17 SDGs, across both developed and developing markets.

The potential for positive impact is huge. Over the next seven years, 1.4 billion people will start using the mobile internet for the first time, bringing the total number of mobile internet subscribers globally to five billion by 2025 (over 60 percent of the population).[28] Growth in connectivity is helping the mobile industry increase its impact across all the SDGs, and accelerating impact in other sectors. The industry's progress is captured in an annual SDG Impact Report. The 2018 report found that the industry's impact had increased across all 17 SDGs.[29] Some of the highlights included:

- In 2019, the number of globally registered mobile money accounts surpassed the one billion mark, facilitating access for individuals who would otherwise be excluded from using financial services.
- A total of 1.4 billion people use mobile to improve their education or that of their children.
- Five million more people have used mobile-enabled agricultural services supported by the GSMA's mNutrition Initiative, giving farmers access to vital information that allows them to improve agricultural productivity and incomes.[30]

An important objective of GSMA is to work with governments to ensure that its focus on the SDGs is supporting the right objectives. According to Mats:

> As an industry, we are constantly partnering with governments and regulators, across the world, in our outreach and meetings and capacity building. It really shows the positive impact we have as an operator. Obviously, we are doing it because (a) we are providing good value for society but (b) it is a way for us to increase the reputation of the industry. We are not on the back foot but viewed as more forward-thinking and more positive in our meetings with governments. I think it sets up an environment for productive conversations.

The mobile industry's work on the SDGs demonstrates that any industry has the ability to provide solutions that can be transformative and dramatically affect the outcome of the Goals. Working together within an industry can result in a vision for true scale-up and impact. Doing this effectively hinges on a common industry-wide agenda, broad collaboration, and working closely with governments to be certain that industry initiatives and public-private partnerships are truly meeting the most critical challenges. We encourage business leaders to look at the SDGs from an industry perspective to get more scale and impact.

Judging by current trends and data, it will be even more critical to have initiatives where business steps up the pace and depth of the industry contribution. Importantly, there is a great deal of business value at stake. The SDGs are designed to encourage government leaders and policymakers to adopt long-term thinking and integrated decision-making—something that business leaders who want transformational change also aspire to.

On a personal note, while Mats is quick to acknowledge the importance of every Goal, he says he thinks there is something in his Swedish background that fuels a strong personal commitment to SDG 5: Achieve gender equality and SDG 10: Reduce inequality within and among countries, and he has tried to make that a priority throughout his career. According to Mats: "I certainly think that has to do with my upbringing in Sweden and my emphasis throughout my career to always look for and champion the great female leaders. Both in the business context and in society, greater gender balance makes for better, more profitable businesses, an enhanced world and more impact on sustainability challenges."

Managing Trade-offs

As well as generating co-benefits, it is important to consider downsides and avoid, or mitigate, possible trade-offs or negative secondary impacts from actions a company takes in support of one SDG at the possible expense of another.

The 2030 Agenda is described as "indivisible," which means that all the Goals have to be achieved for sustainable development to ultimately occur. For example, SDG 8 (Decent Work and Economic Growth) could be addressed with a rise in GDP but if that economic growth was secured through land clearing, deforestation, habitat, and biodiversity loss, it would be at the expense of SDG 15 (Life on Land). Further, long-term economic productivity would be undermined through loss of topsoil, genetic diversity, and carbon sinks, among other land impacts.

Prioritizing action on the Goals based on where a company can make the most difference through its core business is a smart way to go. At the same time, the full set of SDGs form a valuable checklist for understanding the full range of risks and impacts of business activities and how to manage these impacts effectively.

Being open and transparent about possible negative effects and trade-offs is critical for credibility. Talking about progress toward the SDGs without discussing challenges and downsides undermines real progress.

Taking a Business-as-unusual Mindset

We believe there is substantial business value in acting on the 17 goals. Among other things, it puts a company's actions and commitments in the context of the broader society in which it operates. The SDGs can create a powerful framework for determining how a company can construct a meaningful societal ecosystem. When an industry engages with the 2030 Agenda, which is ambitious and transformative, the results can be equally so. It is not about business-as-usual. Achieving the SDGs means being bold and sometimes making tough decisions. When companies and entire industries set their sights on this level of ambition, it is possible to transform not just a company or an industry, but even the world. This is the kind of leadership mindset that's called for in 3.0.

As long as business leaders are thoughtful and credible in how they work with the SDGs, there is a strong business case for action. It will be increasingly difficult to do business in a hotter, more unstable, unequal, resource-constrained world. Laggards also face regulatory risks since the SDGs are a reflection of future policy at international, national, and regional levels. There is also the risk of market disruption as forward-thinking businesses forge ahead with transformational new business models that threaten to radically reshape markets. For companies who want to stay in business, inaction is not an option—which is an underlying principle in this book.

One of Elaine's roles as a member of the Board of Directors of the Whitaker Peace & Development Initiative (WPDI), see the box below, has been to galvanize the active engagement and support of the private sector for WPDI, whose mission is to support Goal 16. At first glance, this Goal, with its focus on peace and justice, does not appear to be business friendly. But on second glance, it's amazing what a force for good business can be for promoting peace and justice.

Empowering Youth as Agents of Change

We live in a time where we have the largest youth generation in human history, with 1.8 billion young people alive today between the ages of 15 and 29.[31] Of this 1.8 billion, 90 percent live in developing countries, and almost one in four, or approximately 408 million, are living in settings directly affected by armed conflict or organized violence. These young women and men are often portrayed as victims or perpetrators of violence.

Forest Whitaker believes otherwise. The artist, SDG Advocate, and UNESCO Special Envoy for Peace and Reconciliation founded the Whitaker Peace & Development Initiative (WPDI) in 2012 because he believes these youth can be empowered to become agents of change, peace-makers, and entrepreneurs. With the right support, they can help bring peace to their communities and create small business that deliver relevant services while providing jobs to local youth.

Youth around the world face incredibly challenging situations that threaten a bright future, from gangs to drug trafficking to war and conflict, leading to displacement or life in a refugee camp. As a result, many have lost years of education to poverty and marginalization. The WPDI's mission is to provide these young people, as troops on the ground, with tools and resources so that they can take initiatives to transform their communities. Empowering young people in these fragile and conflict-affected settings is fundamental to achieving SDG 16 (Peaceful and Inclusive Societies). In the US, Africa, and Latin America, WPDI has to date reached over 300,000 people through its peacemaking and conflict resolution and youth leadership programs.

Elaine, who serves on the board of WPDI (as does Hans Vestberg, CEO of Verizon), and previously worked with Forest on a number of partnerships to help train youth in ICT skills, has seen the power of this approach up close. Today the relatively small initiative started by Forest has become a globally recognized example of best practice in the pursuit of peace and conflict resolution and a testament to what a single individual can accomplish by shining a spotlight and galvanizing action on a pressing societal challenge.

In future, business could well see the UN push for more substantive private sector action on the SDGs. This could include: (1) accountability for and verification of all corporate claims; (2) adding up all the commitments, and (3) facilitating partnerships.[32] Increasingly, too, consumers will be looking to spend their money with companies who are part of the solution: environmental issues were the top concern for global consumers according to The Tetra Pak Index 2019,[33] and "Green Pressure" is the number one emerging consumer trend for 2020, according to TrendWatching.[34]

All of these factors present a strong invitation for entrepreneurs to take initiative, which brings us back to Niklas Adlaberth and his vision of what startups can bring to the daunting challenge of achieving the SDGs. In addition to the impact investment fund, he founded the $1 million Norrsken Award, the largest prize for impact startups in the Nordics, presented in collaboration with the UN, awarded to the startup recognized for its work to "make the world a better place." And with the Swedish government and the Stockholm Resilience Center, Norrsken is also looking into working with the public sector and academia to form the SDG Impact Accelerator, focusing on empowering "systems entrepreneurs" and innovators providing impact at scale.

Niklas' story is just one example of how partnerships, the essence of Goal 17, can help to ramp up the speed of action. When companies think about the SDGs they need to think about both the impact the company can make and the broader national and global agenda of which they are a part—in order to make the most meaningful contribution. If companies find opportunities to advance the SDGs through their core business activities, partner with others to unravel complex problems, and report transparently and credibly on their progress, the world has a much better chance of staying on course to achieve the Goals. But to make the most ambitious global agenda ever adopted a reality, business leaders need to flip to a business-as-unusual mindset.

Key Takeaways

1. Use the SDGs as a societal and planetary lens to better understand your company's impact on society, and where you can make a difference, but make sure your business commitments are fact-based and actionable.
2. The SDGs cannot be achieved without the resources, skills, innovation, and economies of scale of the private sector. Demonstrate on-the-ground ways of how your company or even your industry can help achieve the Goals.

3. Commit to the Global Goals, but start with the SDGs closest to your core business and where you can really influence step-change and transformation.
4. Make sure you analyze any trade-offs; that is, avoid supporting one Goal at the possible expense of another.
5. The SDGs are the most complete, internationally recognized summary of sustainable development challenges facing humanity. Even if written for and by governments, leverage them to help frame and anticipate current and future market and societal needs by working proactively with governments.
6. Communicate company contributions to the Goals credibly and authentically and avoid SDG-washing. And remember, sometimes supporting a Goal is simply the right thing to do.

Notes

1. Louise Lindberg, "How Klarna Won Over 80 Million Shoppers' Hearts," Dec 6, 2019, https://www.klarna.com/knowledge/articles/how-klarna-won-over-80-million-shoppers-hearts/.
2. Jonathan Shieber, "With Norrsken House, ex-Klarna executive envisions a global network of co-working spaces focused on impact," Techcrunch, Dec 2, 2017, https://techcrunch.com/2017/12/12/with-norrsken-house-ex-klarna-executive-envisions-a-global-network-of-co-working-spaces-focused-on-impact/.
3. Richard Milne, "Swedish start-up founders raise Europe's biggest social impact fund," *The Financial Times*, Dec 23, 2019, retrieved from https://www.ft.com/content/f7da046c-233f-11ea-b8a1-584213ee7b2b.
4. Kim Darrah, "Klarna cofounder Niklas Adalberth's Norrsken Foundation launches €100m impact fund," Sifted, Dec 23, 2019, https://sifted.eu/articles/klarna-norrsken-impact-fund/.
5. UN Global Compact, Global Goals for People and Planet, accessed August 5, 2019 https://www.unglobalcompact.org/sdgs/about.
6. United Nations, Sustainable Development Goals, accessed August 5, 2019 https://www.un.org/sustainabledevelopment/development-agenda/.
7. Transforming our World: The 2030 Agenda for Sustainable Development, Sustainable Development Goals Knowledge Platform, accessed March 15, 2020, https://sustainabledevelopment.un.org/post2015/transformingourworld.
8. António Guterres, *Remarks to High-Level Political Forum on Sustainable Development, Sept 24, 2019,* https://www.un.org/sg/en/content/sg/speeches/2019-09-24/remarks-high-level-political-sustainable-development-forum.
9. CEO Guide to The Sustainable Development Goals, WBCSD, 2017, www.wbcsd.org.

10. IAEG-SDGs, Tier Classification for Global SDG Indicators, accessed August 5, 2019 https://unstats.un.org/sdgs/iaeg-sdgs/tier-classification/.
11. Creativity versus plastic, Adidas, June 2019, https://www.adidas.com/us/blog/361041.
12. Michael H. Keller and Gabriel J.X. Dance, "Child Abusers Run Rampant as Tech Companies Look the Other Way," *The New York Times*, Nov 9, 2019, https://www.nytimes.com/interactive/2019/11/09/us/internet-child-sex-abuse.html.
13. Michael H. Keller and Gabriel J.X. Dance, "Child Abusers Run Rampant as Tech Companies Look the Other Way."
14. Statement by John F. Clark, President and Chief Executive Officer, National Center for Missing and Exploited Children, for the United States Senate Committee on the Judiciary, "Protecting Innocence in a Digital World," July 9, 2019, accessed August 5, 2019, https://www.judiciary.senate.gov/imo/media/doc/Clark%20Testimony.pdf.
15. Netclean.com, accessed February 10, 2020, https://www.netclean.com/.
16. Netclean.com, https://www.netclean.com/.
17. Netclean.com, https://www.netclean.com/.
18. Indicators and a Monitoring Framework, SDSN, accessed February 10, 2020, https://indicators.report/targets/16-2/.
19. SDG Index, 2019 Sustainable Development Report, Bertelsmann Stiftung and the UN Sustainable Solutions Development Network, accessed March 16, 2020, https://sdsna.github.io/2019GlobalIndex/2019GlobalIndexRankings.pdf.
20. Swedish Leadership for Sustainable Development, The Swedish International Development Cooperation Agency (Sida), updated 7 October 2019, https://www.sida.se/English/partners/Resources-for-specific-partner-groups/Private-sector/Collaboration-principles/swedish-leadership-for-sustainable-development/.
21. The Government adopts Sweden's action plan for the 2030 Agenda, The Government of Sweden, June 18, 2018, accessed February 10, 2020, https://www.government.se/press-releases/2018/06/the-government-adopts-swedens-action-plan-for-the-2030-agenda/.
22. Millennium Development Goals, United Nations, accessed March 15, 2020, https://www.un.org/millenniumgoals/.
23. Millennium Villages, The Earth Institute, Columbia University, accessed March 24, 2020, https://www.earth.columbia.edu/articles/view/1799.
24. One Million Community Healthworkers Campaign, accessed March 19, 2020, http://1millionhealthworkers.org/.
25. Mobile Communications to revolutionize African weather monitoring, June 18, 2009, https://www.ericsson.com/en/press-releases/2009/6/mobile-communications-to-revolutionize-african-weather-monitoring.

26. Ericsson, Zain and the GSMA to save lives on Lake Victoria by extending mobile coverage, Ericsson.com, March 3, 2008, https://www.ericsson.com/en/press-releases/2008/3/ericsson-zain-and-the-gsma-to-save-lives-on-lake-victoria-by-extending-mobile-coverage.

27. Transformative Solutions for 2015 and Beyond Manifesto, Broadband Commission on Sustainable Development, accessed March 19, 2020, https://broadbandcommission.org/Documents/publications/BBComm-ManifestoNames.pdf.

28. The Mobile Economy 2019, GSMA Intelligence, accessed March 19, 2020, https://www.gsmaintelligence.com/research/?file=b9a6e6202ee1d5f787cfe bb95d3639c5&download.

29. 2019 Mobile Industry Impact Report: Sustainable Development Goals, GSMA, accessed March 19, 2020, https://www.gsma.com/betterfuture/2019 sdgimpactreport/wp-content/uploads/2019/09/SDG_Report_2019_ ExecSummary_Web_Singles.pdf.

30. 2019 Mobile Industry Impact Report: Sustainable Development Goals, GSMA.

31. World's 1.8 billion youth must 'have a say in the future of the planet,' UN News, Sept 20, 2019, https://news.un.org/en/story/2019/09/1046882.

32. Mark R. Kramer, Rishi Agarwal, and Aditi Srinivas, "Business as usual will not save the planet," *Harvard Business Review*, June 2019.

33. The Convergence of Health and Environment, Tetra Pak Index 2019, accessed April 5, 2020, https://assets.tetrapak.com/static/documents/about/tetra-pak-index-2019.pdf.

34. 5 Trends for 2020, Trend Watching, accessed March 26, 2020, https://trend-watching.com/quarterly/2019-11/5-trends-2020/.

12

The Next Sustainability Frontier Is Digital

Up Close: Elaine Weidman Grunewald, Co-founder of AI Sustainability Center on Tempering the Positive Exponential Impacts of Technology With Its Ethical and Sustainability Implications

In 2007, in the dusty village of Dertu, Kenya, a remote settlement near the border of Somalia, in one of the poorest regions of the country, Elaine met with a group of village elders as they admired a simple but life-saving improvement for the village. A small refrigerator, using excess power from an off-grid radio base station site Ericsson had built, could store anti-venom and other medicines villagers desperately needed, saving a two-day walk to the nearest large town. "It was eye-opening to see how connectivity could tackle challenges related to energy, health and connectivity in one fell swoop," according to Elaine. "We saw these kinds of impacts on people's lives repeated again and again, in places as diverse as South Sudan, the Amazon and Myanmar."

Part of the Technology for Good concept that Elaine and her team pioneered at Ericsson, the Community Power solution in Dertu[1] was among the earliest "ICT for development" initiatives, aimed at a range of pressing development needs—from access to health care and education to safety and security. The projects included the Millennium Villages, connecting some 500,000 people in rural poverty across 11 countries in sub-Saharan Africa,[2] the family-tracing platform REFUNITE from Refugees United,[3] the education program Connect to Learn,[4] and the use of connectivity and sensors to protect mangroves in Malaysia.[5] At the time, there really was no business case to bring infrastructure to these remote locations and the poorest communities on Earth, but the projects became a way for Ericsson to explore and research the transformative impact of connectivity in remote communities, and its potential to provide access to markets as well.

© The Author(s) 2020
H. Henriksson, E. Weidman Grunewald, *Sustainability Leadership*,
https://doi.org/10.1007/978-3-030-42291-2_12

Fig. 12.1 Elaine, left, with Jennifer Suleiman in Dertu, Kenya, in 2007 (photograph by Elaine Weidman Grunewald). Jennifer is mobile operator Zain Group's Chief Sustainability Officer; at the time, she was with pan-African mobile operator Celtel. Ericsson and Celtel partnered to bring connectivity for the first time to this remote village, one of the poorest in the country

Technology, as these programs illustrate, has delivered enormous progress for society. Today mobile communications technology is deeply integrated into the core business of many sectors, unleashing a surge of new services and applications. With 50 percent of the world now benefiting from internet access, ICT continues to be a catalyst for economic growth and progress, and a crucial enabler for achieving the SDGs, as discussed in Chap. 11 (Fig. 12.1).

A lot has changed since that day in Dertu. The early days of working with mobile technology were about explosive subscriber growth and coverage expansion. The principle stated by Ericsson founder Lars Magnus Ericsson more than 140 years ago—that access to communication was a basic human need—became increasingly recognized in the context of global development. It was only later that Elaine began to realize the downsides of technology. She recalls in 2011 rumors surfaced about the government of Sudan shutting down mobile communication networks in Darfur to silence protesters.[6] Later widespread availability of the internet, mobile phones, and social media fueled the pro-democracy protests known as the Arab Spring in the Middle East and North Africa in 2010 and 2011. But it also gave repressive regimes a means to silence digital channels for dissent.[7] In 2013, whistleblower and former analyst for the US National Security Agency (NSA) Edward Snowden dropped the bombshell of NSA's massive secret surveillance programs.[8] In 2016, extensive meddling by Russian hackers in the US presidential election was exposed,[9] and in 2018, the Cambridge Analytica scandal broke, revealing widespread improper harvesting of personal Facebook data from 50 million people to profile and target users with personalized political advertisements.[10] And the list goes on.

Most of these events were distant from Ericsson, and technology—its use and misuse—has been evolving since the First Industrial Revolution. But what emerged for Elaine and her colleagues was the impact of telecom on human rights, and the realization that Ericsson, with its immense global reach, had a responsibility to do more to address the emerging downsides of the technology and to work proactively to support human rights. According to Elaine: "We knew that, just as technology could be an enabler, it could also be misused for unintended purposes, and that much more needed to be done. I was determined to continue to straddle both worlds—promoting tech as a force for good while redoubling efforts to prevent tech for bad."

Future-Proofing Your Vision

Digitalization now pervades every aspect of our modern, global world. Every industry, sector and organization is undergoing some phase of a digital journey. Digital technologies will be a powerful accelerator for creating and scaling sustainable solutions and thus a fundamental component for 3.0 of our leadership model, and exponentiality, as discussed in Chaps. 9 and 10.

In this chapter, we go further to explore this in more detail but also the other side of the coin: technology's potential downsides. We look at some of the exponential technologies such as artificial intelligence (AI), and highlight the value of applying a precautionary approach when introducing these technologies to scale a vision, achieve sustainability aims, and realize business ambitions (which are typically framed in terms of cost efficiencies or revenue gains).

The unintended consequences and fallout from misuse of technology are only just beginning to be understood, ushering in public unease and growing skepticism around the ability of the tech industry to protect our data and handle other challenges in the digital age. According to research from the Pew

Center, the share of Americans who believe tech companies have a positive impact on society plummeted from 71 percent in 2015 to 50 percent in 2019.[11] Some 89 percent of consumers wish companies would take additional steps to protect their data.[12] This is particularly evident among younger Americans, where 84 percent of Gen Z Americans (born between 1996 and 2010) believe that data privacy is a fundamental human right and 54 percent want control over what information they share.[13] Business leaders should pay attention to this growing apprehension—and the escalating public calls to do something about it.

Moving forward, all companies and organizations will be data-driven, with huge implications for sustainability, trust, and responsibility. With data now considered more valuable than oil,[14] those with access to it wield increasing economic power: the five largest global companies are those with the largest data coffers—Alphabet (owner of Google), Amazon, Apple, Facebook, and Microsoft.[15] But data-driven risks no longer apply only to the tech sector—all business leaders need to carefully consider how they deploy technology, be aware of the pace at which data and information are scaling, stay informed about emerging ethical dilemmas, and be prepared to take on the responsibility these developments imply. Any company not yet thinking about the risks and societal impacts of data-driven technologies or digital pollution as the next big sustainability challenge is exposing themselves to vulnerability.

A Massive Paradigm Shift

The breakneck speed of digitalization and technology adoption is affecting all facets of society. The resulting paradigm shift, the Fourth Industrial Revolution (4IR),[16] is blurring the lines between the physical, digital, and biological spheres. At the same time, pressing global challenges like biodiversity loss, species extinction, and climate change demand breakthrough transformations. The momentous scale of these challenges, with time running out, means that people are looking to technology for transformative change and disruptive innovation.[17]

Technologies like artificial intelligence (AI), robotics, the Internet of Things, autonomous vehicles, 3-D printing, augmented or virtual reality, and others offer the exhilarating and even exponential promise of new products and services, improved efficiencies, and productivity across operations, logistics, and supply chains. This, in turn, could open new markets and spur economic growth. And while controversial, technologies like facial and video recognition could play a significant role in creating safer, more secure societies.

Examples of Exponential Technologies

Artificial intelligence (AI): An area of computer science that emphasizes the creation of intelligent machines that work and react like humans. Includes machine learning, which allows computers to handle new situations via analysis, self-training, observation and experience.

Robotics: An industry related to the engineering, construction and operation of robots where any physical constructed technology system can perform a task or play a role in any interface or new technology.

The Internet of Things: A computing concept that describes the idea of everyday physical objects being connected to the internet and being able to identify themselves to other devices.

Autonomous vehicles: A vehicle that can guide itself without human conduction.

3-D printing: A manufacturing process through which three-dimensional (3D) solid objects are created.

Augmented or virtual reality: A type of interactive, reality-based display environment that takes the capabilities of computer-generated display, sound, text and effects to enhance the user's real-world experience or to simulate a person's physical presence in a specific environment that is designed to feel real.

Source: Techopedia[18]

Delivering exponential benefits is a key component of 3.0 of our Leadership Model. There are different predictions when it comes to the financial and sustainability benefits of AI. Current predictions from PwC suggest that by the end of the decade, AI could unlock a \$5.2 trillion contribution to the global economy, as well as a 4 percent reduction in GHG emissions. Promising innovations include "digital water" systems powered by IoT sensors and smart meters, precision-based AI analytics systems to make agriculture more sustainable and efficient, and AI prediction models for balancing energy demand, among others.[19] AI can contribute significantly to conservation and ecology, for example, with algorithms that track species of wildlife from seismic vibrations.[20] AI systems allow for earlier and better disease detection.[21] In education, AI-based learning systems are enabling a fully tailored and personalized educational approach.[22]

The business benefits have made companies hungry for data. Customer analytics are considered vital for helping businesses acquire, retain, satisfy, and engage their clientele. Smart products and services are driving companies to rethink operations, organizational structures, and customer interactions. For Scania, for example, connectivity is less about the vehicle itself and more about the intelligence the data reveals, highlighting new ways to improve efficiency and reduce carbon dioxide emissions. For global appliance leader Electrolux, the digital transformation is shaping product development for the smart home, that is, connected appliances that provide better control over energy and water consumption.

Swedish retail and industrial leader Axel Johnson considers digital transformation among its six business-critical areas, anticipating that e-commerce will change commerce more in the next decade than it has in the past century. As CEO Mia Brunell Livfors explains: "Digitalization helps bring us closer to the customers; we're able to learn much more about the product and about the customer and ways to run our business. In short, it makes us much smarter, in many areas of the operations. One example is that we launched a CO_2-emissions labeling in Mat.se, one of our online grocery stores, nudging customers to choose more climate-friendly food."

This rapid pace of digital development highlights the importance of having strong data management and governance routines in place. Without proper data management, in the best case you can end up with duplicate records, incorrect information, wasted time and storage space, and a host of other problems that come with poor organization. In the worst case, you could have all these problems, but also be creating unintended risks that can emerge due to poor data governance, data quality, training data, architecture, algorithm design, and so on. Such risks are described further in the box below: "AI Pitfalls and Risks."

In the age of digitalization every industry faces transformation. Yet there remains a worrisome lack of understanding among business leaders, governments, and citizens about the impact of data-driven technology and solutions on people and society. In this data-driven world, new sustainability challenges are emerging—in particular in the domain of privacy. While the societal lens can help frame the discussion, and the societal ecosystem can help to figure out what to do about risks, the next section explores the implications of this headlong rush toward using new digital technologies without regard for their sustainability, societal, or ethical implications.

A New Type of Pollution Emerging

The prevailing premise is that technologies like AI bring exponential benefits. However, if adopted unchecked, they also carry the potential for exponential harm. As AI is a self-learning, self-scaling, and self-propagating technology, it poses an entirely new level of risk, for example, in the form of privacy intrusion, discrimination, and the amplification of bias, or, in other words, "digital pollution." There is a lot of hype around AI but currently no robust and systematic approach to evaluating the potential downside impacts on people and society—as cases and examples in this chapter illustrate.

Digital or data pollution is when the use of data or data-driven technologies has harmful or negative, unintended consequences on people as a result of unattended risks, or poor data management.

This lack of guidance available to help companies navigate these tricky waters led Elaine to co-found the AI Sustainability Center (AISC) in Stockholm in 2018 with digital economist Anna Felländer.[23] The AISC is a multidisciplinary hub to address the scaling of AI and data-driven technologies in broader ethical and societal contexts. The Center has developed an operational framework to help organizations identify and proactively mitigate data-driven risks. At present, most applications of AI lack fundamental measures to address issues like explainability, transparency, accountability, and governance.

AI Pitfalls and Risks

An array of challenges and risks can arise from the use of data-driven solutions and AI. All of these can erode trust. The AI Sustainability Center has characterized four categories, or pitfalls, that can lead to risks[24]:

1. *Misuse or overuse of data*: the AI application/solution could be intrusive (using overly broad or deep open data) or data could be used for unintended purposes by others. An egregious example is the Cambridge Analytica case mentioned at the start of this chapter, where data was monetized by a third party.
2. *Bias of the creator*: when values and bias are intentionally or unintentionally programmed by the creator who may lack the knowledge/skills to appreciate how the solution could scale in a broader context. An example would be racial bias in assessing the risk of future crimes, as revealed in a 2016 investigation by ProPublica.[25]
3. *Immature data or AI*: when the data the algorithm is working on is insufficient or not structured enough, or the AI model is not trained or tested enough for market-readiness. Insufficient training of algorithms on data sets as well as lack of representative data could lead to incorrect and unethical recommendations. For example, facial recognition systems that don't recognize dark skin or Asian eyes.[26]
4. *Data bias*: the data available is not an accurate reflection of reality or the preferred reality and may lead to incorrect and unethical recommendations. Amazon's AI recruitment tool, for example, learned to prefer white men, and was later scrapped.[27]

If these pitfalls are not managed well they can lead to a wide range of risks. These include privacy intrusion, amplified discrimination and inequality, capitalizing on dopamine, addictions, and other forms of vulnerabilities, social exclusion, and segregation, as well as faulty conclusions, recommendations and predictions, and misinterpretations.
Source: The AI Sustainability Center

Data is the new gold, and the tech sector monetizes what people search for, what they say and do, what they "like," and basically everything about them. In the best case, analytics reveal valuable customer insights; in the worst, they can become highly privacy-intrusive. And the debate over this skewed business model continues: who should hold the keys to our data: an individual, a company, or an organization? As Anna Felländer explains: "Many digital services present an integrity paradox or an integrity tradeoff—I give you my data, and you give me the convenience. But the balance is not in the favor of the individual or the citizen or the consumer, creating a new kind of pollution which is about privacy, discrimination, and bias."

The potential misuses of technology in a digital world can also present a dystopian scenario. This includes use of technology to manipulate elections,[28] the dopamine addiction of "likes," and the pervasive "fake news" and "filter bubbles" that reflect back one's own views rather than unbiased information.[29] These developments have grave implications for trust and democracy. There is concern about AI being deployed by the military to create autonomous systems with the ability to use lethal force—risky if these fall into the hands of autocratic regimes or terrorists.[30] The dark web, an encrypted network and collection of hidden sites not accessible via a regular browser, can be a breeding ground for criminals, terrorists, extremist groups, and perpetrators of online child sexual abuse.[31]

What can be done about it? A number of companies are taking steps to secure the privacy of data. For example, Swedish investment company Kinnevik places emphasis on the importance of digital commerce, particularly as some of its portfolio companies work within what the EU would designate "high-risk sectors," meaning that they handle sensitive information. One of these is micro insurance firm Bima (see Chap. 10). CEO Georgi Ganev recognizes that some of their companies will have different levels of maturity as regards data privacy. He says: "We are building to protect data and privacy. Our decision will always be no if it increases the risks of the service and trustworthiness. We train our people not to take those shortcuts."

Georgi continues:

When we look at the way we provide services, we have very strict governance on access to personal data on all our accounts and Bima in particular. We don't sell any personal data to any third parties and the personal health data that is gathered through the telemedicine services can only be accessed by doctors providing that consultation at that particular time. If you want to build a long-term company you have to respect integrity, respect data records and make sure that you cannot allow anyone else access without a real consequence from the end user. I'm not talking about a long disclaimer that you never actually read but what it means to actually share the data and for what purpose.

A similar precautionary approach is taken by Axel Johnson, according to Mia Brunell Livfors. "Integrity and privacy around the way we use data is a very important issue and something you need to be very aware of. You need to create the right boundaries around which information you collect, what you do with it and how you handle it. You need to find the balance between using the tools made possible by digitalization but being responsible about how you do it."

Lack of a Harmonized Approach

Managing the risks and pitfalls are compounded by regional differences. AI systems developed, for example, in China or the US could be inherently biased against, or non-representative of, Africa, for instance. AI tools can deliver great innovations; there's no doubt. Yet the digital divide—a concern over the past two to three decades in terms of affordable internet and mobile access—could be exacerbated by AI. The result could be that an entire continent such as Africa could be left behind, lacking the skills for a twenty-first-century job market. AI systems built by designers and coders in the Western world, with issues like "bias of the creator" coded in, and without the proper precautions, could amplify discrimination and social exclusion rather than reduce or eliminate it.

For decades, many governments have had laws in place to regulate classic forms of pollution, such as chemical use and air emissions. Over time, as regulatory frameworks kicked in, business has been forced to account for these costs on the balance sheet. The same is inevitable with digital pollution; it's only a matter of time. Today, while some countries are trying to rein in the negative impacts of technology, regulatory frameworks are still largely lacking, and the technology is evolving faster than governments can respond. The UN Secretary General has named "taming the Wild West" of the digital world as one of his top priorities. In Europe, a precautionary approach to the technology is preferred, while other regions believe that because these technologies are so new, and so valuable, they should not be inhibited as that could hamper innovation. What role legislation can and should play in helping to manage this disruption is unclear. Policymakers need to minimize the risks to people and society while encouraging technological advancement for economic and societal benefit. Whether AI-specific legislation is needed, or whether existing regulation around, for example, privacy and other areas, can be effectively applied to AI, remains to be resolved. Global companies can operate with more certainty if regulations are harmonized but to date regulations around AI at the national and regional levels have varied significantly.

In 2019, the EU also developed a broad set of ethical principles for "trustworthy AI," but no real practical guidance on how to implement them. In its white paper on artificial intelligence published in February 2020, the EU Commission put forward a strategic direction for a future regulatory framework for AI[32] that advocates for "an eco-system of trust," which means AI should be human centric, take a societal perspective, and have strong ethics. The Commission introduced seven specific requirements which should apply to "high-risk" AI applications. These are human agency and oversight; technical robustness and safety; privacy and data governance; transparency; diversity, non-discrimination, and fairness; societal and environmental wellbeing; and accountability. While a number of the requirements are covered under existing legislation and regulations, there are significant gaps, for example, with transparency, traceability, and human oversight. While the white paper certainly takes a societal perspective, there is no clear means of how to implement the requirements, and the lack of regulatory certainty could hamper innovation. In other words, it addresses the *what*, but not the *how*. The same could be said for many voluntary AI ethical principles being adopted by companies like Microsoft, Google, and Telia, among others. Many stakeholders recognize that there could be a problem, but how to implement the right measures is not entirely clear.

In contrast, the US is creating a national AI strategy which entails a "light-touch regulatory approach" which is designed to achieve three goals: ensuring public engagement, limiting regulatory overreach, and promoting trustworthy technology. However, the US approach, unlike the EU, is taking a hands-off approach to protect innovation. The ultimate intent is to ensure that agencies avoid "regulatory or non-regulatory actions that needlessly hamper AI innovation and growth," according to US Chief Technology Officer Michael Kratsios.[33]

China does have ethical AI principles, although the notion of privacy in China is markedly different; many Europeans would consider it surveillance.

Despite these different regional approaches and emergent regulations, regulatory gaps remain. Not only privacy legislation, but product security and consumer protection are also lagging when it comes to understanding the societal effects of future technologies. In the future, privacy will be an increasingly important trust differentiator for companies, as a growing concern among consumers, policymakers, and legislators continues to evolve. Rather than waiting for regulation, there is an opportunity for companies to make privacy protection and preservation part of their business model from the outset. Applying a societal lens early on is key to succeeding in this effort. In fact, our advice would be for business leaders to start to consider and proactively address privacy (and ethical AI and data-driven risks more broadly) in the same way they would any other risk, that is, financial, business continuity, compliance, or even climate change risks, and to start to take proactive actions. We outlined some of these new sustainability risks in Chap. 5.

Telecoms and media company Telia, as illustrated later in this chapter, is a good example of this proactive approach, making data privacy a key feature in its use of data to improve safety and security in cities with its Crowd Insights offering.

What Companies Can Do

The bottom line is that in the face of regulatory uncertainty, there could be an opportunity for companies to show their ability to self-regulate. At a minimum that would include adopting voluntary policies and guidelines and applying the relevant principles around transparency, governance, accountability, and explainability to their data-driven solutions and strategy. It would also be prudent to measure, and act to minimize, the risks of any potential harms caused, the same way you would in managing other sustainability issues. This circles back to setting a strong foundation based on values and purpose, as we described in Chap. 4. Combining these practices with the application of the societal lens then makes it possible to understand how technology is scaling in a broader societal context. The societal ecosystem would help to explore new types of partners and value creation opportunities, and also set a foundation for minimizing and mitigating risks.

The cases presented in this chapter look at how two leading Swedish companies—Telia and Scania—are taking advantage of the exponential possibilities of digitalization as an accelerator, while also using a societal lens and adopting a precautionary approach to avoid or manage the downsides. In their handling of data privacy risks and evaluation of the use and maturity of data, among other considerations, they demonstrate how to address the four risk areas identified earlier.

According to Johan Dennelind, former CEO of Telia Company, a major telecoms and media company operating across the Nordics and Baltics and founding member of the AI Sustainability Center:

> The underlying technology moves so fast, and we want to explore that to the fullest, but also to make sure that as part of technology and innovation, we have sustainability embedded. It's so easy to lose trust with consumers if you do things wrong with technology. You need to make sure you do things responsibly and use private data in the right way. And that's why we're part of the AISC, because then you have this thinking early, because the dilemmas will only increase, these technologies will test our human integrity and how we define the rules. We need to define those rules in a human-centered way, otherwise we may end up in a very negative spiral. It is paramount to have this knowledge in your fingertips, not just the CEO or the management team or the Board but it needs to be there in the organization; otherwise as a company you'll be too slow to react to any warning signs that arise.

Telia: Responsible Use of Data for Smart, Sustainable Cities

By 2050, 68 percent of the world population will live in cities.[34] While cities generate most of the world's economic growth, they are also responsible for 70 percent of global CO_2 emissions.[35] Rapid urbanization and population growth in cities require innovative, sustainable solutions within transport, power, water, and waste systems, and digitalization will help generate many of those solutions, from smart grids to electric vehicles to autonomous driving and other developments. Yet as use of data extends into both private and public domains, governments and companies need to be cognizant of the need to balance digitalization's promise with its perils.

Telia Company's approach is to ensure that the dilemmas around the sustainability and ethics of AI are part of product development at an early stage, as well as making sure that the ethical aspects of new technologies are embedded in the organization.

As part of its efforts to gain insights to help cities improve traffic congestion, city planning, safety, and security, Telia is intent on preserving consumer privacy. The unprecedented amount of data available through individual use of smart devices like mobile phones requires a thoughtful approach in collecting and using citizen data. As an example, an investigation by *The New York*

Times Privacy Project recently revealed the existence of a file of information holding more than 50 billion location pings from the phones of more than 12 million Americans as they moved through several major American cities, seen by many as hugely privacy intrusive.[36]

These are the kinds of considerations that come into play for Telia's Division X, which focuses on developing new businesses. Telia introduced nine ethical AI principles in January 2019[37] and wanted to make sure they were being applied in practice. Keen to develop and test advanced privacy preservation techniques such as the generation of synthetic data as a trust differentiator, Telia decided to apply the AI Sustainability Center framework as a way to assess and mitigate data-driven risks. The project involved city officials in Malmö in southern Sweden, the country's third largest city, where officials want to show how distinct actions can contribute to improved perceptions of safety for citizens.

A use-case was defined building upon Telia's Crowd Insights offering which provides insights about how people move around a city, drawn from mobile network data. To ensure privacy, the data is aggregated and irreversibly anonymized before it can be used in any Crowd Insights case, which limits the level of location granularity and demographic profiling that can be used.

In the innovation case with the city of Malmö, Crowd Insights is used to generate information that can support a city when planning for better solutions and interventions that improve the safety of certain areas, or perceptions of safety for certain demographics, in order to help the city become a more open and inclusive city, without revealing the identity of the citizens (Fig. 12.2).

How it works: Telia's mobility data is used to generate a synthetic data set that resembles the characteristics of the real population (presence, movement, trends, and deviations over time) but creates "fake" composite profiles so that no real subscribers are used in the solution. This removes privacy risks, while allowing analysts to work with more detailed information than today's current aggregation and anonymization techniques permit. The goal is to create a more open and inclusive Malmö while sufficiently safeguarding the privacy and integrity of citizens.

The risks identified included misuse of the solution, for example, if it was used for unintended purposes such as unethical surveillance or that results in discrimination of certain groups of citizens, for example, limiting access to public services. Telia and AISC have characterized risk scenarios and are evaluating and implementing both technical and non-technical measures to mitigate the risks.

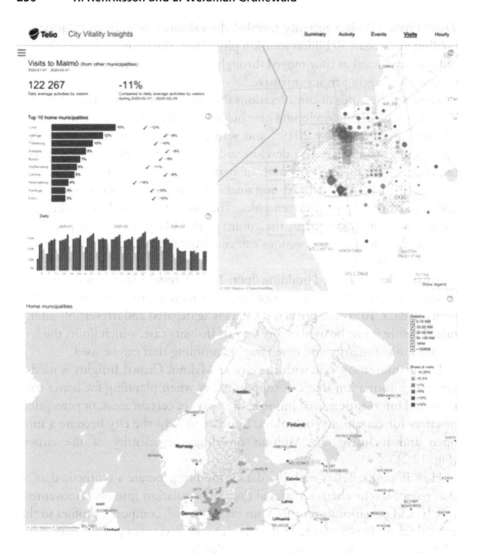

Fig. 12.2   Telia Crowd Insights offering uses location data to provide unique insights to cities and municipalities (© Telia Company & Tableau). It's based on aggregated and anonymized data from Telia's mobile network and enables strategic and data-driven decision-making and impact measuring through people movement patterns, without compromising on privacy

Scania: Smart and Safer Transport

In another example of how digitalization can be an accelerator, Scania is using technology to help with more sustainable movement of goods. Greater demand for transport and mobility will be required in the future both within cities and for long-distance transport. Digitalization is key to both meeting that demand and addressing sustainability. Since 2011, Scania has connected all its vehicles on the road, today over 460,000 vehicles, a key accelerator to meeting the company's science-based targets and sustainability goals more generally.

From a safety perspective, Scania is using connectivity to boost vehicle safety. For instance, in a partnership with Sony, a smart watch interface provides added safety for drivers when loading and off-loading goods. The watch detects if the driver has a fall, if the pulse is abnormal, and includes a panic function for immediate help. It also monitors driver fatigue by monitoring pulse and movements. The vehicle's connectivity also activates the global Scania Assistance Center or emergency numbers for first responders. By using AI to detect pattern and behavior, cameras and sensors can also detect if drivers are falling asleep or texting while driving which can help prevent accidents.

Another example of how digital solutions can play a critical role in public safety is linked to April 7, 2017. On that day, a terrorist drove a stolen truck onto Drottninggatan, the main shopping pedestrian street in Stockholm, killing five people and injuring 15 others[38]—Sweden's worst terrorist attack in decades. Shortly after the attack, Scania and other heavy truck manufacturers started a dialogue with city law enforcement and policymakers on how to use connectivity to help avoid a similar situation in the future. The solution eventually adopted uses geofencing via built-in GPS and the vehicle's connectivity. When a vehicle enters a certain part of the city, its speed is limited to typically 10 kilometers per hour. This is technically possible, with impressive accuracy, and can be used to limit speed, for example, in an area designated for pedestrians. The solution can also limit emissions by turning off the combustion engines in emissions-free zones, switching to electric battery in hybrid vehicles. The balance for Scania and policymakers is to use these functionalities in a way that benefits society, without jeopardizing the privacy and integrity of the individual, in this case the everyday truck driver.

While there are positive use cases of digitalization, at the same time, there needs to be consensus around the ethics of technological applications, how they are used for mobility, and the potential new risks. For example, autonomous vehicles promise greater safety and emissions reduction but also present new safety risks. Autonomous self-driving trucks and buses are a fairly new challenge for Scania, especially for future vehicle operation in cities, presenting new dilemmas. For instance, how these "intelligent" vehicles, which use algorithms for setting the parameters in the vehicles' software, handle traffic situations. The vehicles might face "one-way situations" where it must turn left or right; that decision could potentially injure people or damage property.

The challenge is how to build the right decision-making into the vehicles' intelligence, built on accurate, reliable data. In such a scenario, algorithms may carry the weighty responsibility of deciding who lives or dies, even though when a mistake is made, all the vehicles can learn, as opposed to just one.

Eventually new norms and regulations will provide guidance but in the meantime, in the virgin territory of new technology, companies in the vehicle industry face a ramp-up period where they need to take on considerable responsibility for making the right decisions. This demands strong values and leadership and an emphasis on the precautionary approach. For Scania, addressing these data-driven risks is top of mind for Henrik and his management team.

The New Basics

Clearly, there are a host of complex issues for business leaders in all sectors to consider in this era of digitalization and data-driven solutions. This chapter has highlighted some of the issues for further consideration, and for balancing the positive aspects of digitalization with the potential downsides. Adopting a societal ecosystem perspective can help leaders to better understand the implications of their increasing use of data and algorithms, and find new ways to increase returns while also preserving integrity and values.

That might involve considering how the data could cause harm, how to protect rights to avoid the risk that rights might be exploited or violated, and whether societal impacts can be integrated into the way of working and business model. Governing use of data and managing the ethics around technology are fast becoming a new kind of basic expectation for sustainability leadership—the next frontier in sustainability.

The Cautionary Tale of Thomas Midgley Jr.

Sustainability pioneer and thought leader John Elkington, founder and chief pollinator of the consultancy Volans, predicts that

> whether it's drones, or autonomous vehicles, the internet of everything, synthetic biology, or artificial intelligence, the economy is about to change ferociously fast. And if I have *one* really big concern, set aside loss of species, set aside climate collapse and all the rest of it, it's that the sustainability industry is still looking backwards. We're fixated on the big players in the old fossil fuels industry, the Exxon Mobils, or the General Motors or whatever it may be. We're not putting remotely enough effort into engaging the industries of the future.

(continued)

(continued)

So, when he travels to places like Silicon Valley, he asks people two questions: "The first is, who are you dealing with in the sustainability area? And very often it doesn't go to proper sustainability, it goes to toxics, or stuff that is a bit more specific and local. And the second question I routinely ask is: Have you ever heard of Thomas Midgley Jr.? Typically, they haven't."

Midgley was a brilliant engineer and chemist with General Motors and then DuPont, personally holding over 100 patents, at his peak in the 1920s and 1930s. He came up with leaded gasoline (a breakthrough in anti-knock technology [to reduce engine knocking], but one that had immense unforeseen consequences in terms of children's nervous systems) and he also synthesized early Freons, chemicals that went on to help tear a hole in the stratospheric ozone layer.[39] After Midgley contracted polio he developed an automatic bed, using ropes and pulleys to get him in and out of bed without nursing care. In 1944, the bed strangled him.[40]

Moral of the story? For John: "Even geniuses often unwittingly trigger cascades of unintended consequences. Thomas Midgley has been described as the single organism in the earth's history that has done the most damage to the planet, and yet we haven't heard of him! I tell his story to say: however brilliant Mark Zuckerberg {founder and CEO of Facebook} or Larry Page {co-founder of Google}, or whomever it might be, our future is going to be full of unexpected, unintended consequences. It would make a lot of sense to be thinking about, and planning for them, now."

These concerns also preoccupy the next generation of tech innovators, including Niklas Adalberth, the tech billionaire founder of Swedish e-commerce firm Klarna, now heading the Nordic region's largest social impact tech incubator, Norrsken Foundation. You'd think Niklas would be an unabashed tech optimist. But his view is more nuanced:

Technology could be the end of the world, but it could be used for good as well, it depends on how you use it. It gives us the power of the gods, but we also need the wisdom of the gods to be safe stewards to navigate this world. And that makes me a little worried, if we don't use this power in the right way. I look around and I still see current tech industry leaders measuring impact only on a few KPIs, like growth of the company and profit and turnover. As a result, you continue to have these perverse incentives because this is how we have always optimized business. But the consequences of that to the world and the planet could be disastrous. We need to create a world that is optimized for both people and planet. We face monumental, catastrophic risks if we don't. I don't know if those risks are existential, but there are multiple collapse scenarios for sure, if we don't handle this in a good way.

With technology, digitalization, and a myriad of wicked global challenges confronting us, the pace of change has never been greater. Future-proofing your vision begins where we started: leading with purpose and values and a solid foundation. Purpose and a strong societal lens can help make sense of the risks associated with new developments, even if they can only be glimpsed on the horizon. Without that ethical compass, business leaders are more likely to trip up, risking brand, reputation, and even the very foundation on which their business is built.

In conclusion, business leaders should consider tempering their tech optimism with a healthy dose of caution. Many companies have been riding a tech for good wave, but collectively business is now being flooded with a tsunami of dilemmas and other implications around the use of technology. Technology has continued to evolve rapidly, connecting families and homes, cities, and every aspect of our lives. This raises a host of new issues around privacy and security. Every company will need to go back and start to rethink tech for good.

Given the complexity of these issues, the need for collaboration and stakeholder dialogue—and unconventional partnerships—has never been greater. The issues are too complicated for any one actor to solve. In the age of data-driven technologies and transparency, information is available at one's fingertips and spreads with lightning speed—facts, rumors, and both good and bad information. A multidisciplinary and multi-stakeholder approach, together with dialogue and action, gives business leaders the platform to co-design a technology future that is founded on good.

Key Takeaways

1. Digital may be one of your most important accelerators, but exponential solutions carry the potential for exponential risks: know the effects of the digital solutions you deploy and scale on people and society.
2. In the future, everything will be data-driven but be aware of digital downsides, too. If your business is based on data, exercise caution. Consider how you are using it, and how it is being used by others (intended or unintended use).
3. Privacy regulation and AI ethics is an evolving field, and more regulation is likely. In the face of regulatory uncertainty, explore proactive and voluntary measures to self-regulate.
4. Be mindful of the emerging field of digital pollution, and what you can do to actively prevent it. Start to identify and measure unintended risks and pitfalls, and establish criteria to decide acceptable risk levels.

5. Ensure that AI Sustainability fundamentals like governance, transparency, explainability, and accountability are in place and recognize that AI and data-rich products evolve with learning and data, so risk assessments and governance need to be continuous, not set and forgotten.
6. Consider how responsible use of data can deliver exponentiality, but also how you can make good governance your trust premium.

Notes

1. Community Power Solution brings power to people and wins GSMA award, Ericsson.com, Feb 15, 2011, https://www.ericsson.com/en/press-releases/2011/2/community-power-solution-brings-power-to-the-people-and-wins-gsma-award.
2. Millennium Villages, The Earth Institute, Columbia University, accessed December 10, 2019, https://www.earth.columbia.edu/articles/view/1799.
3. Refunite.org, accessed December 10, 2019, https://refunite.org/partners/.
4. Connect to Learn deployments, Ericsson, accessed December 10, 2019, https://www.ericsson.com/en/about-us/sustainability-and-corporate-responsibility/technology-for-good/access-to-education/connect-to-learn-deployments.
5. Ericsson launches world's first Connected Mangroves initiative in Malaysia, November 2015, available at: https://www.ericsson.com/en/press-releases/7/2015/ericsson-launches-worlds-first-connected-mangroves-initiative-in-malaysia.
6. 2011–2013 protests in Sudan, Wikipedia, accessed March 3, 2020, https://en.wikipedia.org/wiki/2011%E2%80%933_protests_in_Sudan.
7. Mark I. Wilson and Kenneth E. Corey, "The role of ICT in Arab spring movements," NETCOM26, no 3–4 (2012).
8. Edward Snowden: the whistleblower behind the NSA surveillance revelations," The Guardian, 2013, https://www.theguardian.com/world/2013/jun/09/edward-snowden-nsa-whistleblower-surveillance.
9. Abigail Abrams, "Here's What We Know So Far about Russia's 2016 Meddling," Time, April 18, 2019, https://time.com/5565991/russia-influence-2016-election/.
10. Vivian Ho, "Facebook's privacy problems: a roundup," The Guardian, 2018, https://www.theguardian.com/technology/2018/dec/14/facebook-privacy-problems-roundup.
11. Carroll Doherty and Jocelyn Kiley, "Americans have become much less positive about tech companies' impact on the U.S.," Pew Research Center, July 29, 2019, https://www.pewresearch.org/fact-tank/2019/07/29/americans-have-become-much-less-positive-about-tech-companies-impact-on-the-u-s/.

12. Megan Sullivan-Jenks, "Digital advertising trends survey," Choozle.com, July 10, 2018, https://choozle.com/blog/digital-advertising-trends-survey/.
13. The Truth about Privacy, McCann World Group, 2018, https://cms.mccann-nworldgroup.com/wp-content/uploads/2017/05/MWTC_TAPrivacy_ExecSummary.pdf.
14. The world's most valuable resources is no longer oil but data, The Economist, May 6, 2017, https://www.economist.com/leaders/2017/05/06/the-worlds-most-valuable-resource-is-no-longer-oil-but-data.
15. Data is more vulnerable than oil, how is how we manage it, May 2017, https://www.hipb2b.com/blog/data-is-more-valuable-than-oil-best-practices-for-managing-it.
16. Klaus Schwab, *The Fourth Industrial Revolution*, World Economic Forum, 2017, https://www.weforum.org/about/the-fourth-industrial-revolution-by-klaus-schwab.
17. "How technology can fast-track the global goals," World Economic Forum, 2019, https://www.weforum.org/agenda/2019/09/technology-global-goals-sustainable-development-sdgs/, accessed December 4, 2019.
18. Techopedia, Dictionary, accessed March 3, 2020, https://www.techopedia.com/.
19. "Artificial Intelligence: Transforming the Future of Energy and Sustainability," World Future Energy Summit, Jan 13–16, 2020.
    https://www.worldfutureenergysummit.com/__media/WFES%202020/Download%20Centre%20Page/Artificial-Intelligence%2D%2D-Transforming-the-Future-of-Energy-and-Sustainability.pdf.
20. Lanisha Butterfield, "How AI can help us save the planet," University of Oxford, 2018, https://www.research.ox.ac.uk/Article/2018-10-15-how-ai-can-help-us-save-the-planet, accessed 4 December 2019.
21. "How technology can fast-track the global goals," World Economic Forum, 2019, https://www.weforum.org/agenda/2019/09/technology-global-goals-sustainable-development-sdgs/, accessed 4 December 2019.
22. Lasse Rouhiainen, "How AI and Data Could Personalize Higher Education," Harvard Business Review, 2019, https://hbr.org/2019/10/how-ai-and-data-could-personalize-higher-education, accessed 4 December 2019.
23. AI Sustainability Center, https://www.aisustainability.org.
24. AI Specific Unintended Pitfalls, AI Sustainability Center, accessed February 11, 2020, http://www.aisustainability.org/.
25. Julia Angwin, Jeff Larson, Surya Mattu and Lauren Kirchner, "Machine Bias," ProPublica, May 23, 2016, https://www.propublica.org/article/machine-bias-risk-assessments-in-criminal-sentencing.
26. Steve Lohr, "Facial recognition is accurate, if You're a White Guy," *The New York Times*, Feb 9, 2018, https://www.nytimes.com/2018/02/09/technology/facial-recognition-race-artificial-intelligence.html.

27. Jeffrey Dastin, "Amazon scraps secret AI tool that showed bias against women," Reuters, Oct 9, 2018, https://www.reuters.com/article/us-amazon-com-jobs-automation-insight-idUSKCN1MK08G.

28. Facebook data misuse and voter manipulation back in the frame with latest Cambridge Analytica leaks, 1Business World, Jan 6, 2020, retrieved from https://1businessworld.com/2020/01/business/facebook-data-misuse-and-voter-manipulation-back-in-the-frame-with-latest-cambridge-analytica-leaks/.

29. As fake news spreads, algorithms and 'filter bubbles take centre stage, Business Standard, July 14, 2018, retrieved from https://www.business-standard.com/article/technology/as-fake-news-spreads-algorithms-and-filter-bubbles-take-centre-stage-118071400102_1.html.

30. Michael Horowitz, The promise and peril of military applications of artificial intelligence, Bulletin of the Atomic Scientists, April 23, 2018, retrieved from https://thebulletin.org/2018/04/the-promise-and-peril-of-military-applications-of-artificial-intelligence/.

31. Aditi Kumar and Eric Rosenbach, "The Truth about the Dark Web," International Monetary Fund, Finance & Development 56, no. 3, available at: https://www.imf.org/external/pubs/ft/fandd/2019/09/the-truth-about-the-dark-web-kumar.htm.

32. "On Artificial Intelligence—A European approach to excellence and trust," European Commission, Feb 19, 2020, https://ec.europa.eu/info/sites/info/files/commission-white-paper-artificial-intelligence-feb2020_en.pdf.

33. Brandi Vincent, "White House proposes 'Light-Touch Regulatory Approach' for Artificial Intelligence, Nextgov.com, Jan 7, 2020, https://www.nextgov.com/emerging-tech/2020/01/white-house-proposes-light-touch-regulatory-approach-artificial-intelligence/162276/.

34. 68% of the world population projected to live in urban areas by 2050, UN, Department of Economic and Social Affairs, https://www.un.org/development/desa/en/news/population/2018-revision-of-world-urbanization-prospects.html.

35. McKinsey and Company, Sustainable Cities, Webpage. https://www.mckinsey.com/business-functions/sustainability/how-we-help-clients/sustainable-cities.

36. Stuart A. Thompson and Charlie Warzei, "Twelve Million Phones, One Dataset, Zero Privacy," The New York Times Privacy Project, Dec 19, 2019, https://www.nytimes.com/interactive/2019/12/19/opinion/location-tracking-cell-phone.h.

37. Guiding principles on trusted AI ethics, Telia Company, January 2019, https://www.teliacompany.com/globalassets/telia-company/documents/about-telia-company/public-policy/2018/guiding-principles-on-trusted-ai-ethics.pdf.

38. Christina Anderson, "Sweden Mourns Stockholm attack victims; suspect is formally identified," *The New York Times,* April 10, 2017, retrieved from https://www.nytimes.com/2017/04/10/world/europe/sweden-terror-attack.html.

39. John Elkington, "John Elkington: Tomorrow's Boards Need More Robotic Members," Sustainia, 2018, https://sustainiaworld.com/john-elkington-tomorrow-boards-need-more-robotic-members/.

40. John Elkington, "Saving the Planet from Ecological Disaster Is a $12 Trillion Opportunity," *Harvard Business Review,* 2017, https://hbr.org/2017/05/saving-the-planet-from-ecological-disaster-is-a-12-trillion-opportunity.

13

Finding Your Personal Influencing Platform

Up Close: Hans Vestberg, CEO of Verizon on Using His Platform to Energize an Organization and Put Business and Sustainability on a Global Stage

In August 2018, when Hans Vestberg became CEO of Verizon, one of the world's largest communication technologies companies, he was determined that sustainability should be a key element of "Verizon 2.0," a new strategy to position Verizon in leading its industry on the global stage and shape the conversation around what business can do to tackle global challenges.

Hans is no stranger to using his platform to influence change, whether within the company he leads, or on a broader societal level. As a leader in the ICT industry, Hans long advocated for how connectivity and mobile broadband could be gamechangers in tackling global challenges like poverty, health, education, and climate change. This conviction now underpins Verizon's efforts to scale up 5G to accelerate technologies that can enable greater environmental and social impact. Faced with the extraordinary platform of a company the size and scale of Verizon, he wasted no time in setting out to inspire the company's employees to support his vision. He knew he was a virtual unknown and that the first step in establishing the kind of platform he envisioned was by listening and learning from his own organization.

Here's how Hans explains it:

> I needed to create credibility for myself and at the same time come in with totally new initiatives. How do you do that in a successful company with over 140,000 people? I started by asking the 250 top managers to think about three questions about steering a new direction for the company, so we could really leverage our influence: what do we want to preserve? What do we want to strengthen? And what do we want to transform? I sat down with 20 key people across the organization, listening to their thoughts. Taking the time to listen was

© The Author(s) 2020

H. Henriksson, E. Weidman Grunewald, *Sustainability Leadership*,

https://doi.org/10.1007/978-3-030-42291-2_13

a way for me to understand how my own views fit the organization and made me understand the changes I needed to make and how big those changes needed to be. It was about hearts and minds—not just strategy and policy. Once we had our top leaders on board, we held a series of leadership summits for the entire organization.

Taking that kind of leadership to the global level, Hans was the first CEO to sign up to the Global Citizen Private Sector Leaders "CEO Coalition" in support of Global Citizen, the international advocacy organization that engages millennials around the world in the movement to end extreme poverty and achieve the Global Goals by 2030. It is expected to cost $350 billion annually over the next ten years to get the world's 59 poorest countries on track to achieve the UN SDGs.[1] Global Citizen partnered with the UN in 2019 on Global Goal Live: The Possible Dream, to raise those funds.[2] As co-chair on behalf of the ICT sector for the CEO Coalition, Hans personally called more than two dozen of his industry peers and partners to get them onboard to back the campaign. The Global Citizen movement brings together a huge variety of people from all walks of life, from business leaders to politicians to actors and artists. With tens of thousands of people attending the Global Citizen benefit concert in 2019, this kind of platform can turn up the volume on a company's position and bring new types of stakeholders into the fold (Fig. 13.1).

Whether it is leading his peers in a global development campaign or serving as a board member of the UN Foundation or as a member of the leadership council of the UN Sustainable Development Solutions Network, Hans has continued to use his platform to reinforce company purpose and values and drive change. At every opportunity, whether at a CEO summit, business strategy event, internal leadership training, or external forum, he emphasizes the importance of the SDGs and why more companies should see sustainability as core business. "I engaged with the UN very early on because I think technology is important and also because it was linked to our strategy at Ericsson, and now at Verizon. I bring to the table my business insights and skills, which serves two purposes: taking responsibility and fulfilling Verizon's strategy."

Hans' influencing platform evolved over time, but early on he saw the link between business and sustainability. We believe more business leaders can, and should, use the platform of their company, industry, or a personal conviction to amplify their voice. Among other things, this is a reflection of the sheer economic power of business: 69 out of the 100 richest entities in the world are companies.[3] In the past 20 years, the number of companies with a

Fig. 13.1 Hans Vestberg, CEO of Verizon, speaks to participants at Global Citizen in 2019 in New York City's Central Park (© Verizon). Global Citizen, an international advocacy group engaging millennials worldwide in ending extreme poverty, is partnering with the UN. Their goal is to raise the $350 billion needed annually over the next ten years to helps the world's poorest countries achieve the UN Sustainable Development Goals, and Hans is co-chair of the CEO Coalition working to make that happen

market capitalization above $100 billion has more than doubled (from 37 in 1999 to 98 companies in 2019).[4] And with this power comes responsibility.

Enter the Activist CEO

Today's CEOs and other C-suite leaders are increasingly expected to use the influence that comes from their privileged positions for good. In the past, it might have been enough for leaders to know their financial numbers and be a good salesperson. Today's CEO must also be aware of the implications of policy trends and complex, global issues to future-proof their strategy, manage non-financial risks, and stay attuned to society's emerging needs.

As a result, we are starting to see the emergence of the activist CEO, as today's pioneering business leaders step up and speak out. If done credibly and authentically, leaders can add significant momentum to the search for solutions to the increasingly complex issues affecting business and society. We would also argue that this is becoming a fundamental aspect of leadership. The emphasis on culture, values, and purpose at the heart of Chap. 3 comes full circle here, to how an individual leader drives that purpose through his or her own platform.

Now, companies are expected to provide real solutions to sustainability challenges and business leaders are expected to hold an informed and proactive position on the environmental and social issues that most concern their companies and stakeholders. Beyond just delivering financial returns, we argue that there is great business value in convening a wide range of stakeholders to grapple with complex challenges like climate change, growing inequalities, and transitioning to a circular and bio economy.

In this chapter we look at how business leaders can find the cause and platform that best reflects their purpose and values and use that agenda to define their ambition level and advance a vision for sustainability transformation. It's a matter of having an impactful and authentic voice and presence, knowing the facts, being open and transparent, and backing up words with action. We share examples of companies, individuals, industry groups, cross-sector alliances, and public-private partnerships that are successfully moving the needle on sustainability.

Every leader's voice matters in creating a new corporate narrative on sustainability. We encourage leaders to stand up and engage from the platform in which they can make the greatest difference. Against the backdrop of the huge challenges we face today, captured so well by the SDGs described in Chap. 11, finding the right platform may demand a new narrative, perhaps a reinvention of the story that has long guided a company or a leader's inner compass.

Readers of this book likely agree that we are truly facing an emergency: not only with our rapidly closing window to act on climate change but also to tackle a range of other planetary and societal challenges. Previously we have seen the world come together to address the global financial crisis in 2008, and the coronavirus pandemic is ongoing in 2020, with many business leaders standing up to help address an unprecedented crisis that governments cannot solve on their own. Sustainability challenges should be no different in setting off alarm bells; in fact, they have been ringing loud and clear for some time.

Our goal is to encourage action in support of the sustainability agenda—we urge leaders to find their burning platform and make it the beating heart of their business. Our admiration runs deep for Paul Polman, Unilever's former CEO and corporate sustainability pioneer. We want to see more Paul Polmans in the world. The third phase, 3.0, of our Sustainability Leadership

Model challenges leaders to find and use the power of their platform to amplify a sustainability strategy and convince others in their wider ecosystem to join them.

An authentic influencing platform first and foremost is about being true to one's own words, always connecting back to purpose and values. That is as true for building credibility within your own organization as it is for reaching out beyond the limits of your company or industry to achieve positive impact at scale. Often this involves finding the right partners and alliances and forming a united front on the issues that you are most willing to fight for. And far from this being an altruistic, charitable act, expanding your sustainability leadership platform should create even stronger competitive advantage.

Taking a Stand

Purpose and platform go hand in hand—recent studies bear this out. According to Professor Michael Toffel of Harvard Business School, in the emerging phenomenon of CEO activism, CEOs are stepping into controversial issues that are values-driven, not bottom-line-driven.[5] Even without external stakeholder pressure, some leaders are seizing the moral imperative to act and make their voices heard, including on controversial topics that could potentially invite customer backlash.

Some 89 percent of consumers believe purpose is demonstrated by how a company benefits society and the environment, and that this has to be consistent to be seen as authentic and avoid "purpose washing."[6] Many leaders find that taking a stand is surprisingly positive for building a brand with purpose. Still others meet criticism when their stand is found to be inconsistent or inauthentic. Here are a few notable examples in both categories:

Apple: Apple CEO Tim Cook has spearheaded the largest tech company in the world to take big actions on sustainability, including 100 percent of its global facilities being powered by renewable energy.[7] Now he has thrown down the gauntlet to other CEOs. He called out to those "who have great power to change the world at their fingertips, and who have so far declined to use it … If you are an executive who has not developed an innovation strategy to address your impact on the climate, then you are failing in your duties as a leader."[8]

Nike: Sportswear company Nike lit up the cultural discourse in 2018 with an ad featuring a close-up of American football player Colin Kaepernick, with the words "Believe in something, even if it means sacrificing everything."

Kaepernick had been at the center of a fierce debate after remaining seated and later kneeling during the national anthem to protest police brutality against African-Americans.[9] It was an example of demonstrating brand purpose by aligning with a controversial cause. The move did not hurt Nike's business—in fact, the company claimed $163 million in earned media, a $6 billion brand value increase, and a 31 percent boost in sales.[10]

Amazon: In 2019, an open revolt of some 8000 employees, including a shareholder resolution over climate inaction,[11] was the catalyst for Amazon CEO Jeff Bezos to pledge that Amazon, the world's largest online marketplace, would become carbon neutral by 2040. The announcement came one day ahead of a global climate strike in which 1500 Amazon employees had planned a walkout. Then in February 2020, Bezos said he was committing $10 billion to address the climate crisis in a new initiative called the Bezos Earth Fund.[12] Rising stakeholder pressure for Amazon to take action on climate change finally forced impressive action. But if the CEO had shown leadership in the first place, the company could have avoided getting caught on the back foot.

Google: Employees at the global search engine have not been shy about making their voices heard. In spring 2018, some 4000 signed a petition to get Google to back off its Pentagon drone AI project, concerned that the warfare technology could be used to kill people—the company dropped the project a month later.[13] A few months later, over 20,000 employees walked out to protest sexual harassment and misconduct at the workplace,[14] and a week later, Google promised to make changes to a number of its policies.[15] Noting that Google's unofficial motto since 2000 had been the simple phrase "don't be evil,"[16] many employees now felt that Google had "lost its way."[17] Whether or not that's true, it is an example of how poor corporate conduct can rub up against purpose and values, and backfire.

Blackrock: The annual letter to CEOs from Larry Fink, Chairman and CEO of the world's largest money manager, makes the financial and business world sit up and pay attention. In recent years, Fink has used that pulpit to stress that companies should do more than pursue profits and urged executives to step into a leadership vacuum in a divided world.[18] His 2020 letter was particularly noteworthy, with a new urgency around climate change: "Climate change has become a defining factor in companies' long-term prospects ... But awareness is rapidly changing, and I believe we are on the edge of a fundamental reshaping of finance," Fink wrote. BlackRock has committed to divest from any company that makes more than 25 percent of its revenue from thermal coal, one of the largest ever divestments from coal, and remarkable for one of the world's largest investors in coal, oil, and gas.[19] Further, BlackRock in 2020 joined the global investor initiative Climate Action 100+ to push 160 of the world's largest corporate greenhouse gas (GHG) emitters to come into alignment on the Paris Agreement.[20] These examples show an admirable use of BlackRock's platform—but it is inconsistent and there remain many skeptics. Investors and environmental groups accuse BlackRock of dragging its feet on the climate crisis. One report found that BlackRock's climate inaction had cost its clients tens of billions of dollars.[21]

So, we have bold examples where companies and leaders took risks, stood for something they believed was important, despite the potential for backlash, and won. And then there are other cases where a leader doesn't take a stand, acts too late or too superficially, or fails to live up to purpose entirely. Being neutral is no longer enough, nor is cleaning up problems after they've occurred. Leaders can use their platform to fix or avoid the problem at the source—or find an alternative route to address it. Actions are what count.

Many Ways to Influence

For leaders intent on sustainability leadership, there are many effective platforms to work from, ranging from public commitments and statements and legislative and government policy engagement, to membership in industry or other associations, participation in major events and global fora, UN and NGO partnerships, as well as unexpected alliances or unconventional partnerships. In our experience it is important to be proactive and progressive in developing and evaluating the different ways in which to wield influence in a positive way. Equally important is being informed and having a broad overview of issues from many stakeholder perspectives.

In Chap. 4, we learned how Henrik temporarily closed down Scania's global operations to run climate training for all employees, inspired by the September 2019 global climate strikes. The event has had ripple effects: Scania's owner, Volkswagen, was inspired by the best practice and plans to hold a climate event for its 650,000 employees. Scania Climate Day was a powerful example of using a high-profile external event as a platform for the company to go beyond and show commitment to tackling climate change in line with the Paris Agreement.[22] It was not a one-off, however. Henrik has long advocated for action on climate change, both within the organization and on a much broader societal platform. Not long after, as noted in Chap. 8, Scania was among 87 companies at the 2019 Climate Action Summit pledging to set science-based targets aligned with a 1.5°C trajectory for a net-zero future. The pledges are part of the Business Ambition for 1.5°C—Our Only Future, a project of the UN Global Compact, Science Based Targets Initiative, and the We Mean Business coalition.[23]

Today Scania is a top of mind for both organizers of forums and events focused on sustainability in the transport sector, as well as customers. Henrik jokes that this is precisely the intention: "We've said we want to be like ghost-busters for anyone looking for sustainable transport solutions ... *'Who you gonna call?'*..."

But in addition to participating and being visible in external events, Henrik and his team wanted to ensure the direct business relevance to his own customers and employees. To do that, Scania created the Sustainable Transport Forum. This multi-stakeholder event is an opportunity to influence and drive the discussion around sustainable transport and to create outcomes to help Scania realize its vision—through the kind of societal ecosystem approach we discussed in Chap. 10. Society as a stakeholder is an underlying impetus for the Forum, which brings together business leaders, policymaker, academia, and other thought leaders to grapple with societal challenges—specifically, climate change. The first forum in 2016 was the moment where Henrik put his stake in the ground, about the role transport must play as part of the solution to climate change. The second forum in 2018, in Stockholm, took that sense of urgency, personified by keynote speaker former US Vice President Al Gore,[24] and put science behind it with the unveiling of the Pathways Report, and by presenting the Pathways Coalition that would put the report's findings into action. The 2020 Sustainable Transport Forum in Stockholm has been postponed to 2021, but the plan is to create even more ripples in the water by continuing to build and invest in coalitions of unlikely and unconventional partners that can help drive the shift in sustainable transport. The earlier forums were about creating awareness and sense of urgency, and a vision of what's possible. The 2021 event will seize on the change already afoot, sharing best practice examples and creating new alliances to further accelerate the transformation.

For her part, Elaine also focused on building coalitions. A strong believer in creating coalitions of the willing, she frequently sought out other fellow influencers that could provide unconventional insights. She turned that into many successful collaborative partnerships, like the global education initiative Connect to Learn, focused on secondary education for girls in developing countries. She also teamed up with (now former) Ericsson CEOs to help them realize the power of using their platforms, identifying opportunities for them to leverage their voice, supported by strategies designed to elevate their messages, backed by real programs. She recalls that in 2007, at a time when very few corporate voices were talking about the role of business in human rights, Elaine and former Ericsson CEO Carl-Henric Svanberg attended a UN human rights event in Geneva, delivering a message about how companies need to put human rights at the top of their agenda. Today with the UN Guiding Principles for Business and Human Rights, more companies speak up on human rights. But at that time, Carl-Henric and Ericsson were a lone voice, a novelty. Yet this message sparked what later became an in-depth commitment to ICT and human rights at Ericsson.

In the runup to establishing the 2030 Agenda that would become the UN SDGs, Elaine and Hans Vestberg for years championed awareness of the role of ICT in accelerating the SDGs. More recently Elaine is focused on using her own platform to raise awareness about the need to better integrate sustainability and ethics into use of artificial intelligence and data-driven technologies (explored in Chap. 12), as well as speaking out on the need for industry to take a stronger stand on preventing the distribution of child sexual abuse material. She also actively supports the agenda of the Whitaker Peace and Development Initiative (see Chap. 11), as a member of the fundraising, crisis management, and program committees of the Board of Directors.

There are several ways companies can engage in shifting or influencing the policy discussion on sustainability. Some Swedish companies have used a range of options to extend their platform, from working in a transparent and effective way with governments, to forming new coalitions and alliances within and across industries, to embarking on public-private partnerships. Fossil Free Sweden, which commits Sweden to being fossil free by 2045, is a good example and is described further below. Industry manifestos and calls to action are another way to signal a firm commitment to policymakers. While trade or industry associations offer strength in numbers, a tendency to adopt broad policy positions can lead to a lowest common denominator approach (depending on the sector)—alternatively, proactive companies can use their membership to push an industry association to adopt a bolder approach on key industry association positions—a tactic adopted by SAS CEO Rickard Gustafson, as we explore later in this chapter.

From a policy perspective, tackling complex sustainability issues like climate change requires long-term stability and continuity, and companies and leaders that have chosen climate as their platform can encounter frustration at the short-term horizons and lack of policy coherence of many national governments. It is difficult to wield influence effectively in the face of policy inconsistency, where the rules put in place by one administration are promptly abandoned by the next. A transformative private sector sustainability agenda benefits most from regulatory certainty and stability. This creates the essential ground conditions for long-term investment that asymmetric and multifaceted risks, such as those from climate change, demand. Therefore, it is important to integrate this long-term thinking approach into company (and leaders') commitments and messaging more broadly, and encourage your organization to fight for that long-term certainty and stability.

Lobbying in a 3.0 Context

In the context of 3.0 of our model, the classic means of companies seeking to influence legislation through lobbying is complemented by a broader, societal, and planetary-infused perspective that reinvents this traditional aspect of wielding influence. In a time of transformative transparency, with information available at one's fingertips, the days of free polluting and hidden lobbying are over. While not all lobbying is bad, ethical, transparent, and constructive lobbying can support policy development. Lobbying is an integral part of a healthy democracy, closely related to universal values such as freedom of speech and the right to petition government. It allows interest groups to present their views on public decisions that affect them.[25]

That said, unfair and opaque lobbying practices can lead to undue influence and represent one of the key corruption risks facing society, according to Transparency International.[26] In today's hyper-transparent world, lobbying of this nature is more easily brought to light, and indulging in this kind of double agenda will erode corporate trust faster than anything. One example was the recent COP25 in Madrid in December 2019, where NGOs and other groups noted how some representatives the fossil fuel industry were publicly stating support for climate policy, while working behind the scenes to disrupt progress.[27]

Leaders must be aware of their companies' lobbying positions, and to keep in mind that positions should not contradict other public commitments or, worse still, company values. To be taken seriously as a sustainability leader, any lobbying, behind the scenes or otherwise, must align with other public positions. At the very least, a CEO must ensure that their regulatory teams are not lobbying to defeat legislation or other related positions that the company publicly says it supports.

We think there is a far more effective approach companies can adopt to leverage their policy positions. As Electrolux CEO Jonas Samuelsson expresses it: "Our policy and approach when it comes to regulation is that we're very much in favor of tougher regulation when it comes to sustainability and we're a driver as long as it meets two criteria: predictability and enforceability. As long as we can meet those two needs, we're generally on the proponent side. We think it's a competitive advantage for us and we think it's the right thing to do."

Electrolux has been consistent with this approach for decades, and has consistently built stakeholder trust over time. One early example of that approach demonstrates the value of being proactive on legislation that could potentially involve great costs for a company, or—as Electrolux saw it—present an industry-leading opportunity. In 2002, the European Union adopted the Waste Electrical and Electronic Equipment (WEEE) Directive,[28] requiring treatment, recovery, and disposal of electrical products to be financed by their producers. Electrolux fought for, and succeeded in, establishing individual, rather than collective, producer responsibility for electronic waste. As an industry leader in developing products designed for recyclability and energy efficiency, Electrolux knew it had a competitive advantage. With their leadership, other companies in the white goods and electronics industries followed suit, and in 2003, Electrolux, Braun, Hewlett Packard, and Sony formed the European Recycling Platform (ERP).[29]

Per Grunewald, now a clean-tech investor, who led the strategy around WEEE in 2003 as Senior Vice President at Electrolux, recalls that

> part of our strategy was to move the industry and take a leadership position. The benefit is that you can be part of shaping the game plan. You can influence and gain greater credibility to influence future legislation. If you have the ability to be proactive you can find a win-win. Policymakers don't have to tighten the laws if they can encourage competition within industry—a race to the top. I think the strongest instrument we have in policy is the innovation, technology and competition that business can offer. That's important for policymakers to keep in mind, rather than making detailed, proscriptive rules. If you let companies figure out a way to do it, and work with them, it can inspire even better results. We showed a certain pride in how well we could design products with sustainability in mind, and that has continued today.

Just as electronic waste and the growing producer responsibility movement preoccupied sustainability leaders in the early 2000s, today the need for a price on carbon is an intense topic of discussion for both business and governments. Carbon pricing is an approach to reducing greenhouse gas emissions that uses market mechanisms to pass the cost of emitting on to emitters. The lack of a true cost for carbon is one of the biggest barriers to making more progress on climate change. While more than 40 countries, including Sweden, have adopted some sort of price on carbon, typically through direct taxes on fossil fuel or cap-and-trade programs, there is debate on how effective countries have been in setting prices that are high enough to spur truly deep reductions.[30] The private sector has an important role to play in setting a price on carbon to lower emissions and a market-based approach is needed to do this in an economically sound way.

Factoring in a product's carbon dioxide emissions when pricing a product would be far more representative of the actual business case. Certainly, choosing fossil fuels, if factored in at the true cost of carbon, would quickly prove to be a non-starter. Business leaders and society would make very different decisions if there was a global price on carbon.

According to Georg Kell, founder and former Executive Director of the UN Global Compact and Chairman of Arabesque Partners, pricing carbon is the best solution across all industries: "Even if we do not have a unified global price, we should grow it bottom up everywhere, so I hope policymakers will redouble their efforts in that area to steer business across all sectors."

Some companies aren't waiting for government action and are setting their own internal price on carbon. Microsoft, for example, introduced a price on carbon in 2012, and recently announced that in July 2020 it would start phasing in its current internal carbon tax to cover our scope 3 emissions. Currently this fee is $15/metric ton and covers all scope 1 and 2 emissions, plus scope 3 travel emissions. Unlike some other companies, Microsoft says its internal carbon tax isn't a "shadow fee" that is calculated but not charged. "The fee is paid by each division in our business based on its carbon emissions, and the funds are used to pay for sustainability improvements."[31] Scania has an internal price on carbon of 100 euros per ton (about $108) which it uses like any other business calculation in making its product development and industrial capital expenditure decisions. The carbon price forces the organization to take the impact of CO_2 emissions into account and has become a standard approach.

What's clear is that many companies are moving on this issue and taking a stand. Others, however, are using their platform in a negative way to keep a price on carbon from becoming a reality. According to Sue Reid, Principal Advisor-Finance at Mission2020, a collaborative platform for addressing climate change, progress on carbon pricing "definitely has been thwarted by some of the entrenched incumbents, for example, major fossil fuel companies. These companies have both directly and through trade associations worked behind the scenes to stop progress and to funnel millions and millions of dollars to stop carbon pricing from going forward even as they publicly in many cases lay out climate objectives."

When an influencing platform is used in this way it makes clear the dangers of an inconsistent and hypocritical approach. Far more productive is to tear down the walls of the "us-versus-them" mentality of government-business antagonism, which is unhelpful. Whether the issue is a price on carbon or a specific government initiative like Fossil Free Sweden, we need more engagement between business leaders and policymakers, to sit around a table and work out their differences and figure out how to get past the hurdles. Abandoning their silos, and taking on a bigger role, there is a far greater chance for all parties to solve these complex challenges together. Being proactive can help bring clarity and certainty on this topic, which will be a win-win for companies and for governments, and, ultimately, society.

A Force for Good

To make their platforms exponential, companies can work within and across sectors and leverage public-private partnerships, and we explore each of these approaches in this chapter. For Professor Jeffrey Sachs of Columbia University, and Director of the UN Sustainable Development Solutions Network,[32] itself a public-private sector initiative to create and implement transformative solutions to achieve Agenda 2030, the private sector has a vital role to play in supporting practical problem-solving for sustainable development at local, national, and global scales.

"The main thing I'm trying to grapple with is how to get more governments to understand the practical pathway to success," he told us.

> The 180 countries in the world are not the technology pioneers. They're not producing the vehicles, for example, but they are responsible for clean energy, and clean power is each country's responsibility, even if it is partly on an interconnected grid. Most countries in the world are the technology users, not the technology producers. We need companies like Scania to be able to show these countries that are users of technology: "This is what should be part of your 2020–2030 strategy and you will be able to decarbonize in this manner." That is my challenge, how to help countries get practical, to know what the range of solutions is, and how we can achieve the practical pathway analysis, country by country.

Jeffrey Sachs believes taking sector-wide approaches and getting a wide range of industry sector partners around the table are key elements of success.

A lot of my own thinking is around getting the sector around the table, so that the sector feels the need and the confidence to move, without feeling the competitive pressure not to move. In Sweden, many companies act because it is the right thing to do, even if China isn't doing it, or your competitors in the US aren't doing it. You want to lead, and you know that you can come up with the solutions. I'm concerned about sectors where we're just not getting that kind of leadership—basically, the hard-to-abate sectors, like aviation, transport, shipping and four or five key industrial sectors like steel, cement, and petrochemicals. We need major solutions for those sectors, and my thought has been to get a sector-wide approach. There is the risk of course that it could lead to the least common denominator, but you have to try.

A specific example on a national level is Fossil Free Sweden, a pioneering government initiative to help meet the country's goal to become one of the first fossil-free nations, with a zero-emissions vision for 2045.[33] Launched ahead of the COP21 climate change conference in Paris in 2015, it is backed by over 400 companies including Scania, Ericsson, SAS, Northvolt, Volvo, IKEA, H&M, Stora Enso, and Telia Company (many of them featured in this book). Business sectors have drawn up their own roadmaps as to how they will be fossil free while also increasing their competitiveness. The initiative has launched four challenges for corporations, municipalities, regions, and organizations aimed at phasing out fossil fuels within the areas of transport, solar energy, business travel, and company car use.

Henrik and other Swedish leaders have found that the constructive dialogue and platform for action presented by Fossil Free Sweden have spurred companies to work within their industries to devise decarbonization roadmaps which they then share with policymakers to de-risk the political decision-making. Swedish politicians are now embracing these roadmaps to create incentives and changes in policy. Sweden has introduced a climate policy framework, a changeover in the transport sector from fossil fuels to sustainable fuels and electrification, and is making major investments in renewable energy and energy efficiency. The Swedish government has invested SEK 2 billion (about $200 million) to date in The Climate Leap (Klimatsprånget), a program for supporting investments in regional and local initiatives to reduce GHG emissions. Investments are being made in charging stations, biogas plants, railway maintenance, and energy efficiency. Support to solar and wind power is being increased, with the goal of 100 percent renewable electricity production. The 2018 budget bill marked the Swedish government's greatest ever investment in climate and the environment: 5 billion SEK (about $500 million)—a doubling since 2014.[34]

Fossil Free Sweden is a great example of how a common agenda between corporations and governments can be implemented on the national level to create results when all partners are committed toward achieving the same goals.

Tackling the Challenge of Sustainable Aviation

As a member of the board of governors of the International Air Transport Association (IATA), Rickard Gustafson, CEO of Sweden-based Scandinavian airline, SAS, found himself increasingly frustrated at the lack of willingness to push the envelope on sustainability. SAS is a sector leader in sustainability, which Rickard describes as "an existential issue" for the industry: stakeholders are demanding clear leadership to transform the industry toward more sustainable aviation. SAS has pledged to reduce CO_2 emissions by 25 percent by 2030 and use advanced biofuels equivalent to all SAS domestic air traffic.

As the trade association for the world's airlines, IATA represents some 290 airlines, or 82 percent of total air traffic. IATA has pledged a reduction in net aviation CO_2 emissions of 50 percent by 2050, relative to 2005 levels. But at the IATA's December 2018 meeting, Rickard told us,

> I stood up and told the IATA Board of Governors: "We should be proud of what we have done in setting targets, but this will not give us a get-out-of-jail-free card. We have to do more or we will face more regulation of our industry, and that will make it very hard for us to operate going forward. We need to demonstrate that a much more aggressive sustainability agenda and not just hide behind fancy 2050 goals. That won't do it." As I was looking around the table, I saw a lot of headshaking and people saying, "Yeah, yeah, yeah." But you have to be persistent. Six months later, when the Board met again, I made the same pitch. And things were different. All the European carriers agreed that the industry was falling behind, that we were about to lose this war. Then Australia and New Zealand joined us, along with Canada and Japan.

At the IATA Annual General Meeting in June 2019, the organization approved a resolution in which they reiterated strong support for the Carbon Offsetting and Reduction Scheme for International Aviation (CORSIA), a carbon pricing instrument for the aviation sector which caps net CO_2 emissions from aviation at 2020 levels.[35] A resolution urged airlines to implement all available fuel efficiency measures and participate fully in a long-term energy transition to sustainable aviation fuels.[36]

"We didn't convince everyone," Rickard accepts, "but gaining support from two-and-a-half continents in six months wasn't bad. Now the next time we meet I know that sustainability will be a major item on the agenda. And my point is, we're far from the biggest carrier, but we can still use the platform available to us to try to push an agenda. And hopefully ignite some change."

In recent months, a number of airlines have been announcing substantial commitments to slash their CO_2 emissions or become carbon neutral. Delta announced that starting March 1, 2020 it would commit $1 billion over the next ten years to mitigate all emissions from its global business going forward. The airline will invest in driving innovation, advancing clean air travel technologies, accelerating the reduction of carbon emissions and waste, and establishing new projects to mitigate the balance of emissions.[37] JetBlue plans to become carbon neutral on all domestic flights by July 2020 and would use an alternative fuel source for flights leaving from San Francisco.[38]

Finding Effective Cross-sector Platforms

Working cross-sector, as opposed to working within a sector, can bring new diversity and shed new light on problems which can in turn deliver new opportunities for catalyzing change. Cross-sector policy platforms can be especially effective mechanisms for action that extends across a system, or, in our words, a societal ecosystem. That's not news to Osvald Bjelland, the charismatic chairman and founder of Xynteo, an advisory firm that specializes in empowering leaders and businesses to transform themselves and their wider systems. For years, Osvald, an entrepreneur academic, and formidable networker, has used his own platform to drive collaborative action to tackle systemic problems and rethink growth models that are no longer future fit. As his experience deepens with time, he says that life is simply too short to spend with people that are not interested in the same high-energy systemic change that is needed to dramatically move the needle on sustainability challenges. And he prefers to hang with a like-minded crowd that shares this passion.

Xynteo committed early on to working with leaders and large organizations to help them navigate toward a type of growth that works for the business, but also satisfies three crucial criteria for that growth: it does not come at the expense of the planet, it does not fuel the power between the few and the many, and it dares to prioritize value in the long term, not just the next quarter. Over time, Xynteo has carved out a position by being able to bring together coalitions for action and through unique, transformational experiences led by its highly capable, empathetic team.

Held annually, the Xynteo Exchange brings together some 500 mission-driven entrepreneurs, business leaders, financiers, politicians, and artists to exchange ideas around finding new and sustainable economic models for the world. Osvald and his team challenges leaders to grapple with a distinct and not insubstantial underlying problem: the world's existing market-led growth model based on relentless GDP growth is no longer working. While the existing growth model has catalyzed enormous progress, in many ways it has become a destructive force, promoting short-term wins over long-term prosperity, depleting natural resources, and widening exclusion. "We need to form new alliances, and work together to basically reinvent economic growth as we know it to solve the biggest human problems. For in the future these problems also represent our biggest commercial opportunities," explains Osvald.

Along with helping to form multi-party coalitions of businesses that share a growth objective across a system, Xynteo hosts specific transformation projects. One of these is the Europe Delivers initiative, focused on four Grand Challenges expected to shape the future of European growth: a new social contract, the future of work, a green and resilient economy, and a global Europe: both Scania and Verizon are part of that work. As a member of the Europe Delivers project, the Scania focus is on the creation of a bioeconomy as part of a green and resilient economy—an outgrowth of its societal ecosystem approach that we examined in Chap. 10.

The bioeconomy initiative presented a clear opportunity for Henrik to use his voice and platform as CEO to join with others who shared that vision to make it happen. Henrik would not have had the opportunity to meet all the players and potential collaborators without the platform that Osvald and his team at Xynteo so effectively created and convened. We think every leader needs to find those types of platforms that can make real change happen.

A Growing Role for Public-Private Partnerships

Public-private partnerships are another influential platform for business that can greatly enhance sustainable development efforts. Because all parties benefit from working together in a public-private partnership, bigger issues can be solved, that no single party would have the incentive or capacity to solve on its own.

With the many daunting sustainable development challenges the world faces, there is a growing realization among NGOs, governments, the UN, and other intergovernmental bodies that they need the resources, innovation, scale, and skills of the private sector. At the same time, if the private sector engages in helping to solve sustainability challenges, it may need expertise in areas that are outside of its core business, so it can be a win-win partnership for all parties.

For Elaine, who has worked with multiple public-private partnerships, that opportunity became clear when establishing Ericsson's Connect to Learn program. A global education initiative launched in 2010 by Ericsson with the Earth Institute at Columbia University and Millennium Promise as partners, the aim was to increase access to education for girls by integrating technology tools and digital learning resources into schools across the globe, with a focus on remote areas in emerging markets.

The program could not have succeeded without the unique assets that each partner brought to the table. Ericsson could provide the technology platform and solutions, but were not educators or content experts. By working with governments and local mobile operators, Ericsson was able to use mobile broadband to solve the access to education part of the program. Then, working with Columbia University's Earth Institute, local schools, and Ministries of Education, it was able to address how to bring in qualified teachers and educators. And by working with mobile operators, Internet usage was made more affordable and accessible. In Myanmar in particular, DFID, the UK government's arm for development assistance, provided significant funding which enabled the initiative to scale up.

Both the cross-sector approach and public-private partnerships can be effective means for business leaders to effectively impact on an issue while taking a stand. There are also significant commercial and practical benefits of engaging in such collaborative platforms, including strengthening the ability to pool and enhance capabilities and distribute risk and share costs. Further, partnering in this way can boost the brand, accelerate learning in the organization, and, in a multitude of ways, result in mutually beneficial value.

Crafting an Influencing Plan

Historically, business has always had a powerful lobby voice, usually activated when there has been something to lose. In contrast, a societal ecosystem perspective underscores that leaders need to better understand how to address their impacts and how they can channel their voice as a force for good, if we are going to overcome the tipping points spelled out so starkly in the planetary boundaries. Effectively addressing climate change and achieving the SDGs demand a more visible collective global agenda, and business can be a powerful change agent.

There are a multitude of ways business leaders can use their platform, including public events, lobbying, public-private partnerships, cross-sector dialogue, and even protests. It may be that a CEO calling on his employees to strike isn't in the cards, as Henrik discovered, but a Climate Day that gets into the day-to-day operations of the company can prove to be an even more powerful way to take a stand. Whatever form it takes business leaders impatient with the pace of change should not be afraid to use their platform, nor should they underestimate its power. The societal ecosystem approach makes it possible to develop an influencing platform with greater clarity and impact, viewed through the societal and planetary lens.

Leaders on this planet, in business or in politics, are expected to take on a larger responsibility than their appointed or elected roles. Every leader has a unique platform to drive change—we urge leaders to seize that opportunity. It comes back to leadership, value, and purpose, and recognizing that leadership affords privilege but also responsibility. Inaction really isn't a choice for a leader who wants to leave a meaningful legacy. There is no shortage of problems demanding urgent solutions. What matters is finding the right cause and the right platform that allows for the most Expönential impact.

Stepping up means that we should not be afraid to take a position and start the conversation and the journey. Don't do this haphazardly. Engage your stakeholders and teams and do it in an orchestrated and consistent way that builds trust among all stakeholders. Dare to be part of the conversations that you might have earlier shied away from.

In this final chapter, we come full circle, from the purpose-driven leadership that is the Foundation of any transformation journey, to the personal influencing platform that is the springboard for making the Leap to the system change that sustainability demands. Using your platform, your voice, and your leadership is the best way—in fact, *the only way*—to future-proof your vision of a more sustainable world. It is what will make this entire journey of Expönentiality worth every bit of time you spend on it.

Key Takeaways

1 Recognize that your privilege as a leader also means you have a responsibility to act. Choose the issues that resonate with both you as a leader, and with the company's purpose.
2. Use the power of your platform to take a bold stand, and, if it doesn't exist, create one.
3. Own the agenda important to you, and be sure messages are backed with concrete action.

4. Know the facts. When you take a position, be prepared to match it with meaningful action and to act with consistency and integrity.
5. Don't align with organizations that conflict with your values. Seize opportunities to help shape policy and legislation fairly, transparently, and constructively—but avoid lowest common denominator traps.
6. Consider industry alliances, and also unexpected alliances to get difficult things done.

Notes

1. William Naughton-Gravette, "9 Essential Organizations Global Citizen's 'Global Goal Live' Campaign Will Support, Global Citizen, Sept 26, 2019, https://www.globalcitizen.org/en/content/global-goal-live-essential-partners/.
2. Global Citizen Launches Biggest Campaign Yet with Global Goal Live: The Possible Dream, Sept 26, 2019, https://www.globalcitizen.org/en/content/global-goals-live-the-possible-dream/.
3. Global Justice Now, 69 of the richest 100 entities on the planet are corporations, not governments, figures show, Oct 2018. https://www.globaljustice.org.uk/news/2018/oct/17/69-richest-100-entities-planet-are-corporations-not-governments-figures-show.
4. PWC, Global Top 100 companies by market capitalisation, July 2019. https://www.pwc.com/gx/en/audit-services/publications/assets/global-top-100-companies-2019.pdf; Top 100 Companies by Market Capitalization, http://fortboise.org/top100mktcap.html.
5. "Why CEOs Are Taking a Stand," Harvard Business Review, 2018, https://hbr.org/ideacast/2018/03/why-ceos-are-taking-a-stand.html, accessed 2 December 2019.
6. 2018 Cone/Porter Novelli Purpose Study: How to Build Deeper Bonds, Amplify Your message and Expand the Consumer base, https://www.cone-comm.com/research-blog/2018-purpose-study.
7. "Apple now globally powered by 100 percent global energy," April 9, 2018, https://www.apple.com/newsroom/2018/04/apple-now-globally-powered-by-100-percent-renewable-energy/.
8. William Feuer, "Apple CEO Tim Cook says he's taking on climate change and needs backup," CNBC, Oct 22, 2019, https://www.cnbc.com/2019/10/22/apple-ceo-tim-cook-accepts-ceres-conference-sustainability-award.html.
9. Steve Wyche, "Colin Kaepernick explains why he sat during national anthem," NFL.com, http://www.nfl.com/news/story/0ap3000000691077/article/colin-kaepernick-explains-why-he-sat-during-national-anthem.
10. Jeff Beer, "One year later, what did we learn from Nike's blockbuster Colin Kaepernick ad?"

11. Julie Bort, "Amazon employees were miffed at Jeff Bezos' response to their climate-change proposal: 'This is not the kind of leadership we need,' Business Insider, May 23, 2019, retrieved from https://www.businessinsider.com.au/jeff-bezos-not-in-room-amazon-employee-climate-change-proposal-2019-5.

12. Karen Weise, "Jeff Bezos Commits $10 Billion to Address Climate Change," The New York Times, Feb 7, 2020, retrieved from https://www.nytimes.com/2020/02/17/technology/jeff-bezos-climate-change-earth-fund.html.

13. ZDnet, Google employee protest: Now Google backs off Pentagon drone AI project, June 2018.

14. Lisa Marie Segarra, "More than 20,000 Google employees participated in walkout over sexual harassment policy," Nov 3, 2018, Fortune, retrieved from https://fortune.com/2018/11/03/google-employees-walkout-demands/.

15. Janelle Griffith, "Google changes sexual harassment policies after employee walkout," NBC News, Nov 8, 2018, retrieved from https://www.nbcnews.com/tech/tech-news/google-changes-sexual-harassment-policies-after-employee-walkout-n934046.

16. Kate Conger, "Google removes 'Don't Be Evil' clause from its Code of Conduct,' May 18, 2018, Gizmodo, retrieved from https://gizmodo.com/google-removes-nearly-all-mentions-of-dont-be-evil-from-1826153393.

17. WIRED, Three Years of Misery Inside Google, the Happiest Company in Tech, August, 2019. https://www.wired.com/story/inside-google-three-years-misery-happiest-company-tech/.

18. Purpose & Profit, Larry Fink's 2019 Letter to CEOs, retrieved from https://www.blackrock.com/corporate/investor-relations/larry-fink-ceo-letter.

19. Michael Brune, "What one of BlackRock's Biggest critics thinks about Larry Fink's letter," CNBC, Jan 15, 2020, retrieved from https://www.cnbc.com/2020/01/15/one-of-blackrocks-biggest-critics-on-larry-finks-climate-letter.html.

20. BlackRock. Joins Climate Action 100+ to ensure largest corporate emitters act on climate change, Ceres, Jan 14, 2019, retrieved from https://www.wemeanbusinesscoalition.org/press-release/blackrock-joins-climate-action-100-to-ensure-largest-corporate-emitters-act-on-climate-crisis/.

21. Attracta Mooney, "BlackRock lambasted over wasteful fossil fuel investments," Financial Times, Aug 1, 2019, https://www.ft.com/content/c4ff0b55-b165-34ba-9154-97f3b402fe87.

22. Scania calls for a Climate Day and halts operations for sustainability training for employees," PR Newswire, Aug 2, 2019, https://markets.businessinsider.com/news/stocks/scania-calls-for-a-climate-day-and-halts-operations-for-sustainability-training-for-employees-1028411910.

23. New leadership group announced at Climate Action Summit to drive industry transition to low-carbon economy, Climate Action Summit 2019, Sept 23, 2019, https://www.un.org/en/climatechange/assets/pdf/release_industry_transition.pdf.

24. Sustainable Transport Forum 2018 gathers world leaders to discuss the shift to a fossil-free transport system," Scania.com, May 18, 2018, https://www. scania.com/group/en/sustainable-transport-forum-2018-gathers-world-leaders-to-discuss-the-shift-to-a-fossil-free-transport-system/.

25. Lobbying in Europe: Hidden Influence, Privileged Access," Transparency International, 2016, http://transparency.eu/wp-content/uploads/2016/09/Lobbying_web.pdf.

26. "Europe: Unregulated Lobbying Opens Door to Corruption," Transparency International, April 15, 2015, https://www.transparency.org/en/press/europes-unregulated-lobbying-opens-door-to-corruption.

27. "COP25 was a success for the fossil fuel industry, governments respond to people's demands with weakest possible decision," 350.org, Dec 15, 2019, retrieved from https://350.org/press-release/cop25-was-a-success-for-the-fossil-fuel-industry-governments-respond-to-peoples-demands-with-weakest-possible-decision/.

28. WEEE Directive, European Commission, https://ec.europa.eu/environment/waste/weee/index_en.htm.

29. European Recycling Platform, https://erp-recycling.org/.

30. Brad Plummer and Nadja Popovich, "These Countries Have Prices on Carbon. Are They Working?".

31. Brad Smith, Microsoft will be carbon negative by 2030, Microsoft.com, January 16, 2020, https://blogs.microsoft.com/blog/2020/01/16/microsoft-will-be-carbon-negative-by-2030/.

32. Sustainable Development Solutions Network: A Global Initiative for the United Nations, https://www.unsdsn.org/.

33. SOU 2016:21 Ett klimatpolitiskt ramverk för Sverige. Delbetänkande av Miljömålsberedningen. (A Political Climate Framework for Sweden. Partial report by the Environmental Goals Committee, accessed Dec 5, 2019, http://www.sou.gov.se/wp-content/uploads/2016/03/SOU_2016_21_webb.pdf.

34. Largest ever investment in climate, the Government of Sweden, Sept 5, 2017, retrieved from https://www.government.se/press-releases/2017/09/largest-ever-investment-in-climate/.

35. Resolution on CORSIA," IATA, 2019, available at: https://www.iata.org/pressroom/pr/Documents/resolution-corsia-agm-2019.pdf.

36. "Resolution on CORSIA," IATA.

37. Driving change for you and our planet, Delta.com, accessed March 19, 2019, https://www.delta.com/us/en/about-delta/sustainability.

38. JetBlue to become carbon neutral in 2020, Reuters, Jan 6, 2020, https://www.reuters.com/article/us-jetblue-environment-idUSKBN1Z5237.

Part IV

Final Thoughts

14

Conclusion: No Time to Lose

We wrote this book because we believe there is an emergency on planet earth and business is in a powerful position to do something about it. There is good reason to look toward Sweden for inspiration. First, because sustainability is such a high priority across every sector of society. But also, because the national traits of consensus, of respecting every voice, and inviting everyone around the table empower people to take ownership of big societal challenges and to innovate and work together to find solutions. But beyond inspiration must also come a deep sense of responsibility to act, and to act soon.

The Sustainability Leadership Model in this book is our attempt to draw from the Swedish experience and guide you on how to build a consistent and impactful approach over time. You can start immediately, if you haven't already. Use the experiences and insights we share and tweak or develop them to fit your own vision of sustainability leadership. Each journey will be unique—what we offer are some guideposts that we wished someone had offered us when we started out.

The journey begins and ends with leadership. Make sure you put a stake in the ground with a clear purpose, that is well anchored in the culture and values of your organization. Build sustainability into your business model and strategy to get everyone onboard, especially your customers. Measure your progress beyond your obvious impact. Do this not just for your stakeholders, but for your own knowledge as a leader—that you're doing everything you can to maximize your positive impacts and minimize the negative ones. You now have a Foundation to stand on and you have started to imbed sustainability into the Core of your company.

© The Author(s) 2020
H. Henriksson, E. Weidman Grunewald, *Sustainability Leadership*,
https://doi.org/10.1007/978-3-030-42291-2_14

To take the Leap toward 3.0 in our model, you need to exponentially boost your individual ambition and that of your organization. That's where the Expönentiality Formula helps you find the missing pieces of the puzzle and your X-Factor. Start by building a deeper scientific knowledge base about your business ecosystem. Apply a societal and planetary lens to broaden your view and see your world unfold into a societal ecosystem. Seek unexpected partnerships in this new world and use digitalization, to leverage your business model.

With Society as a stakeholder you will make more informed decisions to the benefit of your company and society more broadly, and you will ensure that your company stays relevant when we reach the tipping point. That is, when sustainability becomes the norm, a non-negotiable aspect of doing business. At that point it will no longer be possible to run a company that is not sustainable—you simply won't be relevant. Because no one will buy your products, no will invest in your company, and no one will want to work for you.

So, the final question is, what legacy do you want to leave for the next generation of leaders in your company? Those short-term incremental improvements? Or a sustainable legacy with a strong foundation, a customer-focused business model, and an organization fueled with ambition?

Ultimately, it all comes down to leadership and how you use your personal influencing platform to act, to be a role model, to make a difference, and to pay it forward. Writing this book has been our way of paying it forward, to hopefully inspire you, and others, to join us on the path to sustainability leadership (Fig. 14.1).

Even if we get only one business leader to take us up on this challenge, it will still be worth all the hard work we've put into this book.

Join us!

EXPÖNENTIALITY JOURNEY

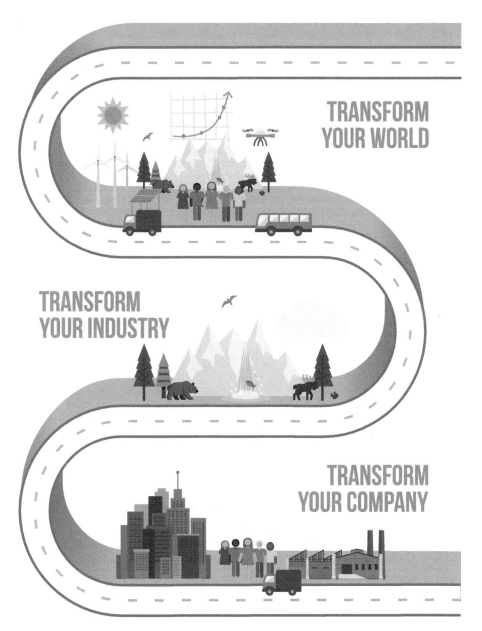

Fig. 14.1 The Expönentiality Journey

About the Authors

Henrik Henriksson joined Scania in 1997. After heading commercial operations in different markets and business areas as well as serving as global head of sales and marketing, he was appointed President and CEO in 2016. Entrepreneurial at heart, he joined Scania to explore global business and remained, thanks to Scania's strong customer focus, the delegated responsibility and the constant aim to do better.

He is a board member of Electrolux AB and Hexagon AB and currently holds the Chairmanship of the European Industry Association for Heavy Commercial Vehicles (ACEA CV).

The transport industry accounts for a significant share of global CO_2 emissions, one of the key issues to be tackled in the UN Sustainable Development Goals Agenda 2030. Henriksson's passion and fierce advocacy for sustainability have become a beacon in the shift toward a fossil-free transport system. He is an advisor to the Swedish government and part of its Agenda 2030 delegation.

He leads Scania from its headquarters in Sweden where the political commitment to decarbonize and the power of innovation and competition within a strong heavy commercial vehicle cluster have enabled significant progress. With a newly defined purpose for the company—to drive the shift toward sustainable transport—he continues to position Scania as a role model in decarbonizing the heavy commercial vehicle sector.

© The Author(s) 2020
H. Henriksson, E. Weidman Grunewald, *Sustainability Leadership*,
https://doi.org/10.1007/978-3-030-42291-2

Henriksson holds a Bachelor of Science in Business Administration from Lund University and has also studied at the Stern School of Business (New York University) and at Edinburgh University.

He is the proud father of two young girls who spur him on, and whom he considers the true judges of his legacy.

Elaine Weidman Grunewald is a co-founder of the AI Sustainability Center, a world-leading center for identifying, measuring, and governing ethical and societal implications of AI and data-driven technologies.

She is an expert on global sustainability and development issues. She has worked for over two decades in the private sector, focusing on digitalization and sustainable development challenges across multiple sectors. She spent nearly 20 years at Ericsson, where she was SVP and Chief Sustainability and Public Affairs Officer, and a member of the Executive Team.

She sits on the Boards of environmental architecture and consulting firm Sweco AB, the Whitaker Peace and Development Initiative, which focuses on the importance of youth empowerment in peace building, and the International Women's Forum, Sweden. She has been actively engaged in the Broadband Commission for Sustainable Development, the UN Sustainable Development Solutions Network, and the Business and Sustainable Development Commission. She speaks frequently at industry and other events, and is a corporate development and sustainability adviser to startups, companies, and CEOs.

She holds a double master's degree in International Relations and Resource & Environmental Management from Boston University's Center for Energy and Environmental Studies. She lives in Stockholm with her husband Per Grunewald, two teenage sons, and her English springer spaniel, Sammy.

About Scania

Scania's aim is to drive the shift toward a sustainable transport system, creating a world of mobility that is better for business, society, and the environment. Founded in 1891, Scania is a world-leading provider of transport solutions, including trucks and buses for heavy transport applications combined with an extensive product-related service offering. Scania offers vehicle financing, insurance, connectivity, and rental services to enable its customers to focus on their core business. Scania is also a leading provider of industrial and marine engines. Scania employs around 52,100 employees in about 100 countries. Scania is part of the listed TRATON SE, a subsidiary of Volkswagen AG.

© The Author(s) 2020
H. Henriksson, E. Weidman Grunewald, *Sustainability Leadership*,
https://doi.org/10.1007/978-3-030-42291-2

About the AI Sustainability Center

The AI Sustainability Center was established in 2018 to create a world-leading multidisciplinary hub to address the scaling of AI (Artificial Intelligence) and other data-driven technologies in broader ethical and societal contexts. It is a collaborative, research-focused environment for piloting and testing AI sustainability strategies and frameworks. The center focuses on helping companies and public agencies to mitigate risks, and it facilitates the realization of the vast gains to organizations, society, and individuals by acting proactively. Its mission is to provide users of AI with practical tools to avoid risks while keeping humanity and fairness at the core.

© The Author(s) 2020
H. Henriksson, E. Weidman Grunewald, *Sustainability Leadership*,
https://doi.org/10.1007/978-3-030-42291-2

Paying It Forward

As we noted in the Conclusion, writing this book has been our way of paying it forward. To make good on that pledge, and in keeping with the principles expressed in our leadership model, we are donating the proceeds from sales of this book to Norrsken Foundation, as featured in this book.

Norrsken Foundation supports entrepreneurs solving some of the world's greatest sustainable development challenges. This is not about charity. The big ideas that Norrsken funds are a perfect embodiment of our X-Factor concept in action, and we hope that our modest contribution can help them achieve even greater impact and scale.

© The Author(s) 2020
H. Henriksson, E. Weidman Grunewald, *Sustainability Leadership*,
https://doi.org/10.1007/978-3-030-42291-2

Elaine's English springer spaniel Sammy and Henrik's Spanish water dog Gracie on the go in Stockholm, refueling oxygen in one of the breaks from writing the book in early 2020

Index

© The Author(s) 2020
H. Henriksson, E. Weidman Grunewald, *Sustainability Leadership*,
https://doi.org/10.1007/978-3-030-42291-2